Bethsaida
Home of the Apostles

Fred Strickert

A Michael Glazier Book
THE LITURGICAL PRESS
Collegeville, Minnesota

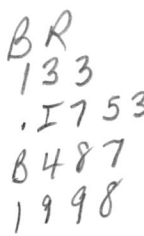

A Michael Glazier Book published by The Liturgical Press

Cover design by David Manahan, O.S.B. Cover photo by Bethsaida excavation site by Fred Strickert.

The Scripture quotations contained herein are from the New Revised Standard Version Bible, Catholic edition, © 1989 by the Division of Christian Education of the National Council of Churches of Christ in the USA. Used by permission. All rights reserved.

© 1998 by The Order of St. Benedict, Inc., Collegeville, Minnesota. All rights reserved. No part of this book may be reproduced in any form or by any means, electronic or mechanical, including photocopying, recording, taping, or any retrieval system without the written permission of The Liturgical Press, Collegeville, Minnesota 56321. Printed in the United States of America.

1   2   3   4   5   6   7   8

Library of Congress Cataloging-in-Publication Data

Strickert, Frederick M.
    Bethsaida : home of the Apostles / Fred Strickert.
      p.   cm.
    "A Michael Glazier book."
    Includes bibliographical references and index.
    ISBN 0-8146-5519-X
    1. Bethsaida (Extinct city)   2. Christian antiquities—Israel--Bethsaida (Extinct city)   3. Bible. N.T.—Antiquities.   I. Title.
BR133.I753B487   1998
225.9'5—dc21
                                                                         98-16536
                                                                                CIP

To Gloria who shares my dreams

Contents

List of Illustrations, Photographs, Maps   vi

Acknowledgments   ix

Chapter 1   Sources   1

Chapter 2   Bethsaida Prior to the New Testament   13

Chapter 3   Home of the Apostles   19

Chapter 4   "Across the Sea . . . to Bethsaida"   31

Chapter 5   Fishing Village   47

Chapter 6   Houses of Fishermen and Others   65

Chapter 7   Philip as Ruler   77

Chapter 8   The Founding of Bethsaida-Julias   91

Chapter 9   The Disciples of John the Baptist   109

Chapter 10   The Multiplication of Loaves and Fishes   115

Chapter 11   The Healing of the Blind Man   125

Chapter 12   Woe Saying against Bethsaida   131

Chapter 13   Early Christian Community in Bethsaida   139

Chapter 14   The Gathering of Sayings of Jesus   155

Chapter 15   The Destruction of Bethsaida   161

Index of Ancient Sources   178

Index of Names and Places   185

Illustrations, Photographs, Maps

Illustrations

Topographical Plan of et-Tell   11

Clay Figurine with *Atef* Headgear   14

Peter's House in Capernaum   23

Lead Weight   50

Seine Net   52

Basalt Ring Weight   52

Common Fish in the Sea of Galilee   54

Fishing Equipment: Hook and Needle   55

Clay "Fisherman's" Seal   56

Migdal Boat   59

The Simple House   66

"The Fisherman's House"   68

Possible Reconstruction of Courtyard House   69

Hellenistic Cooking Pot   70

Hellenistic Fine Ware   70

The "Winemaker's" House   71

Roman Key   74

Illustrations, Photographs, Maps vii

Gold Earring   75

Iron Sickles   75

Philip Coin—1 C.E.: Augustus and Philip   80

Pedestal from Si Containing Nabatean Inscription   81

Philip Coin—30 C.E.: Augustus and Livia   85, 101

Hasmonean Coins   87

Julia Coins of Procurator Gratus—15 to 17 C.E.   96

Pontius Pilate Coin—29 C.E.   97

Philip Coin—30 C.E.: Image of Livia   98

Philip Coin—30 C.E.: Image of Philip   100

KTIS Coin of Philip: Tiberius—30 C.E.   100

Plan of "Livia Temple"   104

Clay "Livia" Figurine   106

Philip Coin: Julia—30 C.E.   146

Pontius Pilate Coin—30 C.E.   146

Agrippa 1 Coin—42/43 C.E.   147

"Cross" Pottery   150

Anchor Handle   153

Photographs

Aerial photograph of Tel-Bethsaida   10

Lead Weights   51

Ring Weights   53

Courtyard of "Fisherman's House"   67

Street passing by "Winemaker's" House   72

Wine cellar with complete jars   73

Incense Shovel, Livia Cult   105

"Cross" Pottery   151

Twisted wall in "Winemaker's" House—earthquake damage   168

Maps

Fishing Cities on the Sea—Joshua 19:35   15

Bethsaida According to Josephus   32

Harbors on the Sea of Galilee   34

The Road System Near Bethsaida   37

The Battle of Bethsaida—67 C.E.   38

The Beteiha Plain   42

Bethsaida: Geological Development   43

The Bethsaida Area in 2nd–5th Centuries C.E.   44

The Sea of Galilee during the Jewish War—67 C.E.   61

The Territory of Philip   78

The Feeding Episode: A Possible Route   121

The Evangelical Triangle   135

Fault System: Jordan Rift Valley   166

Later Sites Near Bethsaida   176

Acknowledgments

A project such as this cannot be accomplished without the support and assistance of many individuals. It is appropriate therefore to begin with the many unsung heroes of archaeological digs, the volunteers. These individuals give up their own time and comfort to spend long hours at hot, dirty, and tedious work at their own expense merely for the joy and satisfaction in uncovering a short chapter of history. In many cases they never fully appreciate the impact of their own contributions, not realizing how their pieces fit into the larger picture while the area supervisors and associated scholars carry out subsequent analysis and publication. If fortunate, they may read about one of their own finds under the name of another.

Over the previous decade, I have sincerely appreciated my association with the many "nameless" volunteers who demonstrated curiosity, patience, and good humor while carrying out their tasks. In particular, I recognize over two hundred students from Wartburg College who have joined me and my colleague Chip Bouzard for our May Term adventures along the Galilean shore. It is with them in mind, and also many lay visitors and armchair students of Bible and archaeology, that I write this less technical study.

The Bethsaida excavations project has developed from meager beginnings when on May 1, 1988, Israeli archaeologist Rami Arav sat by the side of the road near the unexplored tell equipped with a rented jeep and borrowed tools awaiting our group of inexperienced diggers to begin breaking the surface and revealing the elusive city. It is Rami who has provided the expertise and kept the total picture in his mind while the rest of us have done our small parts. Our colleagues who have been there from the beginning, Heinz-Wolfgang Kuhn, John Greene, Mark Appold, and the sainted John Rousseau, have joined season after season to see a fascinating picture emerge. Their camaraderie has been most enjoyable; their discussion and insights, most helpful; and their learned papers and articles most illuminating. Subsequently joined by Dell Hutton, John Mark Nielson, James Olsen, Elizabeth McNamer, Toni Tessaro, Sandra Fortner, Denny Clark, Mark Smith, Gordon Brubacher, Charles Page, John F. Shroder, Michael Bishop, Mina Cohn, and Monika Bernett, we have become a formidable team.

We have all appreciated the administrative leadership of Richard Freund and the University of Nebraska at Omaha who have organized our consortium and facilitated budgets and publicity, as well as research, presentations, and publication—especially through the multivolume reports published through Thomas Jefferson University Press in Kirksville, Missouri.

In the particular endeavor of writing this book, I appreciate the sabbatical assistance granted by President Robert Vogel and Dean Jim Pence of Wartburg College and my colleagues who covered for me during my absence; the Albright Institute in Jerusalem which opened to me their library and research facilities; and the Evangelical Lutheran Christmas Church in Bethlehem which provided office space and computer resources.

Finally, I am indebted to wife Gloria and children Angela, Ben, and Rachel, who have demonstrated loving patience during long absences from home and who have offered support and encouragement. It is good fortune to have a spouse who enjoys and shares in one's research interests, especially when that individual has the knack for uncovering some of the most exciting finds.

The following illustrations and maps were reprinted by permission from the pages indicated of *Bethsaida: A City by the North Shore of the Sea of Galilee*, eds. Rami Arav and Richard Freund, Kirksville, Mo.: Thomas Jefferson University Press, 1995. Illustration 1: "Topographical Plan of et-Tell" (revised from John Mark Nielsen), p. 4; Illustration 2: "Clay Figurine with *Atef* Headgear," p. 18; Illustration 4: "Lead Weight," p. 28; Illustration 8: "Fishing Equipment: Hook and Needle," p. 28; Illustration 9: "Clay 'Fisherman's' Seal," p. 20; Illustration 14: "Hellenistic Cooking Pot," p. 37; Illustration 15: "Hellenistic Fine Ware," pp. 109–15; Illustration 18: "Gold Earring," p. 34; Illustration 19: "Iron Sickles," p. 33; Illustration 31: "Clay 'Livia' Figurine," p. 21; Map 6: "The Beteiha Plain," p. 74; Map 7: "Bethsaida: Geological Development," pp. 92–3; Map 13: "Fault System: Jordan Rift Valley," p. 68.

Illustration 5, "Seine Net," p. 52, was reprinted with permission of Jo Moore.

Illustration 7, "Common Fish in the Sea of Galilee," was reprinted with permission from *Jesus and His World*, Rami Arav and John J. Rousseau, Minneapolis: Fortress Press, 1995, p. 95.

Illustration 21, "Pedestal from Si Containing Nabatean Inscription," was reprinted with permission from *The Princeton Expedition of Southern Syria (1904–1909)*. Division III. Inscriptions. No. 101, p. 80.

Chapter 1

Sources

Bethsaida is one of the more prominent towns in the Gospels. Only Jerusalem, Capernaum, Nazareth, and Bethany are mentioned more often.[1] However, the importance of this city in the first century is attested by its frequent mention among first-century authors, both Christian and secular. It occurs both in the local Hebrew designation "Bethsaida" and in the Roman name "Julias" given by the first century ruler Herod Philip.

Secular Literary Sources

The city of Bethsaida is mentioned in secular literary sources only in the first and second centuries of the common era. It receives the most attention from the late first-century Jewish historian Josephus[2] who refers to it no less than seven times. To be precise, Josephus uses the name Bethsaida itself only once when he mentions that Herod's son Philip rebuilt the city in the early part of the century:

> Philip for his part made improvements at Paneas, which is situated at the headwaters of the Jordan, and called it Caesarea; he further granted to the village Bethsaida on the Sea of Galilee both by means of a large number of settlers, and through further expansion of strength, the rank of city and named it after Julia, the daughter of Caesar (Josephus, *Ant.* 18.28).

---

1. Jerusalem occurs 65 times, Capernaum 16 times, Nazareth and Bethany 12 times. The name Bethsaida occurs eight times in most textual traditions although it also does occur in variant readings for John 5:2.
2. Josephus texts are taken from the ten volumes in the Loeb classical series translated by H. St. J. Thackeray, Ralph Marcus, Allen Wikgren, and L. H. Feldman. Josephus, *The Life, Against Apion, Jewish Antiquities, Jewish War*, Loeb Classical Series (Cambridge, Mass.: Harvard University Press, 1926–65).

In this text in the *Jewish Antiquities* he notes that Philip also gave the fishing village a new name, Julias, by which it is known among other secular writers. In fact, in the parallel passage in *Jewish War*, Josephus himself refers to the founding of the city only by that later name:

> On the death of Augustus, who had directed the state for 57 years six months and two days, the empire of the Romans passed to Tiberius, son of Julia. On his accession, Herod Antipas and Philip continued to hold their tetrarchies and respectively founded cities: Philip built Caesarea, near the sources of the Jordan in the district of Paneas, and Julias in lower Gaulanitis; Herod built Tiberias in Galilee and a city which also took the name of Julia in Perea (Josephus, *War* 2.168).

He notes its importance as one of two cities built by Philip and as the place where Philip died and was buried in the tomb that he himself erected:

> Now it was at this time that Philip, Herod's son, died in the twentieth year of Tiberius' reign and after 37 years of his own rule over Trachonitis and Gaulanitis . . . he died in Julias. His body was carried to the tomb that he himself had erected before he died and there was a costly funeral (Josephus, *Ant.* 18:4-6, 106-8).

Because of his interest in the Herodian dynasty, Jospehus also provides much information about Philip in sections where Julias is not specifically mentioned, yet which shed light on our understanding of the city.

In describing the territory of Philip's successor, Agrippa 1, he notes the city Julias at the southern extremity:

> That Kingdom beginning at Mount Libanus and the sources of the Jordan, extends in breadth to the Lake of Tiberias, and in length from a village called Arpha to Julias; it contains a mixed population of Jews and Syrians (Josephus, *War* 3.57).

Because of its position on the northeast side of the Sea of Galilee near the point where the northern Jordan River entered the sea, Josephus refers to Julias on several other occasions in the descriptions of the geography of this area:

> After issuing from this grotto at Paneas, the Jordan River, whose course is now visible, intersects the marshes and lagoon of Lake Semechonitis, then traverses another 120 furlongs, and below the town of Julias enters the Lake of Gennesar (Josephus, *War* 3.515).

> Opposite to it and flanking the Jordan lies a second range, which beginning at Julias in the north, stretches . . . to Petra in Arabia (Josephus, *War* 4.454).

The fact that Julias can be mentioned in passing as a landmark confirms its stature in the first century.

Josephus' knowledge of this city is especially significant because it is based on his own experience in this region. In fact, he notes that during his days as commander of the Galilean forces in the Jewish revolt of 67 C.E., he fought a battle outside the city to the west:

> After this time reinforcements arrived from the king, both horse and foot, under the command of Sulla, the captain of his bodyguard. He pitched his camp at a distance of five furlongs from Julias, and put out pickets on the roads leading to the fortress of Gamla to prevent the inhabitants of Julias from obtaining supplies from Galilee. On receiving intelligence of this, I dispatched a force of 2,000 men under the command of Jeremiah, who entrenched themselves a furlong away from Julias close to the River Jordan, but took no action beyond skirmishing until I joined them with supports, 3,000 strong. The next day, after laying an ambuscade in a ravine not far from their earthworks, I offered battle to the royal troops, directing my division to retire until they had lured the enemy forward; as actually happened. Sulla, supposing that our men were really fleeing, advanced and was on the point of following in pursuit, when the others emerging from their ambush, took him in the rear and threw his whole force into the utmost disorder. Instantly wheeling the main body about, I charged and routed the royalists; and my success on that day would have been complete, had I not been thwarted by some evil genius. The horse on which I went into action stumbled on a marshy spot and brought me with him to the ground. Having fractured some bones in the wrist, I was carried to a village called Cepharnocus. My men, hearing of this, and fearing that a worse fate had befallen me, desisted from further pursuit and returned in deepest anxiety on my account . . . Sulla and his troops, learning of my accident again took heart . . . they did not follow up their success; for on hearing that reinforcements shipped at Tarichaeae had reached Julias, they retired in alarm (Josephus, *Life* 398–406).

This occasion was fixed in his memory because he was injured when his horse stumbled, at which point the tide turned in favor of Agrippa's troops. His description of this battle includes a number of details about geography which are critical for identifying the presently excavated et-Tell with the city described in literature as Bethsaida-Julias.

Following the Jewish revolt of 66–70 C.E., the city does not appear to play a significant role in historical events. In geographic reports of this region, Pliny the Elder in 77 C.E. notes simply the prominence of this city:

> There are four lovely cities on the Sea of Galilee: Julias and Hippos in the east and Tarichaeae and Tiberias in the west (Pliny, *Natural History* 5.15.71).

The second-century geographer Ptolemy likewise includes a short report:

> The four main cities of Galilee are Sepphoris, Capernaum, Tiberias, and Julias (Ptolemy, *Geographia* 5.16.4).

Because of the demise of Bethsaida-Julias, it is not mentioned by later secular writers.

Early Christian Sources

Although the name Julias is absent from early Christian literature, the name Bethsaida occurs eight times in the Gospels. It is significant that it occurs in various strata of the Gospels from the early sayings source Q to late Gospel according to John. The earliest reference to the city Bethsaida is the Q saying of Jesus recorded in both Matthew 11:20-24 and Luke 10:13-15:

> Then he began to reproach the cities in which most of his deeds of power had been done, because they did not repent. "Woe to you, Chorazin! Woe to you, Bethsaida! For if the deeds of power done in you had been done in Tyre and Sidon, they would have repented long ago in sackcloth and ashes. But I tell you, on the day of judgment it will be more tolerable for Tyre and Sidon than for you. And you, Capernaum,
> > will you be exalted to heaven?
> > > No, you will be brought down
> > > > to Hades.
>
> For if the deeds of power done in you had been done in Sodom, it would have remained until this day. But I tell you that on the day of judgment it will be more tolerable for the land of Sodom than for you" (Matt 11:20-24).

> "Woe to you, Chorazin! Woe to you, Bethsaida! For if the deeds of power done in you had been done in Tyre and Sidon, they would have repented long ago, sitting in sackcloth and ashes. But at the judgment it will be more tolerable for Tyre and Sidon than for you. And you, Capernaum,
> > will you be exalted to heaven?
> > > No, you will be brought down
> > > > to Hades" (Luke 10:13-15).

Although this saying of woe places Bethsaida in a negative light, it points to the centrality of the town in the ministry of Jesus—along with Capernaum and Chorazin—since most of his miracles were done there. As the only Galilean cities mentioned in Q, this points to the area around the north shore of the Sea of Galilee, known as "the evangelical triangle," as the center of Jesus' ministry.

The two references in Mark likewise point to miracle activity. In one of the few episodes included only in Mark, Jesus heals a blind man outside Bethsaida:

> They came to Bethsaida. Some people brought a blind man to him and begged him to touch him. He took the blind man by the hand and led him out of the village; and when he had put saliva on his eyes and laid his hands on him, he asked him, "Can you see anything?" And the man looked up and said, "I can see people, but they look like trees, walking." Then Jesus laid his hands on his eyes again; and he looked intently and his sight was restored, and he saw everything clearly. Then he sent him away to his home, saying, "Do not even go into the village" (Mark 8:22-26).

In Mark 6:45, the name is cited in the transitional verse between the miracles of the feeding of the 5,000 and the walking on the water:

> Immediately he made his disciples get into the boat and go on ahead to the other side, to Bethsaida, while he dismissed the crowd (Mark 6:45).

Luke, who omits the episode of the walking on water, does not include this reference to Bethsaida at the end of the feeding story. Instead Bethsaida is introduced at the beginning of the feeding:

> On their return the apostles told Jesus all they had done. He took them with him and withdrew privately to a city called Bethsaida. When the crowds found out about it, they followed him; and he welcomed them, and spoke to them about the kingdom of God, and healed those who needed to be cured (Luke 9:10-11).

This creates something of a problem since the two accounts portray Jesus going in opposite directions. Matthew does not mention Bethsaida in connection with the feeding episode.

The Gospel according to John differs from the Synoptic tradition in that citations to Bethsaida are not directly related to Jesus' miracle activity. Rather, Bethsaida is mentioned as the home of a number of the apostles. In the call narrative of the disciples in John 1:43-44, Philip is introduced as a disciple from the city of Bethsaida, the home of Andrew and Peter:

> The next day Jesus decided to go to Galilee. He found Philip and said to him, "Follow me." Now Philip was from Bethsaida, the city of Andrew and Peter (John 1:43-44).

Likewise, in John 12:21, the importance of this location is emphasized as the reader is reminded once again that Philip originated from Bethsaida:

> Now among those who went up to worship at the festival were some Greeks. They came to Philip, who was from Bethsaida in Galilee, and said

to him, "Sir, we wish to see Jesus." Philip went and told Andrew; then Andrew and Philip went and told Jesus (John 12:20-22).

The connection of Bethsaida to the miracle tradition is only indirect since both Philip and Andrew are main characters in the feeding miracle of chapter 6. A later scribe has also linked this site with the miracle story of the healing of the lame man in chapter 5 by changing the place name Bethzatha to Bethsaida:

> Now in Jerusalem by the Sheep Gate there is a pool, called in Hebrew Bethsaida, which has five porticoes (variant reading John 5:2).

The focus in the Book of Acts on the city of Jerusalem as the center of post-Easter activity of the disciples results in the absence of attention to the Galilean church and thus the mention of Bethsaida—as also other cities of the Gospels such as Capernaum, Chorazin, and Nazareth—is missing. The name never occurs in the rest of the New Testament.

In second-century Christian literature, however, interest in Bethsaida continues. In the Jewish-Christian Gospel of the Nazareans, the woe saying from Q is expanded to note that the miracles worked by Jesus there were 53 in number. On the other hand, 2 Esdras 1:11—written shortly after the Bar Kochba revolt in 132–5 C.E.—mentions the fulfillment of that woe saying, citing the destruction of Bethsaida as one more in a series of mighty works of God:

> Did I not destroy the city of Bethsaida because of you, and to the south burn two cities, Tyre and Sidon? (variant reading 2 Esdras 1:11).

However, even this important reference to the fate of the city is not without complication since one family of manuscripts omits reference to this New Testament city.

In later centuries, Bethsaida continues to be mentioned by interpreters of the gospel traditions and by pilgrims who visited the site. Among the more significant references is the report of the sixth-century visitor Theodosius:

> From Seven Springs [Tabgha] it is two miles to Capernaum. From Capernaum it is six miles to Bethsaida, where the Apostles Peter, Andrew, Philip, and the sons of Zebedee were born. From Bethsaida it is fifty miles to Pancas, that is the place where the Jordan rises from the two places Ior and Dan.[3]

Two centuries later Willibald wrote:

---

3. John Wilkinson, *Jerusalem Pilgrims Before the Crusades* (Westminster: Aris and Phillips, Ltd., 1977) 63. P. Donatus Baldi, *Enchirdion Locum Sanctorum* (Jerusalem, 1982), Section 381, 266.

From there [Capernaum], they went to Bethsaida, the city of Peter and Andrew; there is now a church there in the place where originally their house stood.[4]

In some cases one must allow for the possible preservation of authentic independent traditions, yet the tendency to speculative elaboration is often evident.

Rabbinic Literature

The names Bethsaida and Julias do not occur in rabbinic literature. However, there are a number of references to a place called Tzaidan, which have resulted in considerable debate. There are a number of issues to be dealt with. First of all, one is faced with the relatively late date of these sources even though they refer to figures from as early as the first century. Second, there are questions how this information fits evidence concerning the destruction of Bethsaida. One must consider the possibilities of a rebuilding of the former city as well as the relocation to a nearby site. Third, one is faced with a different name for this site, Tzaidan. Just as Christian sources preferred Bethsaida, and secular sources used Julias, it may be that rabbinic sources provide simply a variation in name. Fourth, there is confusion with the name Sidon for the prominent city on the Phoenician coast. Many older studies have assumed that location for the majority of texts. In some cases, one can judge from context which city is more likely, but, more often than not, that remains a difficult task.[5]

A number of significant readings are included which identify names of prominent rabbis. Among the earliest is one referring to Rabbi Yehudah ben Batayrah, a contemporary of Akiba at the very beginning of the second century:

> And it happened Rabbi Eleazar ben Shamoa and Rabbi Yohanan ha-Sandlar were going to Netzivim to study Torah with Rabbi Yehudah ben Batayrah. They arrived in Tzaidan and remembered the Land of Israel. Their eyes opened and filled with tears and they ripped their clothes . . . .They returned to their original place and said that living in the Land of Israel outweighs all the commandments in the Torah (Sifrei Devarim, Reeh 80:4.80).

---

4. Wilkinson, *Jerusalem Pilgrims Before the Crusades*, 128.
5. These issues are thoroughly discussed by Richard Freund, "The Search for Bethsaida in Rabbinic Literature," *Bethsaida: A City on the North Shore of the Sea of Galilee*, eds. Rami Arav and Freund (Kirksville, Mo.: Thomas Jefferson University Press, 1995) 267–311. See also Dan Urman, "Jews in the Golan," *Ancient Synagogues: Historical Analysis and Archaeological Discovery*, eds. Urman and Paul V. M. Flesher, (Leiden: E. J. Brill, 1995) 2:378–85.

The location of Bethsaida just to the east of the upper Jordan River is a fitting setting for this episode.

One of the names most frequently connected with Tzaidan is the important second-century Rabbi Simeon ben Gamaliel 2. Among the more significant passages relating his name is one that deals with fish:

> Rabbi Simeon ben Gamaliel said, "It happened that I went to Tzaidan, and they put before me more than three hundred kinds of fish in a single dish" (PT Sheqalim 6.2,50c).

Others describe legal concerns:

> If a man says this is your Get on condition that you give me two hundred Zuzim, she is divorced thereby and she has to give . . . Rabbi Simeon ben Gamaliel said: "It happened in Tzaidan that a man said to his wife, 'This is your Get on condition that you give me my robe,' and his robe was lost, and the Sages said that she should give him its value in money" (Mishnah Gittin 7:5).

> Rabbah bar Hanah said in the name of Rabbi Yohanan: "Wherever Rabbi Simeon ben Gamaliel gives a ruling in our Mishnah, the Halachah follows him, save in the matters of Surety, and Tzaidan, and of a later proof" (BT Gittin 75a).

Several passages refer to Rabbi Simeon ben Yohai, a student of Akiba and contemporary of Simeon ben Gamaliel:

> What is an Asherah? Any tree under which is located an idol. Rabbi Simeon says: "Any that people worship." It happened in Tzaidan, there was a tree that people worshipped, and they found a pile of stones underneath it. Rabbi Simeon said to them, "Investigate the type of pile of stones." They did investigate it and found an image in it. He said to them, "Since they are worshipping the image, let us permit them to make use of the tree" (Mishnah Avodah Zarah 3:7).

A later commentary provides yet a further incident from Tzaidan:

> It happened that there was a non-Jew in Tzaidan who used to write scrolls of the Law and the incident came before the Sages and they said it was permitted to buy from him (Tosefta Avodah Zarah 3:7).

Both incidents seem to point to settings with mixed population appropriate for Bethsaida. Another passage refers to a couple unable to have children and ends with a miraculous answer to prayer:

> If one has married a woman and lived with her for ten years and not produced offspring, he has not got the right to stop trying. Said Rabbi Idi, "It happened in Tzaidan that one who married a woman and stayed with her

ten years and they did not produce offspring. They came before Rabbi Simeon ben Yohai and wanted to be parted from one another. He said to them, 'By your lives! Just as you were joined to one another with eating and drinking, so you will be separated from one another only with eating and drinking.' They followed his counsel and made a festival and made a great banquet and drank too much. When his mind was at ease, he said to her, 'My daughter, see anything good that I have in the house! Take it and go to your father's house.' What did she do? After he fell asleep, she made gestures to her servants and serving women and said to them, 'Take him in the bed and pick him up and bring him to my father's house.' Around midnight he woke up from his sleep. When the wine wore off, he said to her, 'My daughter, where am I now?' She said to him, 'In my father's house.' He said to her, 'What am I doing in your father's house? But I have nothing in the world as good as you!' They went to Rabbi Simeon ben Yohai and he stood and prayed for them and they were answered (and given offspring)" (Song of Songs Rabbah 1. 4:89).

This passage and others above are characterized by the formula "It happened in Tzaidan." In Hebrew this construction includes the single letter ב to denote the preposition, thus resulting in the reading "BeTzaidan," extremely similar in pronunciation to Bethsaida.

A final passage mentions a figure who spent most of his life in the Golan region, Rabbi Judah ha-Nasi, the son of Simeon ben Gamaliel II:

> Rabbi Hanina said: "An incident in one wagon of the house of Rabbi that went more than four miles. The incident was brought before the sages and they permitted the use of that wine. They said, 'The incident took place on the highway of Tzaidan and it was completely of Israel'" (PT Avodah Zarah 5:5. 44d).

With good reason, some argue that the city of the apostles became the city of prominent rabbis. It may be that a conclusion will be possible only through further archaeological research.

Material Sources

Interest in the material remains of Bethsaida began as early as 1838 when the American explorer Edward Robinson[6] first visited the site of et-Tell, located a quarter of a mile east of the Jordan River and one and a half miles north of the Sea of Galilee. Although Robinson saw no problem in designating this site as the biblical city, a number of later explorers and

---

6. Edward Robinson, *Biblical Researches in Palestine and Adjacent Regions: A Journal of Travels in the Years 1838 & 1852* (2nd ed.; 3 vols.; London: Murray, 1856).

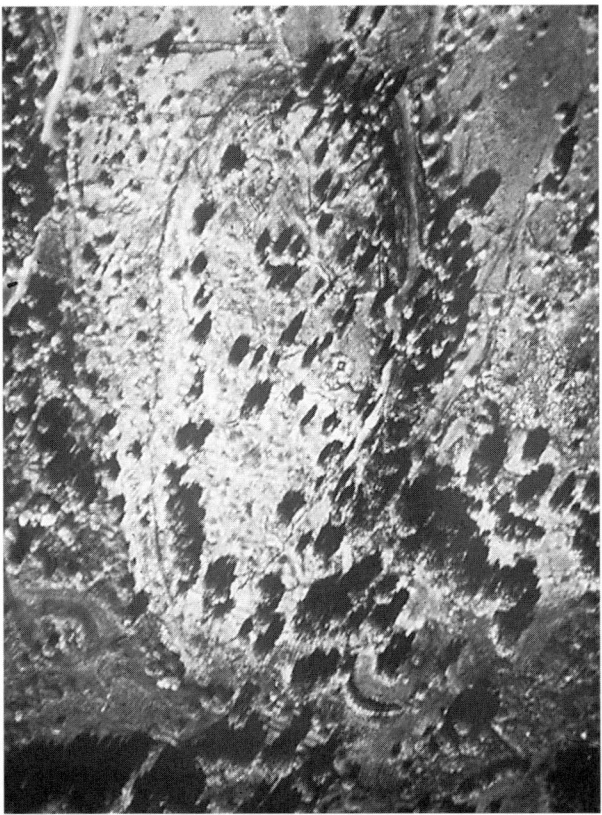
Aerial photograph of Tel-Bethsaida (north at top)

surveyors, such as Gottlieb Schumacher[7] and Dan Urman,[8] preferred a location on the modern shore line at either el-Araj or Mesadiye. Renewed interest in et-Tell came about primarily through the careful analysis of Benedictine Father Bargil Pixner[9] in the 1980s.

Because of geographic and political complexities, scientific stratified archaeological excavation began at et-Tell only in 1987. A decade of research has now been completed under the direction of Dr. Rami Arav.[10]

---

7. Gottlieb Schumacher, *The Jaulan* (London: R. Bentley, 1888).

8. Dan Urman, *The Golan: A Profile of a Region during the Roman and Byzantine Periods* (BAR International Series 269; Oxford: B.A.R., 1985).

9. Bargil Pixner, "Searching for the New Testament Site of Bethsaida," *BA* 48 (Dec. 1985) 207–16.

10. The excavations are presently organized as the Bethsaida Excavations Project with a consortium of schools under the direction of Dr. Richard Freund and the University of Nebraska at Omaha.

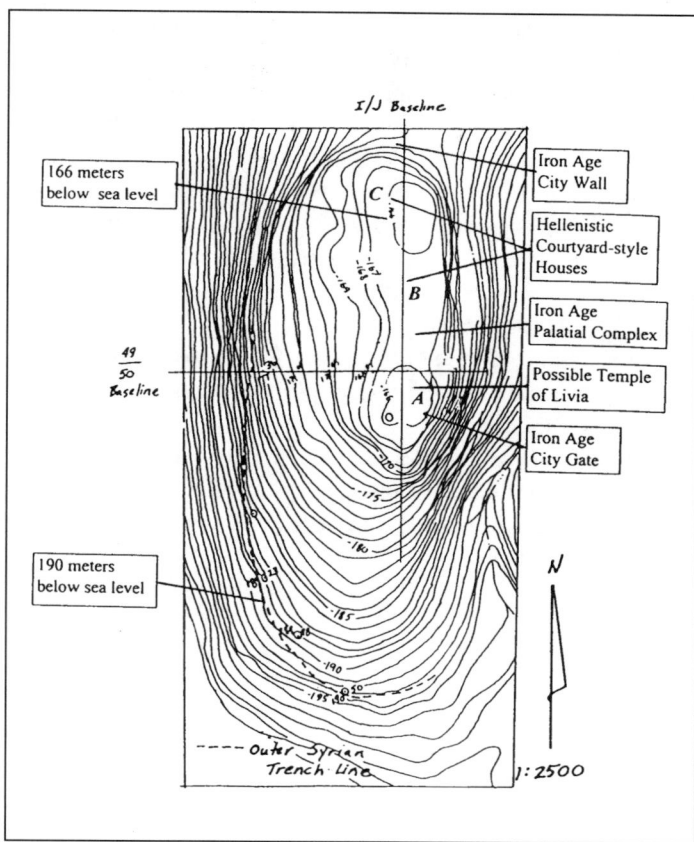

Topographical Plan of et-Tell

The findings of the Bethsaida Excavations Project are now being published in a series of reports by Thomas Jefferson University Press under the title *Bethsaida: A City by the North Shore of the Sea of Galilee.*[11]

Archaeology today involves a number of different disciplines to recover information about ancient sites like Bethsaida. Geological study is extremely important to this particular location because it is located on the major Jordan River rift where there is both gradual shifting of continental plates and where more dramatic earthquake activity has brought about changes throughout history. As we shall see in chapter 3, this is of special significance since the present geography of the site can be misleading with the remains of the fishing village located over a mile from the coastline of the sea.

11. Rami Arav, and Richard Freund, eds., *Bethsaida: A City by the North Shore of the Sea of Galilee,* volume 1 (Kirksville, Mo.: Thomas Jefferson University Press, 1985).

Archaeological excavation reveals much about the first-century city including information about city planning, the construction of houses, daily labor, lifestyle, diet, and trading patterns. Artifacts such as pottery shards, implements of work and war, ornaments of dress, building stones, bones, and a few statuettes provide a wealth of information about these inhabitants when analyzed carefully.

Unfortunately, there have been no significant inscriptions uncovered from this first-century site. Coin finds are always helpful sources of information concerning contact with other regions. This is even more significant during the first four decades of the first century when the ruler of this particular area, Philip, minted his own coins. Nineteen different coin types provide important clues concerning religion, politics, and culture as well as economics for this period.

While literary and archaeological sources are very different in nature and often lead to variant conclusions, it is crucial that our search for understanding ancient Bethsaida be carried out with a book in one hand and a trowel in the other.

Chapter 2

Bethsaida Prior to the New Testament

Josephus credits Philip, son of Herod, as the founder of Bethsaida-Julias. However, he makes it quite clear that Philip did not build the town out of nothing. Rather he took an already existing village and expanded it through additional settlers and building projects (Josephus, *Ant.* 18.28). Archaeology demonstrates that this already existing village had a long and rich history for many centuries. In describing this history, we can best refer to three distinct cities existing in different periods.

Bronze-Age Settlement

The site of et-Tell offered two basic characteristics looked for in building ancient settlements. It was located on a hill—presently situated about one hundred feet above the surrounding plain—and it had a fresh water spring at the southwest base of the hill. In addition, it was accessible to the Sea of Galilee with its resources for fishing and travel by boat. The Jordan River was situated less than a quarter mile to the west. An abundance of basalt stone for building is strewn throughout the area from earlier volcanic activity. The tell itself was relatively large comprising an area of nearly twenty acres.

The first settlement at Bethsaida comes from the early Bronze Age (3050–2700 B.C.E.). This is rather typical for the entire Golan region which was densely inhabited before a period when the population became quite sparse. Little is known about the city from this period—partly because excavators have concentrated on iron and Hellenistic levels—except that the city was surrounded by a stone wall.

Bethsaida During the Israelite Monarchy

The second settlement occurs in Iron Age II (1000–586 B.C.E.) or roughly the time of the Israelite monarchy in the Old Testament. This was a rather substantial settlement enclosed by an impressive city wall, now uncovered on both the northern and eastern sides of the tell. Sections of the wall appear to be over twenty feet wide, a figure which exceeds that of Jerusalem from this period. A magnificent four-chamber gateway, with paved entry and a well-preserved threshold, is located on the southeast. Visitors were greeted with an altar and three four-feet high stele, one of which shows the relief of a bull-headed man wearing a dagger.

The settlement centered around a large public building complex to the north of the gateway with a palatial structure and possibly a temple joined by a paved plaza area.[1] The discovery of a figurine with an *atef* headdress, similar to that described in 2 Samuel 12:30 of the Ammonite Milcom, a stamped jar handle depicting a figure in a prayer posture, upright stones resembling matzevoth, and perhaps the burned remains of an Asherah, all point to cultic activity in the 64 feet by 35 feet structure at the south end of the plaza. On the north end of the plaza was located a palatial structure known as Bit Hilani in the Assyrian-Aramean style which yielded numerous pottery vessels as well as clay loom weights. The discovery of a ninth-century Phoenician-style bulla (used to seal letters) demonstrates the importance of the city, its influence by Phoenician culture, and connections with Samaria the capital of the Northern Kingdom of Israel.[2] The

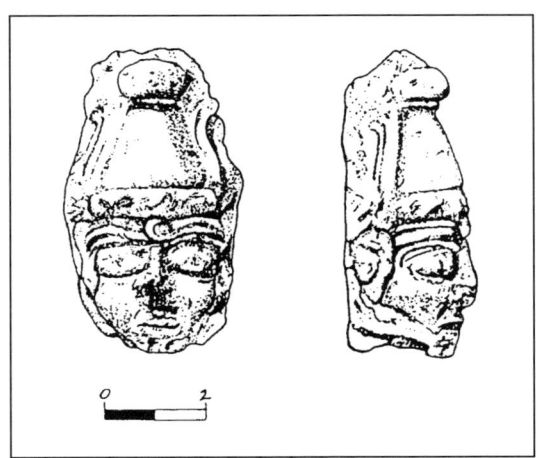

Clay Figurine with Atef *Headgear*

---

1. Rami Arav, "Bethsaida Excavations: Preliminary Report, 1987–1993," *Bethsaida* (1995) 7–18, 24–6.
2. Baruch Brandl, "An Israelite Bulla in Phoenician Style from Bethsaida (et-Tell)," *Bethsaida* (1995) 141–64.

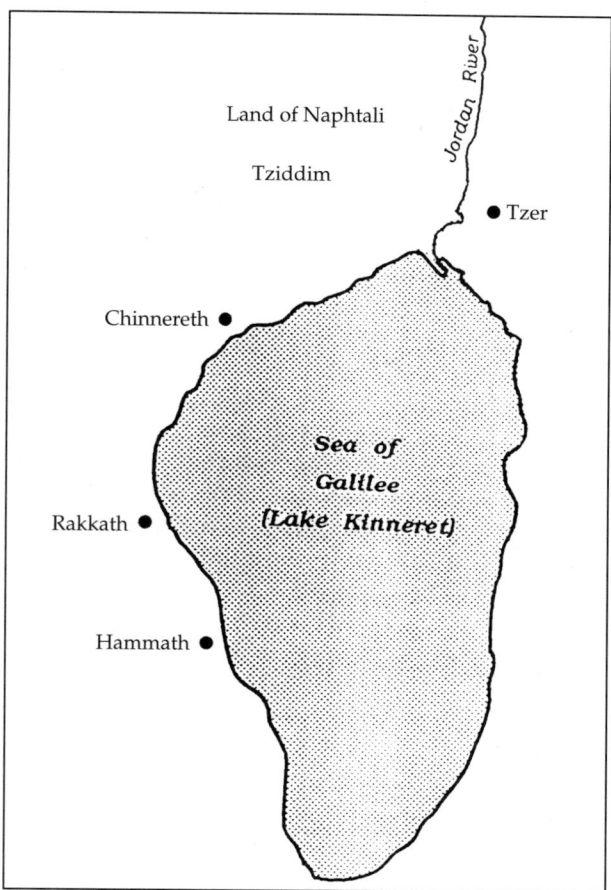

Fishing Cities on the Sea—Joshua 19:35

presence of a *Pataikos* statuette suggests trade relations also with Egypt.[3] These finds point to a rather substantial settlement during the Iron Age period for which there is no rival nearby.

One would expect a site so prominent to have been mentioned in the Old Testament. Yet the name "Bethsaida" is absent. The mention of the fortified city Tzer in Joshua 19:35 fits both in terms of location and possible description as a fisherman's city in the land of Naphtali, Tziddim. Because of similarity in the formation of letters *resh* and *dalet*, it is not difficult to see how Tzer in the Biblical manuscripts was originally

---

3. Rami Arav, "An Iron Age Amulet from the Galilee," *BAR* (Jan./Feb. 1995) 44. Rami Arav and Monika Bernett, "An Egyptian Figurine of Pataikos at Bethsaida," IEJ (1997, 47:3-4) 198–213. IEJ=Israel Exploration Journal.

Tzed—a name linguistically similar to Bethsaida.[4] At the time of the early monarchy, this region was known as the land of the Geshurites. This is especially significant since the Geshurite King Talmai gave his daughter Maacah's hand in marriage to David (2 Sam 3:3). Their son was the well-known Absalom, who led a popular revolt against his father using the Geshurite capital for three years as his base (2 Sam 13:37-39). When one compares the size of et-Tell (20 acres) with sites excavated in the "Land of Geshur Project," such as Hadar (2.5 acres) and Soreg (1 acre), one must seriously consider the likelihood that Talmai's Geshurite capital has been discovered at Bethsaida.[5] The continuation of the name Maacah among wives of later kings of Judah suggests the persistence of the close relationship of these two kingdoms (1 Kgs 15:2, 10, 13; 2 Chr 11:20; 15:16). The Geshurite kingdom was probably at some point incorporated into the Northern Kingdom of Israel although it appears to have later fallen under the sway of Damascus to the north. An eighth-century destruction layer at Bethsaida supports the picture of the Assyrian conquest under Tiglath Pileser and Shalmaneser. Attempts at subsequent rebuilding were modest until the end of the Iron Age period in the sixth century B.C.E.

Bethsaida in the Early Hellenistic Period

The third settlement occurs primarily in the Hellenistic age perhaps as early as the fifth century B.C.E. Although nothing is known about this settlement from literary sources, it appears that Bethsaida was a flourishing city during this period. Coin finds may provide our most important evidence. The first coins come from the mid-fifth century B.C.E. including two from Phoenicia and one from Athens, well before Alexander the Great brought Greek culture east. It was certainly not an isolated city. No less than twenty-eight coins minted in Alexandria and Tyre come from the period when Palestine was under control of the Egyptian Ptolemies (285–21 B.C.E.). On the basis of numbers of coins, one might gather that the high point of this city came in the late third and second centuries B.C.E. when the city was under the control of the Seleucids of Syria. Sixty seven or one third of all coins discovered at Bethsaida come from this period.

Following the Maccabean revolt in 167 B.C.E., Jewish independence was restored once again. Josephus describes the conquests of Alexander Jannaeus in these northern regions in 83–81 B.C.E., not only bringing them

---

4. Rami Arav, "Bethsaida, Tzer, and the Fortified Cities of Naphtali," *Bethsaida* (1995) 193–202.
5. M. Kochavi, T. Renner, I. Spar, and E. Yadin, "Rediscovered! The Land of Geshur," *BAR* (July/Aug. 1992) 31–44, 84–5.

under the political sway of Jerusalem, but also circumcising the males to incorporate them into the Jewish religion (Josephus, *Ant.* 13.393-397) and settling others. Presumably this also includes Bethsaida although it is not specifically mentioned among conquered towns (Josephus, *War* 1.104-105). Coin finds include eighteen Hasmonean coins (136–63 B.C.E.) minted in Jerusalem, which depict Jewish symbols and avoid pagan imagery. Yet there is no evidence of expansion at Bethsaida during this period, nor is there absolute evidence of Jewish practice. There are no synagogues, no ritual baths, no distinctively Jewish architectural fragments or images. In fact, an analysis of bones gathered from the city in Hellenistic layers includes those of the forbidden pig. The description of Josephus is perhaps most instructive that Bethsaida, like the whole region of the Golan, contains a mixed population of Jews and Syrians (Josephus, *War* 3.57).

Chapter 3

Home of the Apostles

Bethsaida, more than any other New Testament town, can rightly be called the home of the apostles. Specific references in the Gospels link three disciples of Jesus to Bethsaida, namely, Simon Peter, Andrew, and Philip. Later traditions also connect James and John, as well as the other James, to Bethsaida. No other location can make such a claim about the disciples.

The Synoptics and the Apostles

From the beginning Jesus was identified in terms of his childhood home: Jesus of Nazareth. However, the Synoptic Gospels show absolutely no interest in identifying the places of origin of the disciples. A possible exception is Judas Iscariot since the Hebrew *Ish* (= man) could possibly connect Judas with the town of Kerioth in Judea. At least as well accepted is the theory that the name Iscariot characterizes Judas as a "man of the dagger" (sicarius) or "man of red hair" (seqar) or "man of lies" (seqarya). This fits more the pattern of the Synoptic writers (Mark 3:16-19; Matt 10:2-4; Luke 6:14-16) who describe Simon as the rock or foundation (Peter); James and John as "sons of thunder" (Boanerges); and the other Simon as Zealot (= Qanana in Aramaic). Elsewhere the Synoptics give patronymics such as "sons of Zebedee" for James and John; "Bar-Jonah" (Matt 16:17) for Simon Peter; and "son of Alphaeus" for James (Mark 3:18) and also for Levi (Mark 2:14). In no case do the Synoptics connect these disciples with particular towns or regions.

The Fourth Gospel and the Apostles

The Fourth Gospel, in contrast, identifies the places of origin of four disciples. In the later appendix, Nathanael is identified as coming from

Cana, presumably located near Nazareth in Galilee (John 21:2)—this in spite of no such identification when Nathanael was first introduced in the opening chapter (John 1:45). In John 1:44, the writer identifies three disciples with the city of Bethsaida: "Now Philip was from Bethsaida, the city of Andrew and Peter."

This identification of Bethsaida as the home of three disciples is interesting for several reasons.[1] First, it raises to prominence Philip, a disciple who does not really play a major role in the Synoptic reports. Second, it mentions Andrew and Peter as if it were already common knowledge that Bethsaida was the home of these two brothers. Third, it is surprising to find Peter mentioned last since the name of Andrew usually follows that of Peter with the notation "brother of Simon Peter." Fourth, the information in this verse is later repeated in the same gospel: "They came to Philip, who was from Bethsaida in Galilee" (John 12:21). The fourth evangelist is clearly presenting a different tradition from the Synoptics. Nevertheless, it need not be treated as a late tradition. John 1:44 is usually attributed to an early signs source which focused on the deeds of Jesus as signs of his messianic role.[2] The information passed on may well have developed in the context of an early Jewish-Christian community in the same area as that of Jesus' ministry.[3]

The Character of the Bethsaida Disciples

The association of these three disciples with Bethsaida is consistent with our knowledge of this community. Philip's name is quite appropriate since the region around Bethsaida was governed by the rather popular son of Herod, also named Philip. The names of all three of these disciples, in fact, are Greek in contrast to all the other disciples who have Semitic names. Although Simeon was a popular Hebrew name, Simon was the Greek form of that name. This is consistent with the description by Josephus that this area contained "a mixed population of Jews and Syrians" (Josephus, *War* 3.57) and that the ruler Philip had elevated Bethsaida to the status of a Greek *polis* (Josephus, *Ant.* 18.28). Presumably a Greek education was made available and the Greek language was spoken. Thus it is not surprising that when Greeks wish to see Jesus, they make use of Philip and Andrew as intermediaries (John 12:20-24). It is difficult to

1. Mark Appold, "The Mighty Works of Bethsaida: Witness of the New Testament and Related Traditions," *Bethsaida* (1995) 229–42.
2. Robert Fortna, *The Fourth Gospel and Its Predecessor: From Narrative Source to Present Gospel* (Philadelphia: Fortress Press, 1988).
3. K. Wengst, *Bedrängte Gemeinde und verherrlichter Christus* (Neukirchen-Vluyn: Neukirchener, 1983).

imagine the success of Simon's missionary journeys to Antioch, Corinth, and Rome without some knowledge of the Greek language. Even the attribution of the name "Peter" by Jesus implies some knowledge of Greek. The connection with the Greek term πετρός meaning "rocky" is appropriate, not just in terms of Simon's subsequent leadership role, but also because the area around Bethsaida is characterized by the rocky soil with volcanic basalt rock scattered everywhere. The connection of Philip, Andrew, and Peter with Bethsaida is thus quite fitting.

Bethsaida in Galilee

The expression "Bethsaida of Galilee" (John 12:21) has been a concern for some since the location of et-Tell was not included in the political realm of Galilee governed by Antipas during the time of Jesus. It has been suggested that this demonstrates the lack of precise geographical knowledge or that it points to the existence of two Bethsaidas, one in Galilee and the other in the Golan.[4] However, one must understand that the expression is used in a Jerusalem context and merely designates the general area in the north away from Jerusalem. In the same way, the Easter directive for the disciples to go to Galilee where they will see Jesus (Mark 16:7) points to a return to the area frequented by Jesus during his ministry along the northern shores of the Sea of Galilee, including both the Galilee and the Golan. In the latter part of the first century, both the Golan and Galilee were connected under the rule of Agrippa 2. Thus it was not unusual for later texts to speak of Bethsaida-Julias as a city of Galilee.[5]

The Call Narratives of the Disciples

Another difficulty with this statement about Bethsaida as home of the disciples is that it occurs in the midst of a call narrative quite different from the more familiar Synoptic accounts. The familiar picture is that of Jesus passing along the western shore of the Sea of Galilee where he sees two pairs of brothers fishing and he calls them to leave their nets to follow him. The Johannine picture also presents Jesus encountering four individuals (John 1:35-51). The names Peter and Andrew are the same, but here are found Philip and Nathanael rather than James and John. There is no motif of fishing and it is through the intervention of Andrew and Philip that Peter and Nathanael are called. Most significant is that the calling takes place before Jesus goes to Galilee (John 1:43).

---

4. Bargil Pixner, "The Search for the Lost City of Bethsaida," *BA* (Dec. 1985) 207–16.
5. Ptolemy, *Geographia* 5.16.4; Pliny, *Natural History* 5.15.71.

On closer analysis, the Synoptic picture is not so fixed as the traditional view assumes. Place names on the western side of the sea are not included in the call episodes. The early Markan account mentions only that "Jesus passed along the Sea of Galilee" (Mark 1:16). It is not until verse 21 that Capernaum is first mentioned. The Matthean and Lukan accounts of the call of the disciples (Matt 4:18-22 and Luke 5:1-11) likewise are not in themselves tied to any particular geographic location on the sea. However, these later accounts make the connection by implication since they have already mentioned Jesus' ministry in Capernaum (Matt 4:13 and Luke 4:31). Matthew is even stronger in creating that impression since Jesus has established his home in this town on the western shore.

A more realistic picture may be that presented by Q in which Jesus travels about within the evangelical triangle of Chorazin, Bethsaida, and Capernaum (Matt 11:20-21 = Luke 10:13-15) "without a place to lay his head" (Matt 8:20 = Luke 9:58).

Excursus: "The House of Peter" at Capernaum

This discussion is important since modern visitors to Capernaum are shown the remains of what is called "The House of St. Peter"—perhaps in conflict with the reports connecting Peter with Bethsaida. The archaeological reports about this house demonstrate that early Christians clearly believed that this house had some significance for the life of Jesus and the Church.[6] This was established by the presence of a fifth-century octagonal structure, which corresponds in style to other church buildings erected during this period to commemorate places and events important in the life of Jesus. This is corroborated by the report of the Spanish pilgrim Egeria who visited this area in the late fourth century and writes:

> In Capernaum a house-church was made out of the home of the prince of the apostles, whose walls still stand today as they were.

These words actually point to a building already existing prior to the octagonal church and found underneath later structures.

When archaeologists dug below these structures they discovered a regular domestic dwelling which was first inhabited in the middle of the first century B.C.E. The structure was built around a central courtyard with smaller rooms both to the north and to the south. A second courtyard existed to the south of the house. The main entrance to the house was on the

---

6. Virgilio Corbo, "The Church of the House of St. Peter at Capernaum," *Ancient Churches Revealed,* ed. Yoram Tsafrir (Jerusalem: Israel Exploration Society, 1993) 71–6. James F. Strange and Herschel Shanks, "Has the House Where Jesus Stayed in Capernaum been Found?" *BAR* (Nov./Dec. 1982) 26–37.

east and there was also located a larger (20 feet by 21 feet) room which had doorways leading to both courtyards. Its floor was composed of unworked basalt stone. This particular house was larger than most that were found in Capernaum, but there was nothing extraordinary during this stage of occupation. The regular assortment of domestic pottery was found throughout the house.

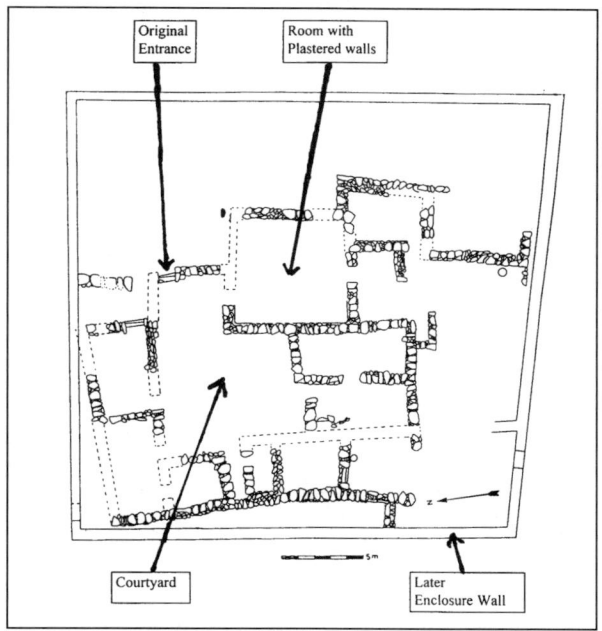

Peter's House in Capernaum

Later in the second half of the first century C.E., a major change took place. The east room was plastered, which is without parallel for structures at Capernaum. There was also a significant change in the pottery found from this time on. Instead of regular domestic pottery, only lamps and storage jars were found. This suggests that this structure was now restricted for public gatherings. While this in itself could be interpreted in various ways, the continuing development of this site clearly suggests that the early inhabitants associated the structure with the life of Jesus.

During the following centuries, the central room was replastered and various graffiti were etched on the walls including crosses and boats and the words "Christ" and "Lord." The inscriptions were primarily Greek although a few were in Semitic languages and one in Latin. Some have interpreted roughly etched inscriptions also to include the name of Peter, but this is not convincing.[7] In the fourth century, the entire house was walled off from the rest of the compound and an atrium 27 feet by 10 feet was constructed on the east side. Within the plastered room, two pilasters were erected on the north and south apparently to support an arch for a new roof. It would be assumed that this is the structure visited by Egeria, which was then replaced a century later by the more elaborate octagonal church. Today a modern church structure is suspended above the archaeological remains.

Although this structure has been labeled as the house of Peter, one must be careful not to make hasty conclusions. There is no hard evidence from the first century linking Peter to this site. However, the finds do present a convincing case that this structure was viewed by early Christians as having importance in the life of Jesus. Normally, early churches were established over places long considered sacred including sites of theophanies, but they are not usually erected over domestic dwellings. Is it possible that this structure simply represented a typical house church with no memorial significance? Perhaps one of the wealthier Christians from Capernaum made it available for gatherings because it was one of the larger structures in this community. If, however, it also had a commemorative purpose, can one be certain it accurately reflects a particular event in the life of Jesus? It was not until the mid-first century that this structure was set apart. Can we be sure that they had accurate knowledge of events taking place a generation earlier? Is it possible that the site commemorated the general work in Capernaum rather than a single event? If it represents one particular event, then which event? These questions are not to say that this building is without importance. It does represent an early gathering place for the church—perhaps one of the earliest that can be established. Yet one can only speculate from that point on.

The conclusion that this house once belonged to Simon Peter is based on a single episode in the Synoptics. Upon Jesus' first visit to Capernaum, after visiting the synagogue on the Sabbath, he was called upon to heal Peter's mother-in-law who was suffering from a fever. A comparison of the Synoptic texts follows:

Matthew 8:14-15	*Mark 1:29-31*	*Luke 4:38-39*
When Jesus entered Peter's house,	As soon as they left the synagogue, they entered the house of Simon and	After leaving the synagogue he entered Simon's house.

---

7. Strange and Shanks, "Has the House Where Jesus Stayed in Capernaum been Found?"

Matthew 8:14-15	Mark 1:29-31	Luke 4:38-39
he saw his mother-in-law lying in bed with a fever; he touched her hand, and the fever left her, and she got up and began to serve him.	Andrew, with James and John. Now Simon's mother-in-law was in bed with a fever, and they told him about her at once. He came and took her by the hand and lifted her up. Then the fever left her, and she began to serve them.	Now Simon's mother-in-law was suffering from a high fever, and they asked him about her. Then he stood over her and rebuked the fever, and it left her. Immediately she got up and began to serve them.

The focus of this account is on Peter's mother-in-law, not on Peter himself. Many have seen this as a way to avoid the discrepancy with Peter's Bethsaida connection. They would argue that Peter merely married into a family from Capernaum. Possibly, because of fishing connections, he relocated to this particular city or he considered Capernaum a second home and visited there often. Still this solution leaves a number of questions unanswered.

The Markan account notes that Jesus' visit to the house occurred as soon as he left the Capernaum synagogue. This has been advanced as an argument for the authenticity of the house church because of its proximity to the synagogue—assuming a first-century synagogue is represented by the black basalt foundation beneath the impressive third century limestone structure. Yet Mark uses the word εὐθύς (immediately, as soon as) some 41 times to convey a sense of urgency for the entire gospel. As is frequently the case both Matthew and Luke have omitted it. So its occurrence at the beginning of this account need not be used to determine the location of the house.

This also raises several questions. Would Peter have possessed a house in such a prominent location? Would it be likely that such a house be more than substantial in size? The excavated house church comprises about 3,500 square feet and includes two courtyards. This stands in contrast to the smaller houses in the insula between the house church and the synagogue. In his book on comparative dwellings from this period, Hirschfeld includes as the best example of a courtyard house from Capernaum one which has an area less than half the size (1,600 square feet).[8] On the other hand, "the house of Peter" at Capernaum is roughly the size of the two excavated courtyard houses at Bethsaida (the house in area B is 4,200

---

8. Yizhar Hirschfeld, *The Palestinian Dwelling in the Roman-Byzantine Period* (Jerusalem: Franciscan Printing Press, 1995) 68–9. See also comparative charts on pages 100–1.

square feet and the house in area C is about 2,700 square feet)—which have been interpreted as homes exhibiting a rather comfortable lifestyle. The excavated house, therefore, is out of character with what we know about and expect of Peter.

There is also a question of why the early Christians plastered the walls on only one room in this structure setting it apart from the rest of the house. It would seem that they wished to designate it as the place where something significant had taken place. In this particular account, the memorable event is the healing of Peter's mother-in-law of a fever. Yet the healing apparently does not take place in the central part of the house. In the early Markan version, "they told him about her," which suggests that she was reclining in one of the side bedrooms—something that would be expected. Thus there seems to be no direct connection between the plastered room and this particular miracle of Jesus.

Finally, there is reason to question whether Peter even owned a house at Capernaum. The point of the call narrative in Mark 1:16-20 is that the disciples have left behind their occupations, families, and possessions. Later Peter proclaims, "Look, we have left everything and followed you" (Mark 10:28). The actual miracle of the healing of Peter's mother-in-law was probably an independent unit (Mark 1:30-31) that was later combined with other materials to present a typical day in the life of Jesus. The introductory verse 29, which ties this episode to Capernaum, appears to be the work of the evangelist Mark. The sentence itself is quite awkward as it provides continuity with the call episode naming again not only Simon, but also Andrew, James, and John. The description that it was the house of both Simon and Andrew creates something of an unusual situation with the presence also of Peter's mother-in-law. The changes in both Matthew and Luke demonstrate that they also see the difficulties of Mark's introduction. They omit reference to the other disciples, James and John, and they describe the house as belonging only to Peter. A more likely scenario is that the house belonged to Peter's mother-in-law and that it was Peter who was merely visiting. The tradition that Peter owned a house at Capernaum, therefore, is suspect. If he does have a link to Capernaum, it is possibly through marriage.

What then is the significance of the house church at Capernaum? The Gospels relate a number of other events which take place in houses at Capernaum. According to Synoptic reports Jesus himself may have had a house at Capernaum. Mark 2:1 reports that when Jesus returned to Capernaum he was ἐν οἴκῳ. This can be translated as "in a house" or "at home." The Matthean tradition is stronger stating that Jesus "made his home in Capernaum" (Matt 4:13). It is here apparently that he taught the crowds so that on one occasion some had to make a hole in the thatched roof (characteristic of Capernaum building) to let down a paralytic before Jesus (Mark 2:1-12). On another occasion, this is the setting for further teaching with the crowds when Jesus' family comes down from Nazareth and seeks to control him (Mark 3:19-35). Is it possible that the Capernaum house church commemorated this teaching activity? Yet again one wonders if this larger house is really fitting for the character of Jesus.

The Gospels, however, do report about two individuals who would be quite at home in such a large house in this prominent location in Capernaum. One is a centurion stationed in Capernaum who sought Jesus' help to heal his slave (Luke 7:1-10). The other is Jairus who sought Jesus' help to save his daughter from the point of death (Mark 5:21-43). In the case of the centurion, Luke writes that "he loves our people, and it is he who built our synagogue for us."[9] In the case of Jairus, all three Synoptic writers describe him as the "leader of the synagogue" (Mark 5:22; Matt 9:18-26; Luke 8:41-56). The excavated house church would be appropriate for either of these men.

The story of Jairus is especially appealing because Jesus actually came to his house and raised his daughter from death. The courtyard setting and the large eastern room provide a proper context for a wake. Thus Mark notes that Jesus "came to the house" and "saw a commotion, people weeping and wailing loudly" (Mark 5:38). Then "he put them all outside, and took the child's father and mother and those who were with him, and went in where the child was" (Mark 5:40). The room where they gathered, therefore, becomes the scene of one of the most dramatic of Jesus' miracles, bringing the child from death to life. Not only does the setting of the excavated house fit the details of the miracle account, but one can easily imagine the possibility that a grateful Jairus later made his house available for the gathering of the early Christian community in Capernaum and that the actual room was eventually marked off in commemoration.

This discussion has attempted to show that there are difficulties with Father Corbo's designation of the Capernaum house church as "The House of St. Peter" and that a number of alternative explanations are just as attractive. Yet there is no way to prove the ownership of this house for the time of Jesus' ministry in Capernaum, whether it belonged to Peter, Jairus, or anyone else. What can be established is that a generation or so later, this building was set apart for a special purpose, probably as a gathering place for the Christian community. The designation of this site as

---

9. The parallel account in Matthew 8:5-13 does not include this detail. A variant account in John 4:46-54 raises questions about historical details.

"the house of Peter" did not come about until the fourth century—after the gospel reports had established a connection between Peter and the town of Capernaum. Since these written reports derive from a single problematical verse in Mark, one must treat them with some degree of skepticism. In no way do they challenge the Johannine report that Bethsaida was the home of Peter and Andrew.

Later Traditions: Bethsaida and Other Disciples

As the era of pilgrimage began, European Christians found interest in establishing the places of the apostles.[10] Constantine allowed a certain Jewish-Christian named Josephos from Tiberias to build churches at Sepphoris, Nazareth, Tiberias, and Capernaum. In the fifth century, the elaborate octagonal church singled out Capernaum for special attention. Just as Egeira reported on the connection of Peter to the house church at Capernaum, so others were attracted to Bethsaida.

In 530 C.E., Theodosius demonstrated that the Bethsaida tradition for Peter and Andrew had not subsided, but that it continued alongside the Capernaum tradition. The account of Theodosius is especially noteworthy because he establishes the geographical information for the sites. He writes about the northern sea of Galilee area as follows:

> From Seven Springs [Tabgha] it is two miles to Capernaum. From Capernaum it is six miles to Bethsaida, where the Apostles Peter, Andrew, Philip, and the sons of Zebedee were born. From Bethsaida it is fifty miles to Paneas, that is the place where the Jordan rises from the two places Ior and Dan.[11]

The distance between Bethsaida and Capernaum as six miles may seem at first too long to the modern traveler crossing from Capernaum to Bethsaida via the modern Aphik Bridge. In reality, it denotes authenticity for the ancient traveler who naturally followed the ancient Roman road via Chorazin. The traditions reported, therefore, seem to be gathered from an on-site visitation.

Theodosius reports that five apostles were born in Bethsaida. The first three names correspond to the Johannine list although Philip is no longer prominent. Peter, possibly because of his reputation, is now mentioned first. By referring to those "born" in Bethsaida, Theodosius seems to reflect knowledge of the complexity of the traditions. Yet the addition of the

---

10. I credit Elizabeth McNamer, who has presented several papers on this topic, with many of the insights which follow.
11. John Wilkinson, *Jerusalem Pilgrims Before the Crusades*, 63. P. Donatus Baldi, *Enchiridion Locum Sanctorum*, Section 381, 266.

two sons of Zebedee, James and John, naturally follows because of the fishing partnership between the four disciples as well as the connection by friendship as the inner circle among disciples of Jesus. It is impossible to know whether this information is derived from independent sources or from a process of deduction using the gospel texts. This report, however, elevates the status of Bethsaida as the home of five disciples.[12] What is striking is that these names occur at the top of all lists of the twelve disciples suggesting their importance (Mark 3:16-19; Matt 10:2-4; Luke 6:14-16; Acts 1:13).

Two centuries later in 725 C.E., Willibald, later the first bishop of Eichstätt in Bavaria, also visited the site and left his report:

> From there [Capernaum], they went to Bethsaida, the city of Peter and Andrew; there is now a church there in the place where originally their house stood.[13]

Here the place of Peter and Andrew has been elevated so that Philip has dropped out of the picture. However, the mention of the church may point to a confusion with a visit to Capernaum. There is no archaeological evidence for such a structure at Bethsaida.

The ninth-century Saxon gospel, known as *The Heliand*, does not mention Bethsaida by name. However, it provides an intriguing version of the call of the disciples:

> He walked along the shore of a body of water where the Jordan has created a sea on the border of Galileeland. There He found the brothers, Andrew and Peter, sitting by the stream at the place where they worked hard setting out their nets on the wide waters as they fished in the current. . . . He told them that He would give them so much of God's kingdom. "Just as you catch fish here in the Jordan river, you will be hauling in the sons of men hand over hand . . . ."

> As they came farther along the seashore, they came across an old man and his two sons, James and John, young men, sitting by the sea. The father and his sons were sitting up on a sand dune. They were hard at work with both hands repairing and reweaving the nets that they had torn the night before on the water.[14]

---

12. The Nestorian Bishop Shelemon of Basra also includes the tradition that these five disciples were from Bethsaida. He cites as his source Eusebius of Caesarea. Ernest A. Wallis Budge, *The Book of the Bee: The Syriac Text* (Oxford: Clarendon Press, 1886) 103–5.

13. Wilkinson, *Jerusalem Pilgrims Before the Crusades*, 128.

14. G. Ronald Murphy, trans., *The Heliand: The Saxon Gospel* (New York: Oxford University Press, 1992) 40–1.

While there is no question that *The Heliand* includes much elaboration to relate the gospel tradition to a Germanic audience,[15] this episode includes several details which point to the possibility of an independent tradition. First, the name Andrew is given prominence over Peter. Second, there is no mention of the town of Capernaum. Third, the linking of this event with the Jordan River is unique since the Gospels never even mention the upper Jordan. Fourth, the geographical description of the mouth of the upper Jordan River opening into the Sea of Galilee is quite accurate in our understanding of first-century geography. Fifth, the account correctly characterizes the upper Jordan as the eastern boundary of Galilee at the time of Jesus. It is impossible to know whether such details originate in an early tradition or whether they came from the reports of pilgrims such as Willibald. However, they point to the fishing activity of disciples nearby Bethsaida.

Later the Syrian author Simon of Bassora mentions a prayer house erected by the apostle Philip.[16] One would tend to give some credibility to such a report because it gives focus to Philip rather than Peter and Andrew. Still, it is not substantiated by other documentation.

One also is faced with the problem in the Middle Ages that the site of Bethsaida became lost and alternative sites were proposed. Maps frequently positioned the city of Bethsaida on the west side of the Jordan near Capernaum. This resulted in a confusion of information rather than solutions. During this period further speculation linked Bethsaida with other disciples including James, son of Alphaeus, and Bartholomew.[17] Clearly Bethsaida had the reputation as "City of the Apostles."

---

15. G. Ronald Murphy, *The Saxon Savior: The Germanic Transformation of the Gospel in the Ninth-Century Heliand* (New York: Oxford, 1989) 58–61.

16. F. M. Abel, *Géographie de la Palestine* (Paris: Librarie Lecoffre, 1967) 2:195.

17. The name Bartholomew is usually thought to be derived from "Son of Ptolemy." However, it is possible that the actual meaning comes from "Son of Talmai," which could be a distant connection with the Geshurite king, grandfather of Absalom. The connection of Bartholomew with Bethsaida is interesting because he has often been identified with Nathanael, mentioned only in the Fourth Gospel. John 1 clearly links Nathanael with Philip from Bethsaida and it is only the later appendix in John 21 which connects Nathanael with the town of Cana.

Chapter 4

"Across the Sea . . . to Bethsaida"

Bethsaida-Julias is consistently depicted in ancient literature as a city by the sea. Pliny notes that Julias was one of four prominent seaside cities and that it was located on the eastern shore:

> There are four lovely cities on the Sea of Galilee: Julias and Hippos in the east and Tarichaeae and Tiberias in the west (Pliny, *Natural History* 5.15.71).

Josephus notes that it is located "in lower Gaulanitis" (Josephus, *War* 2.168) and that the Jordan River entered the lake just "below the town" (Josephus, *War* 3.515). In his own eyewitness report of the battle which took place outside Bethsaida between Galilean and Roman forces in 67 C.E., he includes a number of details which corroborate the location (Josephus, *Life* 398-406). He notes the position of the Jordan River just to the west; he reports the arrival of supporting troops by boat from Tarichaeae (Magdala); and he mentions how he himself had to be transported, presumably by boat, from Bethsaida-Julias to Capernaum (Cepharnocus) when he was injured as his horse stumbled in marshy ground. There is no question about the location of Bethsaida on the northeast shore of the Sea of Galilee.

General Gospel References

In the Gospel accounts, one is struck by the frequent reports of Jesus and his disciples traveling by boat over the northern part of the sea with Bethsaida often included in the itinerary. One interesting sidelight to these reports is that the evangelists often describe the trips to or from Bethsaida as *across the sea*. In Mark 8:13, before Jesus went to heal a blind man at Bethsaida, he got into a boat and "went across to the other side." In this

Bethsaida According to Josephus

case Mark makes clear the points of departure and arrival as Dalmanutha (Magadan in Matt 15:39 = Magdala or Taricheae), half-way down the western coast (Mark 8:10), and Bethsaida on the northeast (Mark 8:22). In contrast, in describing a trip by boat between two locations on the western shore (Capernaum and Dalmanutha), the evangelist merely reports that Jesus "went by boat" (Mark 8:10; Matt 15:39). There is no connotation of crossing.

The Feeding of the 5,000

Likewise the expressions "they went across" or "to the other side" occur in connection with the miracles of the feeding of the 5,000 and the walking on the water. In this context, Bethsaida is mentioned explicitly in both Mark 6:44 and Luke 9:10—the travel descriptions are as follows:

Before Feeding

> Mark 6:32—They went away *in the boat* to a deserted place by themselves.
> Matt 14:13—He withdrew from there *in a boat* to a deserted place by himself.
> Luke 9:10—He took them with him and withdrew privately to a city called Bethsaida.
> John 6:1—Jesus went *to the other side* of the Sea of Galilee.

After Feeding

> Mark 6:45—He made his disciples get *into the boat* and go on ahead *to the other side,* to Bethsaida.
> Matt 14:22—He made the disciples get *into the boat* and go on ahead *to the other side*.
> John 6:16-17—His disciples went down to the sea, got *into a boat*, and started *across the sea* to Capernaum.

Upon Return to Land

> Mark 6:53—When they had *crossed over*, they came to land at Gennesaret.
> Matt 14:34—When they had *crossed over*, they came to land at Gennesaret.
> John 6:21—The boat *reached the land* toward which they were going.

At the beginning of our analysis it is important to make two points. First, Luke contains only a description of the departure because he omits the

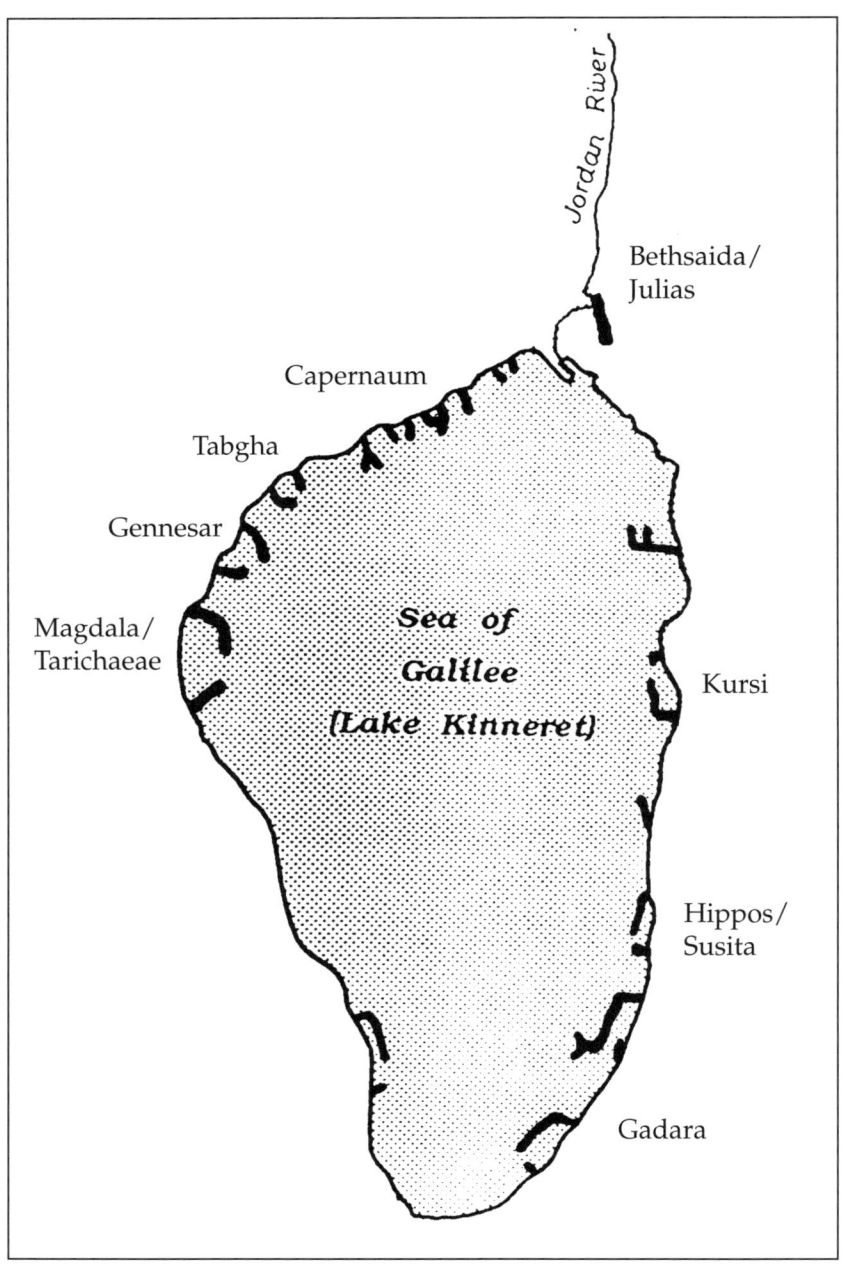

Harbors on the Sea of Galilee

Markan material between the two feeding narratives and proceeds directly to the confession episode at Caesarea Philippi (Luke 9:18-22). Second, there is good reason to question the accuracy of geographical details redacted by Mark. Mark 7:31 betrays a similar confusion in directing Jesus from Tyre to the Sea of Galilee by way of Sidon (to the north) and the Decapolis (to the southeast). A number of scholars, therefore, have suggested that Mark accidentally substituted *Sidon* for *Bethsaidan* in that verse—a reading which would make more sense.[1] The direction of travel in Mark 6:45 "to Bethsaida" contradicts the subsequent report of arrival in Gennesaret in Mark 6:53.[2] By reading "from Bethsaida" in Mark 6:45, the Markan picture is clearer and the four Gospels paint a consistent picture with the disciples traveling from the western shore to Bethsaida and returning to the western shore in the direction of Capernaum, but ending up at Gennesaret.

What is most significant is that Bethsaida is consistently described as "on the other side" or "across the sea" from the various cities on the western shore. Travel to Bethsaida is expressed in terms of "withdrawing" from the crowds and heading towards a deserted place where they could be by themselves. In many ways the picture is more like that of a trip to the far side of the lake as is the case, in fact, in one Synoptic episode: the healing of the demoniac in the territory of the Gerasenes/Gadarenes identified today with Kursi on the eastern shore (Mark 4:35; 5:1, 21; Matt 8:18; 9:1; Luke 8:22, 26, 40). Apparently travel across the lake was common and the expression "as from Tiberias to Susita" became a common metaphor for speed.[3] Yet in the case of Bethsaida, the distance from Capernaum is only a few miles. Nevertheless, there was a great chasm separating these two cities frequented by Jesus.

Bethsaida: Outside the Land of Israel

In one respect the separation was psychological. Bethsaida was not located in Galilee, but in Gaulanitis (the modern Golan). It was under the rule, not of Antipas, but of Herod's other son Philip. To some, it was not considered *eretz Israel*, but the beginning of the diaspora. Although it comes from a later period, one such rabbinic text illustrates this well:

---

1. Julius Wellhausen, *Das Evangelium Marci* (Berlin, 1909) 58; W. C. Allen, *The Gospel According to Saint Mark* (London, 1915) 110; Vincent Taylor, *The Gospel According to St. Mark* (N.Y.: St. Martin's Press, 1957) 353.
2. Variant readings in the manuscript tradition of Mark 6:45 demonstrate a perceived difficulty. *Ms* D includes εἰς Βησσαιδάν rather than πρὸς Βηθσαιδάν. *Mss* P45 and W omit εἰς τὸ πέραν.
3. Genesis Rabbah 31:13; 32:9.

> And it happened Rabbi Eleazar ben Shamoa and Rabbi Yohanan ha-Sandlar were going to Netzivim to study Torah with Rabbi Yehudah ben Batayrah. They arrived at Tzaidan and remembered the land of Israel. Their eyes opened and filled with tears and they ripped their clothes. . . .They returned to their original place and said that living in the Land of Israel outweighs all the commandments in the Torah.[4]

In contrast to the desire on the part of Jesus to withdraw to this place for temporary respite and solitude, such a withdrawal on the part of early second-century Rabbis Eleazar ben Shamoa and Yohanan ha-Sandlar to Tzaidan (quite possibly Bethsaida) was devastating. They were cut off from the land.

Geography

In order to understand properly the expression "across the sea," one must come to know the geography of the area. The Galilee and the Golan are separated by the Jordan River which descends rapidly from the foothills of Mount Hermon to an elevation of 895 feet below sea level at the lake. The river cuts a gorge which rises up quickly on both sides making fording nearly impossible. The only crossing points in the ancient world were the Daughters of Jacob Bridge near Kibbutz Gadot seven miles to the north and, in the Roman period, a bridge slightly north of Bethsaida which led to Chorazin to the west. Today's visitor can easily be misled, as can those relying on biblical maps, who see a natural land connection to Capernaum across a relatively tame Jordan River to the south. Yet the Q woe saying of Jesus does not connect Bethsaida with Capernaum, but rather with Chorazin to the west. Access between Bethsaida and Capernaum in the first century was not by land, but by sea.

The Roman Road

Until recently little has been known about the road system in the lower Golan. Most studies acknowledged that the *Via Maris* passed from Megiddo to the northeast, crossing at the Daughters of Jacob Bridge before continuing on to Damascus.[5] A second north-south road crossed the

---

4. Tannaitic Sifrei Devarim, Reeh 80:4.80. While I tend to agree that this passage refers to Bethsaida rather that Sidon on the Phoenician coast, one must consider the possibility that Tzaidan refers to the region around Bethsaida or even a later settlement somewhat to the north of et-Tell. Richard Freund discusses the basic issues in "The Search for Bethsaida in Rabbinic Literature," *Bethsaida* (1995) 267–311.

5. Michael Avi-Yonah, "The Roman Road System," *The Holy Land: A Historical Geography* (Grand Rapids, Mich.: Baker, 1966); Israel Roll, "The Roman Road System in Ju-

Jordan near Beth Shean and traveled up the eastern side of the Golan. East-west roads connected Tyre on the coast with Caesarea Philippi and Acco with Tiberias and Hippos, crossing the Jordan to the south of the sea, and then continuing east from Hippos. This general picture of roads in the Golan had virtually left Bethsaida isolated.

However, with the excavations at Chorazin, new interest was aroused in the possible expansion of the road system. The discovery of an ancient road passing north of Chorazin led to a more comprehensive survey which made it clear that a major east-west road connected Acco, Chorazin, and Bethsaida.[6] Ilan and Stepanski discovered a major three-mile section of this road near Chorazin which measures from 13 feet to 18 feet in width and includes curbstones and typical techniques of Roman road building. There were also several small bridges which leveled out low spots and provided waterflow through ravines. This confirms earlier reports of portions of the road discovered at Rama to the west and it establishes a junc-

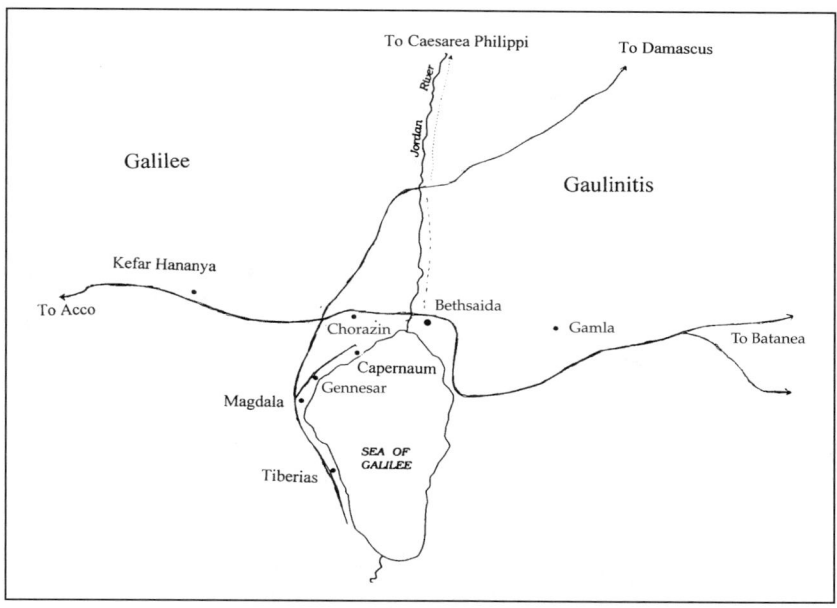

The Road System Near Bethsaida

---

daea," *The Jerusalem Cathedra,* vol. 3 (Detroit: Wayne State University Press, 1983) 136–61; Dan Urman, *The Golan: A Profile.*

6. Zeev Yeivin, "Chorazin," *The New Encyclopedia of Archaeological Excavations in the Holy Land,* vol. 1, ed. E. Stern (Jerusalem: Israel Exploration Society, 1993); Zvi Ilan, "Eastern Galilee, Survey of Roman Roads," *Excavations and Surveys in Israel* (1989/90) 9:14–6. Yosi Stepanski, חורבת משלח, *Hadashot Arkheologiyot,* 104 (1995) 27–9.

tion with the north-south route at Gov Yosef. The survey reports on a side road connecting Capernaum to the south where a milestone has been uncovered, but the precise route of this road is unclear. The critical point is that it links up with the east-west Chorazin road on the heights to the west of the Jordan River which then provides direct access to Bethsaida.

There are a number of uncertainties concerning the exact course of the road as it approaches Bethsaida. Near the ridge overlooking the Jordan River from the west, evidence of the ancient road appears at several places. However, sections of the ancient road appear to have been covered by a new road near Moshav Almagor. This road jogs in a northern direction as it makes its way down to the river at a point about a mile north of et-Tell. Because there are no easy points for crossing the Jordan and because the course of the river has been altered over the centuries, its exact crossing remains uncertain.

Ilan's rough map would suggest that this east-west road passed just to the south of Bethsaida. It is more likely that the road passed about a mile to the north. This would not be unusual since ancient cities were usually constructed a short distance away from the roads which would provide access for passing armies as well as robbers and thieves.[7] The best evidence for reconstructing the ancient route is Josephus' description of Sulla's camp located five furlongs (= 3,500 feet) north of Bethsaida. Sullas's

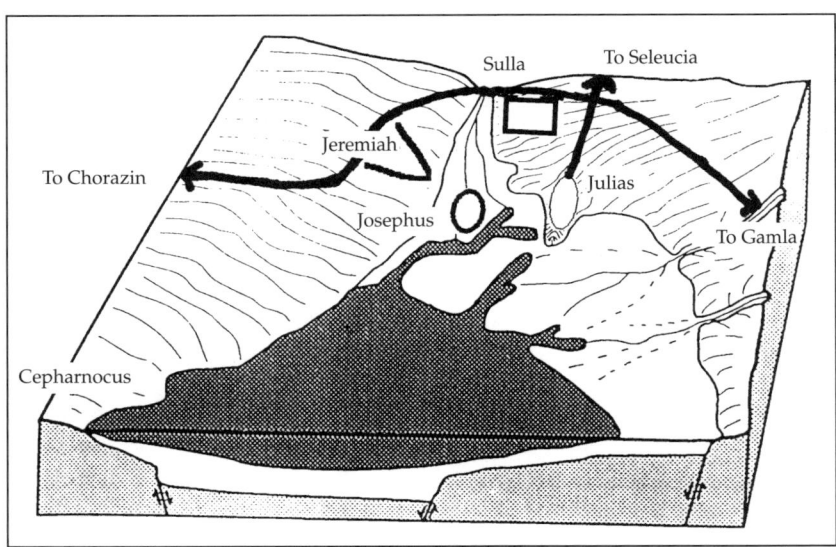

The Battle of Bethsaida—67 C.E.

7. Tosefta Erubin 4.5.

mission was not to besiege Bethsaida, but to cut off the Galilean supply route to the rebellious cities of the Golan (Josephus, *Life* 398-400).

Sulla, therefore, posted guards on the roads leading to Seleucia and Gamla. This statement is very important for our understanding of the road system because it points to roads in three directions: to Galilee in the west; to Seleucia in the north; and to Gamla in the east. If our assumptions about the location of this junction are correct, there would also be a short spur connecting Bethsaida to the south. Although Gamla lies directly to the east of Bethsaida, the course of the road would have been affected by the Wadi Daliot. The course of the road to Seleucia is less clear since three different sites have been suggested for this city: Tell Seleucia, Khirbet Qusbiyye, and Dabura.[8] However, the existence of such a road confirms the connection between Bethsaida and Caesarea Philippi to the north. Avi-Yonah's discovery of a milestone in the area of Dabura, about three miles northeast of the Daughters of Jacob bridge points to the likelihood of a north-south route along the eastern side of the Jordan River gorge. This is consistent with the gospel reports of a stopover in Bethsaida on Jesus' way to Caesarea Philippi (Mark 8 and Luke 9).

There is one further complicating factor. Two Josephus manuscripts offer the reading of *Cana* instead of *Seleucia*. If this reading is correct it would point to the town in the plain of Asochis, about eight miles north of Sepphoris and not far from the Acco-Bethsaida road. Josephus himself spent some time there early in the war (Josephus, *Life* 86). Because it was located near Jotapata, a center for the Galilean forces, it would be a likely point for the origin of the supply route to rebel forces in Gamla. In other words, the statement about Sulla's forces guarding the road between Cana and Gamla would point to its importance as an east-west communications and trade route. It is interesting that Jesus' route from Bethany across the Jordan to Cana in Galilee likewise brought him to Bethsaida (John 1:28, 43-44; 2:1). During the war, this route served to transport military forces to the Golan. Not only was this the case with regard to Sulla's troops, but later following the defeat of Gamla, Titus passed this way with one thousand horsemen in route to Gischala in Galilee (Josephus, *War* 4.87-92).

The role of this route in trade has been the topic of an important study by Adan-Bayewitz.[9] Pottery manufactured at Kefar Hananya, west of Chorazin, has been traced to various sites in the Galilee as well as Gamla, Ein Nashut, and Kanaf. In addition, the influence of the Kefar Hananya

---

8. Tell Seleucia is proposed by G. Schumacher, *The Jaulan*; Khirbet Qusbiyye is suggested by Urman, *The Golan: A Profile;* Dubura is suggested by Ilan.

9. D. Adan-Bayewitz, *Common Pottery in Roman Galilee: A Study in Local Trade* (Tel Aviv: Bar Ilan University Press, 1993).

market on Golan sites resulted in local Golan kitchenware with very similar forms as early as the second half of the first century B.C.E. However, this is not to say that access to the Golan was easy or automatic. These three Golan sites include only 10–20 percent Kefar Hananya ware among samples studied while Galilean sites at a similar distance included around 60 percent of this ware. Especially significant is the contrast with Capernaum where there is a very high percentage of Kefar Hananya ware. This points to some difficulty in accessibility to Galilean trade for Golan sites. Unfortunately, the study occurred prior to the Bethsaida excavations. A preliminary report of late-Hellenistic and Roman cooking pots from the 1992 excavations suggests a high degree of similarity to Kefar Hananya forms.[10] However, further analysis is necessary to demonstrate the degree of impact on this ware from the Galilee upon the Golan site.

Ilan also suggests that the Acco-Bethsaida road continued east to link with Bashan and Hauran. It is only logical that the cities of Caesarea Philippi and Bethsaida would have been linked to these areas on the eastern edge of the territory of Herod Philip. This is especially the case since there was tension between the Nabatean kingdom and Herod Antipas, and fighting broke out shortly after Philip's death. The discovery in this eastern area of a number of inscriptions mentioning the *cohors Augusta* points to a military presence in the first century and the need for access to the west.[11] Interestingly, pottery from Si in the Hauran displays a striking similarity to Kefar Hananya ware[12] and points to the need for further study concerning this trade route.

There is one further piece of literary evidence concerning the Bethsaida road from the second century. In a passage referring to Rabbi Judah ha-Nasi there is a debate concerning the transportation of wine on the Sabbath. At the end it is stated that "the incident took place on the highway of Tzaidan and it was completely inhabited by Israel."[13] While the meaning of the expression "highway of Tzaidan" is not totally clear, it may well point to the road passing to the north of Bethsaida. The settlement of Jews in this area following the New Testament era is supported by the location of the ed-Dikke synagogue from this period.[14]

---

10. Toni Tessaro, "Hellenistic and Roman Ceramic Cooking Ware from Bethsaida," *Bethsaida* (1995) 127–39.

11. Henry Innes MacAdam, *Studies in the History of the Roman Province of Arabia: The Northern Sector*. BAR International Series 295 (1986) 61–7.

12. Adan-Bayewitz, *Common Pottery in Roman Galilee*, 239.

13. PT *Avodah Zarah* 5.5, 44d.

14. Heinrich Kohl and Carl Watzinger, *Antike Synagogen in Galilaea* (Leipzig: J. C. Hinrichs, 1916). Urman, *Ancient Synagogues* 2:503–9.

There was a chasm, therefore, between the Golan and the lower Galilee so that Bethsaida was viewed as "across the sea." Primary access to Bethsaida from the western shores of the Sea of Galilee was by boat. However, an east-west road, passing perhaps a mile to the north, connected Bethsaida with the northern Galilee via Chorazin and provided also a link to the east. Thus the pairing of Bethsaida and Chorazin in Q. Access by road from Capernaum to Bethsaida via Chorazin would have been more difficult as is attested by the six-mile distance noted by the sixth-century pilgrim Theodosius. A north-south road would have linked Bethsaida with Caesarea Philippi.

Geological Findings

Today the visitor is surprised to find Bethsaida located over a mile from the shore. This was not the case in biblical times when Josephus measured the length of the Sea of Galilee as 140 furlongs or about 14 miles, while today it is closer to 12 miles in length (Josephus, *War* 3.506). Two thousand years since the New Testament era have brought major changes. Then the sea came up to the base of the small hill on which Bethsaida is located and a much more dramatic gulf of water separated Bethsaida from the Galilean land to its west.

Geologists John F. Shroder Jr., and Moshe Inbar note that these dramatic shifts are due to three natural causes.[15] First, its location on the Jordan rift fault line led to a gradual passing of two continental plates so that Bethsaida has been moving to the north while the Galilee has been gradually shifting to the south. Second, the instability of the land on this fault line led to periodic earthquakes and to shifting and upward pushing of the land. Third, the natural movement of the Jordan River has carried tons of silt from the northern valley to be deposited in the Beteiha plain below. This can be illustrated in modern times by the flood of 1969 when once-in-a-century rainstorms led to a peak discharge of nearly 6,000 cubic feet per second causing a change of shoreline no less than 1,500 feet. The combination of these last two causes brought about dramatic changes on several occasions when landslides caused by earthquake blocked the Jordan River so that an artificial lake was built up behind it. The subsequent dissolution of these landslide dams brought about a massive force which carried boulders, mud, and debris into the mouth of the river below.

The geologists have found evidence that the Beteiha plain below Bethsaida was once submerged below water. Boreholes dug in the plain paint

---

15. John F. Shroder Jr., and Moshe Inbar, "Geologic and Geographic Background to the Bethsaida Excavations," *Bethsaida* (1995) 65–98.

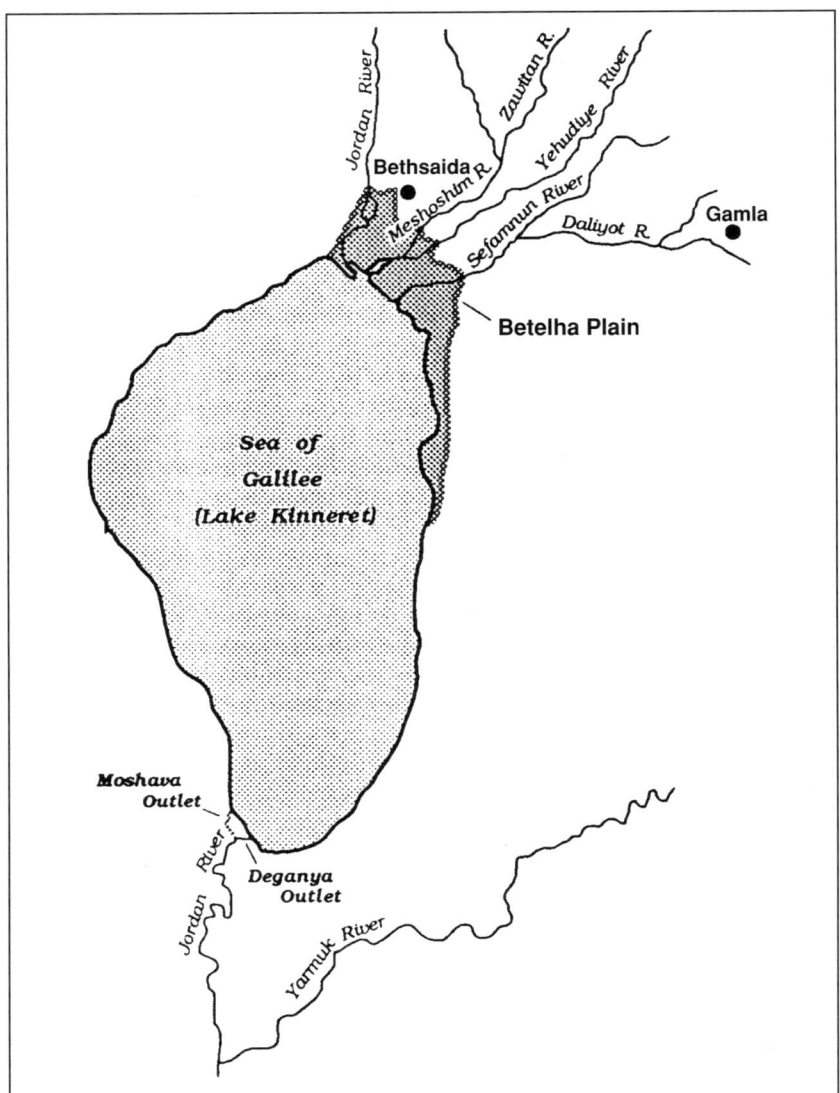

The Beteiha Plain

an interesting history of change. Just 75 feet to the south of the base of et-Tell, there is a dramatic change in soil composition when one digs several feet into the ground. The upper level composed of flood gravel covers a black organic-rich mud characteristic of lakes and lagoons. Deposited in this mud were bones and shells, including ostracods which are found only in quiet waters. Carbon-14 dating of these organic deposits points to the existence of quiet waters below Bethsaida about 2,700 to 1,800 years ago. In other words, there is good reason to believe that Bethsaida had ready access to the sea, whether the shores of the lake itself reached the base of et-Tell or estuaries made their way out to the sea. The maps of Shroder and Inbar suggest something of a development from the time when et-Tell was a peninsula sticking out into the lake—corresponding perhaps to the first habitation of this site—to an estuary model by the end of the New

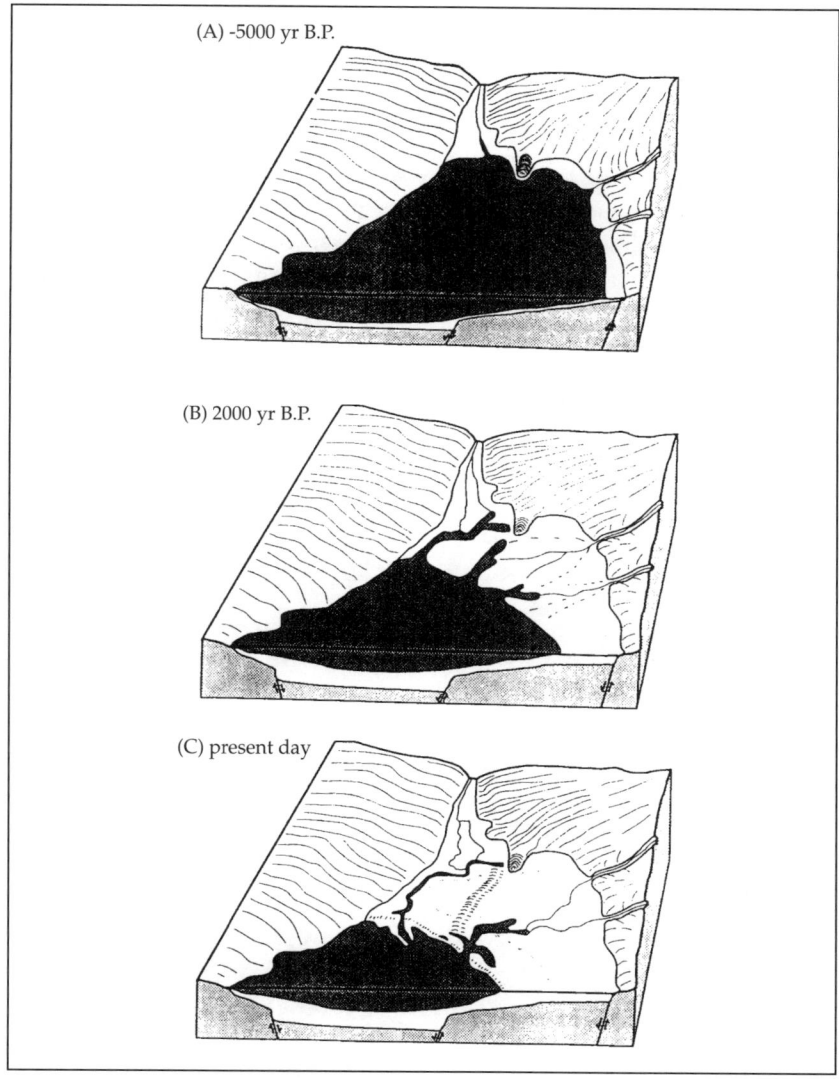

Bethsaida: Geological Development

Testament era. The city of Bethsaida therefore was separated dramatically from the Galilean lands to the west and access by boat was expressed in literary sources as *crossing to the other side*.

The remains of an ancient wall were recently found in a shallow pool presently filled by the nearby freshwater spring which once served the inhabitants of Bethsaida. This yet-to-be-excavated wall may well have served as a mooring point for seagoing vessels of Bethsaida. The fate of the city would easily have been connected to accessibility to the lake. When this passage was blocked by further silting, the role of Bethsaida as a port leading to the cities of Galilee would have come to an end.

Settlements in the Middle Ages

Thus far there is no evidence for a major occupation of et-Tell after the time of the first century and throughout the Middle Ages. On the other hand, in the rabbinic period there was a Jewish settlement with a synagogue at ed-Dikke a mile to the north. The small fishing villages of el-Araj and Mesadiye were constructed in the silted-over Beteiha plain itself. These latter two sites were to complicate the modern search for Bethsaida since the modern reader assumed that it had to be located on the sea.

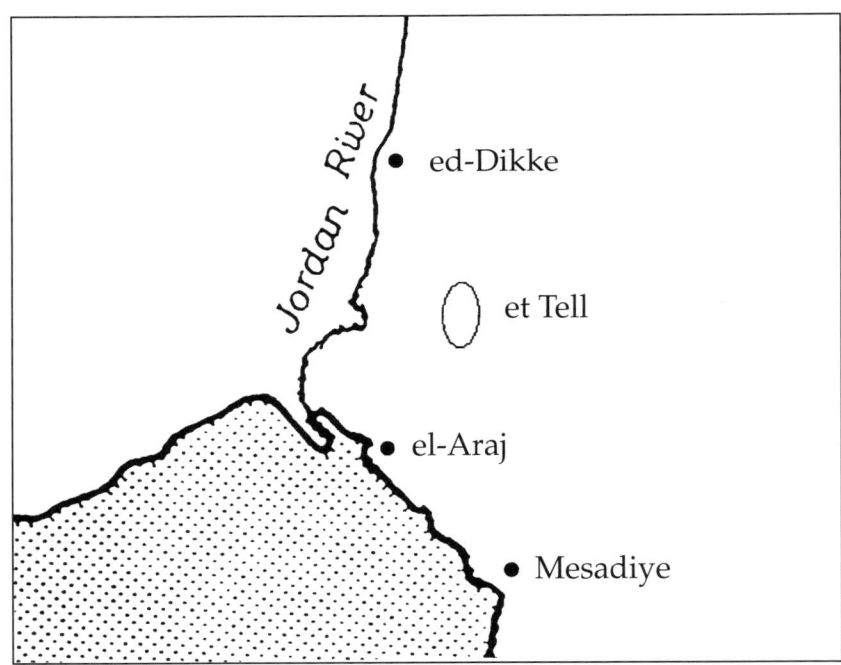

The Bethsaida Area in 2nd–5th Centuries c.e.

Yet in the first century, et-Tell (= Bethsaida) was in fact a city on the sea with the wide Jordan mouth hindering travel connections by land to the cities to the southwest. It was, in fact, on the other side. Its importance was related to its port which provided easy access to these cities by way of boat travel. Literary reports demonstrate regular boat travel connecting Bethsaida with the important city of Tiberias (John 6:23) as well as other locations on the western coast including Capernaum, Gennesaret, and Tarichaeae (Magdala = Dalmanutha). Access was found across the sea.

Chapter 5

Fishing Village

The name Bethsaida means "House of the Fisherman" or, as it might be called today, "Fishertown." In the New Testament it mainly occurs in the form βηθσαίδα although in Mark 8 it is written βηθσαίδαν. Technically, the former form should be translated "fishing," while the latter form means "fisherman" since the final "n" in Semitic languages denotes the person who carries out a particular activity. There is good reason to believe that the name originally was simply Tzaidan, mistakenly written by a scribe as Tzer (Josh 19:35).[1] As in the case of a number of towns, the prefix "Beth," which means "house," was added in the second-temple period. Again, after Bethsaida's destruction, the name Tzaidan appears to have resurfaced in the Rabbinic period for a new settlement near et-Tell.[2]

Hunting Traditions

It should also be noted that Tzaidan can also mean "hunter." Apparently, the same term could be used for both fishing and hunting because nets were employed in both. In a sense both connotations were appropriate for Bethsaida because of the sparsely populated Golan region. When the Emperor Hadrian visited Palestine in 129 C.E., he was fed with pheasants from Tzaidan.[3] Other than this example, however, the theme of hunting is less prominent in the literature about Bethsaida.

---

1. Rami Arav, "Bethsaida, Tzer, and the Fortified Cities of Naphtali," *Bethsaida* (1995) 193–202.
2. Richard Freund, "The Search for Bethsaida in Rabbinic Literature," *Bethsaida* (1995) 267–311.
3. Midrash Kohelet 2.8.

Fishing in the Old Testament Era

From the beginning, Bethsaida, as a city on the sea, seems to have been known for its fishing. In the Old Testament, there was not much attention given to the Sea of Kinneret (= Galilee) area (Num 34:11; Deut 3:17; Josh 12:3; 13:27). The Tribe of Naphtali was given fishing rights. In the allotment of fortified cities in Joshua 19:35, four of them are designated as Tziddim, which may simply mean "fishing towns." The practice of fishing with nets is used by a number of writers for illustration (Eccl 9:12; Job 19:6; Hab 1:15; Ezek 26:5, 14; 32:2; 47:10). Other than these examples, there is little about the fishing industry in the Old Testament.

General Picture from Gospels

The picture is quite different in the Gospels where the fishing motif dominates. At least one parable (Matt 13:47-50) and several miracles are centered around fishing (Matt 17:24-27; Luke 5:1-11; John 21:1-14). Jesus even teaches from a fishing boat (Mark 4:1). It is not surprising that among early symbols are the *ichthus*, representing an early Christian creed, and the anchor. Even among opponents of Christianity, it was noted that Jesus' associates included fishermen.[4] At least four of Jesus' disciples—associated with Bethsaida—were known as fishermen by trade: Peter, Andrew, James, and John. They were called while engaged in fishing and their calling is described in terms of fishing for people (Mark 1:16-20). It was these four who formed an inner circle around Jesus according to the Synoptic reports. Following the death of Jesus, no less than seven disciples are described as returning to fishing (John 21).

Rabbis: Fishing and Tzaidan

In Rabbinic literature there are several sayings about fish connected with Tzaidan. On the one hand, the fish are of high quality as the following tradition states:

> He taught that the fish which comes from Acco is as good a taste as the fish which comes up from Tzaidan and that those fish are not as good as the fish which comes from Paneas.[5]

On the other hand, the fish are plentiful and of various kinds:

---

4. Origen, *Against Celsus* 62. "Jesus collected around him ten or eleven men, the most wicked tax-collectors and sailors, and with these fled hither and thither, collecting a means of livelihood in a disgraceful and importunate way."

5. Sifrei Devarim 4.39.

Rabban Simeon ben Gamaliel said, "It happened that I went to Tzaidan and they put before me more than three hundred kinds of fish in a single dish.[6]

One must be cautious in reading these texts since it is debated whether the city in question is Sidon on the Mediterranean coast north of Tyre or Bethsaida on the Sea of Galilee. In the former reading, one city is clearly coastal (Acco) and another inland (Paneas). However, there may well be a progression from salt water fish from Acco to lake fish from Tzaidan to fish caught in rivers and streams from Paneas. One must also be cautious because these written records are somewhat late. Yet the *maaseh* form (it once happened . . .) is used for the transmission of important traditions.[7] In this case, there were two Rabban Simeon ben Gamaliel, one first century and the other second century C.E. Thus the tradition about Bethsaida's reputation for good plentiful fish may be quite applicable to the New Testament era.

Fishing Artifacts from Bethsaida

During the first decade of excavations at Bethsaida, well over one hundred fishing artifacts have been uncovered at et-Tell. These include stone anchors, both stone and lead net weights, fish hooks, and needles. This collection provides the best selection of fishing equipment from any one site around the Sea of Galilee. Mendel Nun, resident fisherman and expert on fishing practices, has previously published examples of ancient fishing implements. However, they are an accumulation from various sites all around the lake and most have come from the surface.[8] The impressive collection from Bethsaida is extremely helpful in understanding ancient fishing practices and demonstrates conclusively that et-Tell was a fishing village.[9]

Fishing with Nets

The discovery of a large number of net weights points to the preponderance of fishing by net in this region. Much is known about this type of fishing by comparison to modern practice with ancient drawings, especially from tombs in Egypt. In fact, an ancient fishing net complete with lead sinkers was found in an Egyptian tomb and a two thousand-year-old

---

6. PT Sheqalim 6.2, 50a.
7. Richard Freund, "The Search for Bethsaida in Rabbinic Literature," 281.
8. Mendel Nun, *Ancient Stone Anchors and Net Sinkers from the Sea of Galilee* (Ein Gev: Kibbutz Ein Gev Tourist Department, 1993).
9. Even after examining initial finds from et-Tell, Nun denied that this site could represent Bethsaida because of its distance from the shore; Nun, *Ancient Stone Anchors*, 43.

net is among the Bar Kochba discoveries from caves near the Dead Sea.[10] Because of the climate at Bethsaida, one would not expect to find remains of nets, rope, and string. Yet the weights survive.

In his description of fishing practices, Mendel Nun notes three different types of nets used on the Sea of Galilee.[11]

The cast net is operated by a single fisherman and extends twenty to twenty-five feet in diameter. This is the type of net mentioned in the call narratives of the disciples (ἀμφίβληστρον). The disciples have been casting their nets in a circle around them and now Jesus calls them to cast their nets for people (Mark 1:16-20). Throughout the lake area small stones

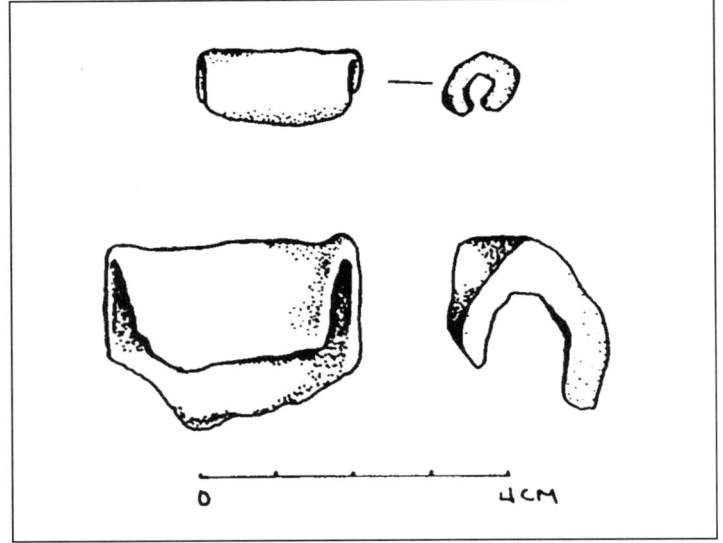

Lead Weight

with bored holes were often used as weights to pull the net to the bottom. However, lead weights were also in use, attached every foot or so along the bottom. Approximately thirty lead weights have been collected at Bethsaida. These were made when molten lead was poured into flat sheets and then cut into strips ¾ inch by 2¼ inch. They were then folded over to create a gap for the string usually measuring less than ¼ inch. The discovery of one unfolded lead strip suggests that these weights were made

---

10. Nun, *Ancient Stone Anchors*, 35, 41.
11. Ibid., 51–5.

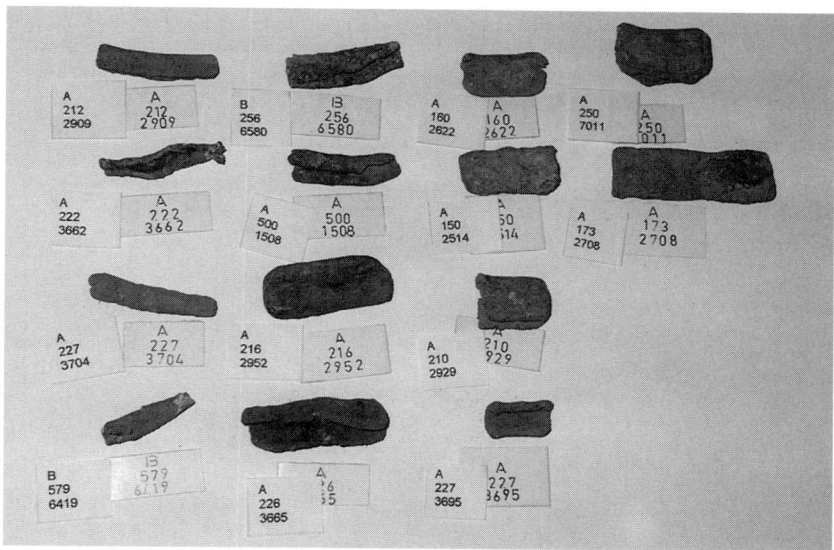

Lead Weights

in Bethsaida itself. Only a few other examples of the folded-lead weight have been found elsewhere, near Capernaum and Magdala. In contrast, about one hundred ring-shaped lead weights were discovered in the ancient harbor at Kursi.[12]

A second type of net is the trammel net, composed of three separate walls of netting of varying mesh so that fish are trapped inside. Today as many as five units, each six feet high and a hundred feet long, are joined together. This kind of net can be laid out in a line or a circle and left for long periods of time. Thus wood floats were used to hold up the top part of the net and stone weights secured the bottom. Among these weights discovered at Bethsaida include examples of irregular-shaped basalt and limestone ranging in weight from one to seven pounds and averaging about three inches in height.

The third type of net is the seine or dragnet. This commonly used type of net creates a long wall of net—in modern times as much as a thousand feet long and from five to twenty-five feet high—which is spread about a hundred yards from shore and then pulled to the shore by two teams of men. The process takes about an hour and is repeated eight to ten times a night.

Again weights are used so that fish cannot escape along the bottom. Irregular-shaped stone weights were often used including some with holes and others with grooves.

12. Ibid., 42.

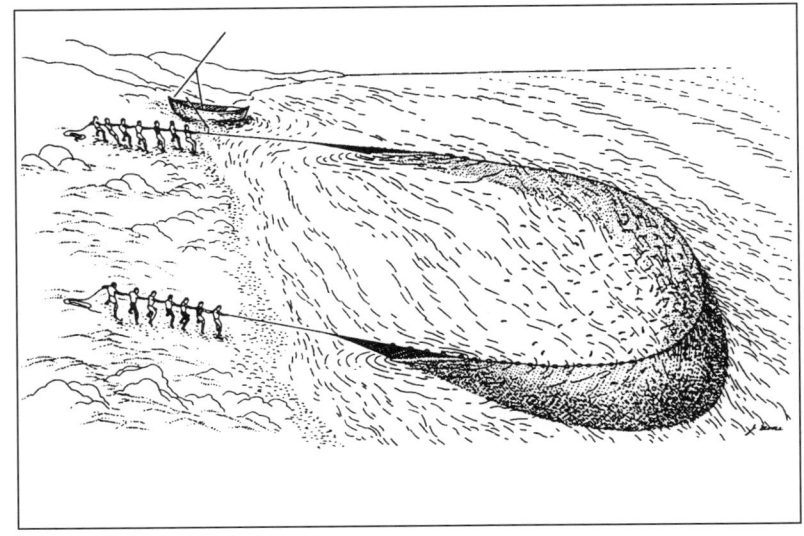

Seine Net

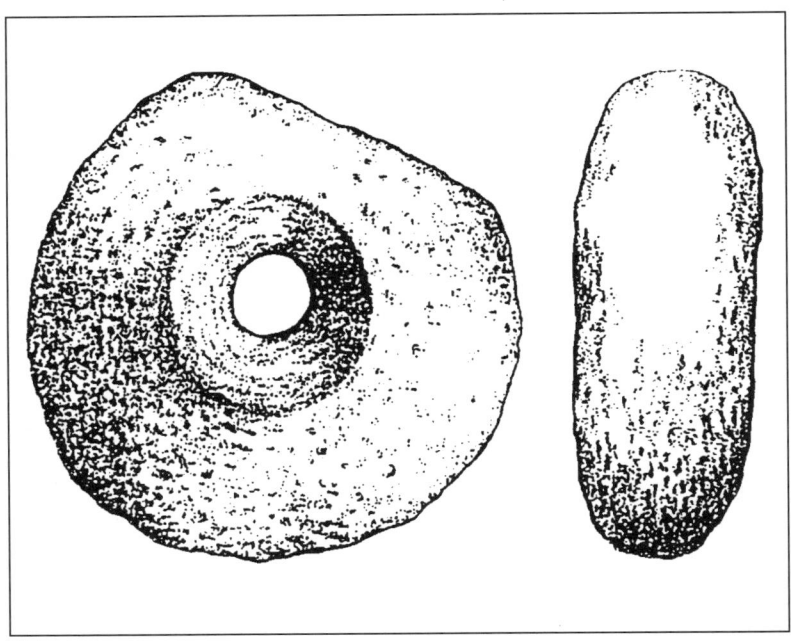

Basalt Ring Weight

However, Bethsaida has produced another type of net weight not previously catalogued by Nun. This is an elaborately dressed basalt ring weight. Three small (one to two inches in diameter) and fifteen large (four to five inches in diameter) examples have been collected. In the case of the large ring weights a uniform-size hole points to the use of a rope slightly less than one inch. It is unclear why the fishermen would go to such an ef-

Ring Weights

fort to work these weights when irregular shaped stones were common on the rest of the lake. This may be explained by the changing north shoreline. We would conjecture that these rings working like wheels facilitated easy pulling of the nets to shore. While most of the lake floor is irregular and rocky, the silt deposits from the upper Jordan would have created a more uniform surface where these rings would have been effective.

The gospel accounts imply familiarity with this type of net. Jesus refers to the σαγήνη, seine or dragnet in the parable of the net where the fishermen must separate out good and bad fish (Matt 13:47).[13] In the account of the miraculous catch of fish, a number of details suggest that the disciples were using a seine. John 21:8 states that the disciples were positioned about one hundred yards off shore and that they were dragging the nets to shore. The team of seven fishermen (John 21:1-2) would be appropriate, as would the use of two boats mentioned in the parallel account (Luke 5:7). The reference to "large fish" (John 21:11) suggests that the

---

13. Lev 11:9-12 forbids certain kinds of fish including the *Clarias lazera* or catfish.

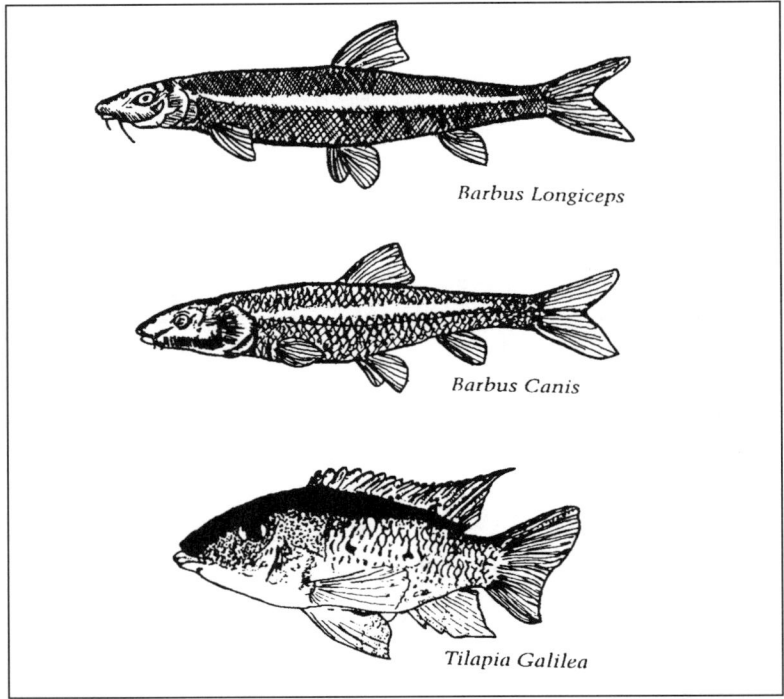

Common Fish in the Sea of Galilee

species was Tilapia Galilea, the long dorsal-finned musht, the largest edible fish in Galilee made popular to modern tourists as "St. Peter's Fish." Nun notes that musht travel in shoals during the winter months toward the warmer water fed by springs in the northern part of the lake.[14] Thus it is not surprising that the disciples find the shoal of fish on the other side of the boat (John 21:6).

This episode also mentions the tearing of nets (Luke 5:6), which must have been common. Thus James and John were occupied with mending their nets (Mark 1:19) when they first met Jesus. Seven large bronze and iron needles (five to six inches long) have been found at Bethsaida. One type with a loop at one end was typical for net repair.[15] The second more common type with a hole in one end may have also been used in repair of both nets and sails. The location of a number of these finds on the floor of a large courtyard house complex in the center of Bethsaida may be significant. The large courtyard would provide ample space for major net and sail repair.

---

14. Mendel Nun, "Cast your Net upon the Water: Fish and Fishermen in Jesus' Time," *BAR* 19 (Nov./Dec. 1993) 46–56, 70.

15. Nun, *Ancient Stone Anchors*, 34.

Fishing with Hook and Line

In addition to fishing with nets, hooks on lines were also employed. Thirteen hooks ranging in size from 1½ inch to 2½ inch have been discovered including several in the two Hellenistic courtyard style houses. While the smaller folded lead weights may have been employed on individual fishing lines, other discovered lead sinkers of various shapes (cube, disc, "k"-shaped) were likely used. This is of special interest because of an episode contained only in Matthew 17:24-27. When Peter reported to Jesus that he was approached concerning the payment of the temple tax, Jesus instructed him to cast a hook into the water and to open the mouth of the first fish that he catches to find a coin with which to pay the tax. In this case, the reference is to a second group of edible fish from the carp family known as the barbels because of the barbs at the corners of their mouths.[16] Since these are predators which feed on small fish, they are often caught by hook—unlike the musht which feed only on plankton.

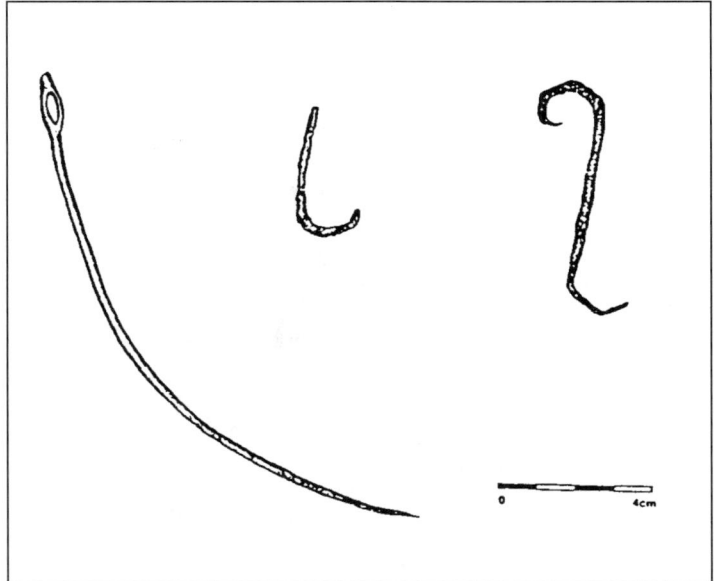

Fishing Equipment: Hook and Needle

---

16. In the Talmud they are referred to as biny from the Semitic binita for hair. Actually there are three types of barbels: (a) *Barbus longiceps*—a long-headed barbel; (b) *Barbus canis*—known as scaly; and (c) *Varicorhines damascinus*. The first two are considered good Sabbath dishes, but the third which feeds on decaying matter has a poor taste. Nun, "Cast your Net," 49.

However, in one respect this story is more characteristic of the musht. Although the musht travel in shoals during the winter, they pair up during the spring months and deposit eggs in the soft bottom near the shore or in lagoons, such as around the mouth of the Jordan River near Bethsaida. After fertilization, the eggs are carried in their mouths for two or three weeks until hatched. Because of this, it is not unusual to find a foreign object in their mouth, such as a coin. It would appear then that Matthew's version of the story betrays signs of confusion about fishing practices on the Sea of Galilee.

The Fishing Seal

One of the most significant finds from the same courtyard house is a clay seal measuring 3/4 inch by 3/4 inch. The seal depicts two men fishing in a small *hippos* boat, like that used by Phoenicians in shallow water.[17] It may be that John 6:22-24 has this type of boat in mind when it mentions that there had been no πλοιάριον at the docks for transporting Jesus by himself to the other side after the feeding episode. This stands in contrast to the regular term for a boat, πλοῖον, which was used to describe

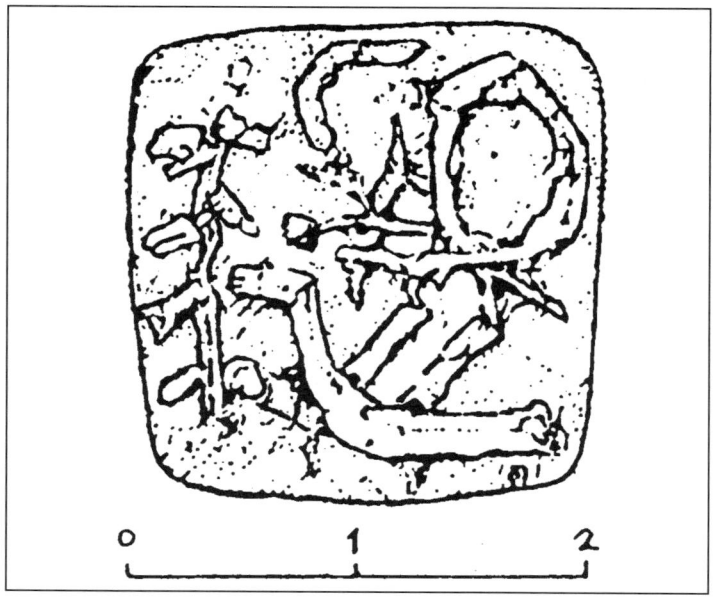

Clay "Fisherman's" Seal

17. Arav, "Bethsaida Excavations: Preliminary Report, 1987–1993," 19.

the transport for the disciples on the previous afternoon. Likewise Josephus also mentions two occasions when he was forced to escape in a boat from Tiberias to Migdal with only two body guards (Josephus, *War* 3.618 = *Life* 96; *Life* 304). Thus the depiction on the seal is consistent with such literary descriptions.

Next to the boat on the left side is a reed which suggests a marshy area which is quite typical of the mouth of the Jordan River today and which was also mentioned in descriptions by Josephus (Josephus, *Life* 398-406). It may be that the reed became a symbol for the city of Bethsaida.[18] The round objects above the men in the boat most likely are depicting the smaller cast nets (ἀμφίβληστρον), similar to that described in the call narratives of the disciples (Mark 1:16-20).

The seal itself was made of clay and has a pyramid-shaped handle. Since it most likely was used to stamp jar handles, it may well be that it denoted the contents of salted fish. This was a very important industry on the Sea of Galilee, especially at Migdal (known also as Magdala, the home of Mary Magdalene). Thus this town was later given the Greek name Tarichaeae, which literally means "the place where fish are salted." John 6:9 refers to the fish in the feeding of the 5,000 as ὀψάριον, the term for dried fish. There is no reason not to think that Bethsaida had this kind of industry as well. Another artifact from Bethsaida is a jar handle with the mark of an anchor, perhaps also used for this purpose.

The fish used for salting are the acanthobrama terrae sanctae, popularly known as the Kinneret Sardine, which today make up 50 percent of the annual catch on the lake or about one thousand tons per year. Presumably this species made up the three hundred fish fed to Rabbi Simeon ben Gamaliel upon his visit to Tzaidan because they are served in a single dish.[19] These fish could be easily caught and handled by a single person using the cast net as depicted on the Bethsaida seal.

Excursus: The Ginnosar Boat

A discussion of fishing practices in connection with Bethsaida is not complete without considering the significance of one other recent archaeological discovery: the Ginnosar boat.[20] In 1986, after a long drought when the Sea of Galilee was at its lowest elevation, members of Kibbutz

---

18. Fred Strickert, "The Coins of Philip," *Bethsaida* (1995) 185. The depiction of a reed occurs only on later coins of Philip.

19. PT Sheqalim 6.2,50c.

20. Shelley Wachsman, "The Galilee Boat: 2,000-Year-Old Hull Recovered Intact," *BAR* 14 (Sept./Oct. 1988) 18–33. Shelley Wachsman, ed., *The Excavations of an Ancient Boat in the Sea of Galilee (Lake Kinneret)*. '*Atiqot* 19, 1990.

Ginnosar discovered a boat in the mud in an area usually submerged. This discovery caused quite a stir, both because it is the only ancient sailing vessel ever found on the lake and because the process was rather exciting with the excavators battling the rising lake water caused by the renewal of rains. The boat proved to be two thousand years old and very helpful for our understanding of first-century life on the Sea of Galilee.

The boat clearly dates to the first century. This was determined by the style of construction with mortise and tenon joints. Among the various objects in the boat were pottery shards including a complete Hellenistic cooking pot of the style which dates from the mid-first century B.C.E. to mid-first century C.E. There was also a complete Herodian lamp which dates to the first century C.E.[21] Carbon-14 dating placed the construction of the boat at 40 B.C.E. +/- 80 years or in a range from 120 B.C.E. to 40 C.E. However, the original construction, using oak for the frame and cedar for the strakes, had been repaired with other woods.[22] In other words, the boat was roughly contemporaneous with the time of the Gospels.

The boat was 25.5 feet in length, 7.5 feet wide, and 4.5 feet in depth. From the markings it appeared that there had been a mast. It had a rounded stern with the fore and aft sections probably decked in, and it could easily seat seven persons. The decking was essential for fishing boats for positioning the seine nets. In the account of the storm at sea (Mark 4:36-41), Jesus is described as sleeping in the stern probably under the decking which provided shelter while the helmsman stationed above was most exposed to the elements. The reference to "the pillow" using the Greek article suggests part of the boat's equipment which, according to Wachsman, was probably a sandbag used for ballast.

An ancient mosaic from Migdal includes a boat of the type discovered near Ginnosar. This foot-long depiction shows a boat with a mast and two oarsman on its left side along with a helmsman holding the rudder in the water.[23] The simplicity of style suggests that the artist was working on the basis of observation rather than from a pattern book. Therefore a crew of five was usual for the typical Galilean fishing boat. This is supported also by the depiction of a boat on a coin minted in Caesarea Philippi.[24] This also fits the report of Josephus concerning his own strategy during the

---

21. David Adan-Bayewitz, "The Pottery," *The Excavations of an Ancient Boat*, ed. Shelley Wachsman, 89–96; and Varda Sussman, "The Lamp," 97–8.

22. Ella Werker, "Identification of the Wood," *The Excavations of an Ancient Boat*, ed. Shelley Wachsman, 65–73.

23. J. Richard Steffy and Shelley Wachsman, "The Migdal Boat Mosaic," *The Excavations of an Ancient Boat*, ed. Shelley Wachsman, 114–8.

24. Coin minted in 220 C.E. under Julia Soaemias. Y. Meshorer, "The Coins of Caesarea Banias," *INJ* (1984–5) 46–7, plate 15:56.

Jewish Revolt when he positioned 230 boats off the shore of enemy-held Tiberias. He reports that each boat was equipped with a skeleton crew of five, which nevertheless brought about a surrender because of the intimi-

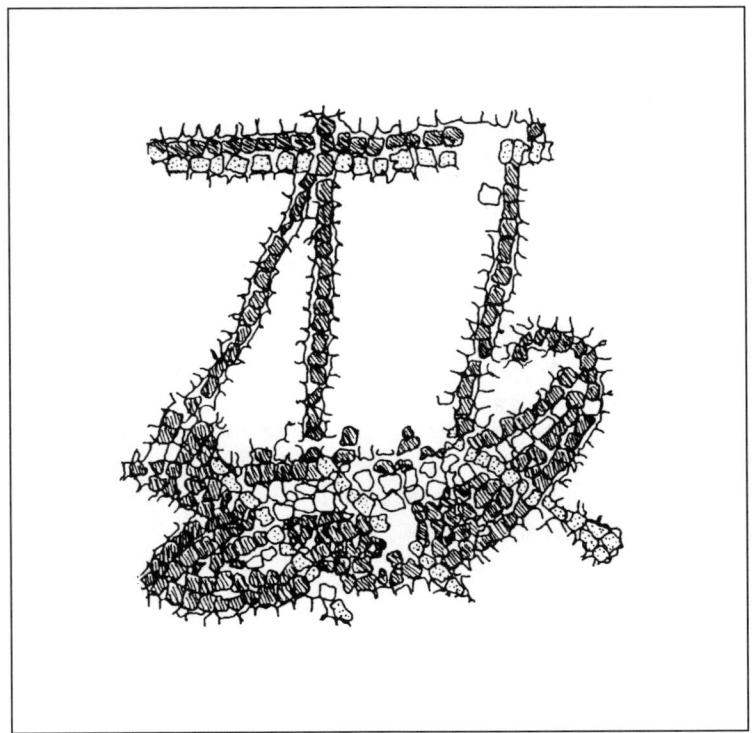

Migdal Boat

dating appearance of the boats some distance from shore near evening (Josephus, *War* 2.632-46 and *Life* 155-78). The typical crew therefore was five.

A larger crew was employed for fishing with others free to handle the seine nets in addition to the five-man crew. In the call of disciples, Mark 1:20 notes that James and John left behind their father Zebedee with the hired men in the boat. In that situation, there were at least five persons and probably more. John 21:2 lists seven disciples who go for a night of fishing. However, Wachsman suggests that the Ginnosar boat may be capable of holding as many as fifteen persons.[25] When Josephus sent ten hostages

25. Shelley Wachsman, "Literary Sources," *The Excavations of an Ancient Boat*, ed. Shelley Wachsman, 111–4.

from Tiberias to Migdal, he explicitly states that they went in a fishing vessel—μιᾷ τῶν ἁλιάδων— (Josephus, *War* 2.639. cf. *Life* 167). In the episode, when he tricked the Tiberians with 230 boats off-shore, he himself landed in a boat with seven soldiers and several friends in addition to the five-man crew. After the surrender, he notes that he transported 2,600 prisoners from Tiberias to Migdal which calculates to eleven prisoners per boat (Josephus, *War* 2.632-46; *Life* 155-178). So the picture in Josephus is consistent with a capacity of fifteen persons per boat. Although the Gospels never state explicitly the number of disciples which accompanied Jesus on his various boat trips, such journeys with twelve disciples aboard are certainly not out of the question.

It may never be known how this boat reached its fate at the bottom of the lake. It is possible that the boat sank during one of the many storms that come up at night. One account of the disciples' nighttime struggle against the winds, which probably began at Bethsaida, describes them eventually reaching shore at Gennesaret (Mark 6:45-53), not far from the recent boat discovery. However, it is significant that partial remains of other boats were also uncovered with the Ginnosar boat. One suggestion is that the boat sank in the nautical battle which took place near Migdal during the Jewish revolt of 67 C.E. Josephus reports that:

> the Jews were sent to the bottom, boats and all. . . . During the days that followed, a horrible stench hung over the region, and it presented an equally horrifying spectacle. The beaches were strewn with wrecks and swollen bodies. . . . The dead, including those who earlier fell in the defense of the town numbered 6,700 (Josephus, *War* 3.392-408, 530).

It is not difficult to imagine that the Ginnosar boat was one of these boats washing ashore slightly to the north of Migdal. However, since the boat was found incomplete, it may be that a boat repair shop was located nearby and that unsalvageable wrecks were simply sunk off shore.[26]

This boat does have a Bethsaida connection. One of the coins discovered in connection with the excavation of the boat is a coin of Philip.[27] The coin depicts both Augustus and Livia and can be dated to the year 30 C.E. when Philip officially founded the town of Bethsaida-Julias.[28] This is significant since Philip's coins were meant primarily for local circulation within the Golan region. Among Philip coins discovered in archaeological excavation, this is the only example thus far found outside the territory

---

26. Wachsman, "The Galilee Boat."
27. Haim Gitler, "The Coins," *The Excavations of an Ancient Boat*, ed. Shelley Wachsman, 101.
28. Strickert, "The Coins of Philip," 179–81.

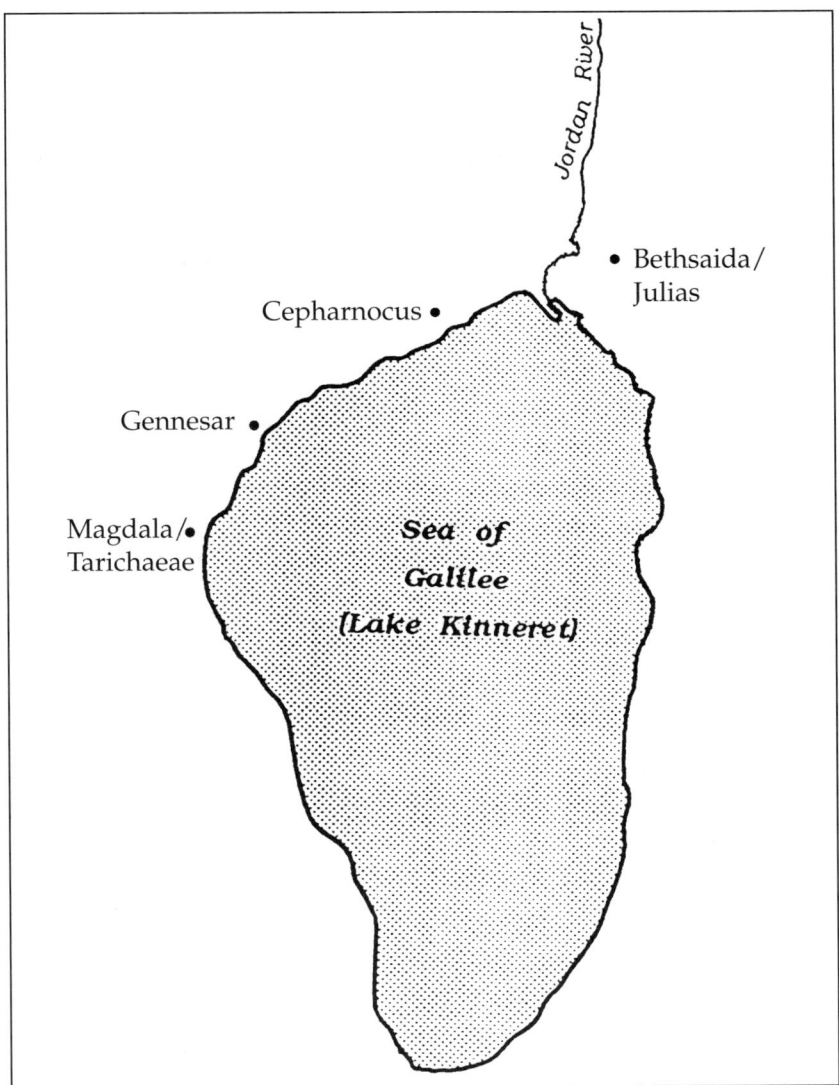

The Sea of Galilee during the Jewish War—67 C.E.

where Philip ruled.[29] It is quite possible that passengers on this boat had embarked from Bethsaida before it sank near Ginnosar.

Anchors

There were two anchors in the Ginnosar boat weighing about 30–40 pounds, one with a hole drilled to secure a rope and the other with a groove

---

29. Philip coins have been discovered at Bethsaida, Gamla, and Tel Anafa. The latter borders on the Golan to the west.

around the center.³⁰ Both types have been found at Bethsaida. Ten basalt stone anchors ranging from thirty to sixty pounds have been discovered at various locations on the top of the tell including the courtyard style houses.³¹ Most are irregular in shape with heights ranging from ten inches to twenty inches and include a single hole in one corner for securing a rope. The rather uniform size of these holes from one to 1¼ inches in diameter suggests the size of ropes used. Such holes were generally drilled with hard flint, many of which have been found at Bethsaida. The discovery also of several large stones with partially drilled holes points to Bethsaida as a place for working anchors. One example has also been uncovered of an anchor with a groove around the middle where the rope was tied.

Missing from Bethsaida is the classical-shaped iron anchor that was common to the Mediterranean. In fact, only one example has ever been found on the Sea of Galilee, pulled up in a fishing net near Capernaum in 1970 and currently displayed at Kibbutz Ginnosar. This iron anchor has a shank five feet long with its arms extending three feet, and it weighs nearly seventy pounds—perhaps too large to be practical for these common fishing boats. Nevertheless, this shape is represented on the jar handle from Bethsaida mentioned previously. Yet this can be explained from the common depiction of anchors on Jewish coinage, influenced by interest in the Mediterranean world.

Excursus: Tabgha

The site of Tabgha on the western shore has long been associated with both the feeding of the 5,000 and the great catch of fish.³² There the visitor is pointed to a stone, where Jesus supposedly laid the loaves and fishes, and heart shaped pillar bases on the shore, where the resurrected Jesus met with his disciples. Although this site is located a short distance south of Capernaum, it is never mentioned in the Gospels. However, the traditions are mentioned as early as the fourth century by the pilgrim Egeria and several churches have been built to commemorate these events.

These associations may well be the result of visits by early pilgrims who were driven less by historical accuracy than by the convenience of a site so near to Capernaum. They also occurred long after the destruction

---

30. Shelley Wachsman, "The Anchors," *The Excavations of an Ancient Boat*, ed. Shelley Wachsman, 107–10.

31. By way of comparison, anchors from the Mediterranean are as large as 450 pounds and several from the Dead Sea weigh two hundred pounds. Nun, *Ancient Stone Anchors*, 17.

32. Bargil Pixner, "The Miracle Church of Tabgha on the Sea of Galilee," *BA* 48 (Dec. 1985) 196–206.

of Bethsaida and after the northeastern shoreline had undergone drastic transformation. The choice of Tabgha is not without reason. It does provide a proper setting with a gradual shoreline and grassy area in the vicinity. Of greater significance is the fact that seven springs are located at this site—thus the ancient name Tabgha, short for Heptagon—which still attract shoals of fish to its shores. The difficulty is that the rocky bottom of the lake at this point is not conducive to use of the common seine net even though numerous details in both Luke 5 and John 21 point to that style of net. While Mendel Nun accepts without question this location for the miracle, he concludes that a trammel net must have been used. With the artifact discoveries at Bethsaida and with the new understanding of geological and geographic changes since the first century, further exploration of the Beteiha plain near Bethsaida may be helpful in learning more about first-century fishing practices.

The mention of 153 fish in John 21:11 recalls the enumerating of three hundred fish served at Tzaidan according to Rabbinic tradition. The particular number 153, however, is so unusual in such a text that it defies explanation.[33] Interestingly, the second-century Jewish-Christian Gospel of the Nazareans includes the detail that Jesus performed 53 miracles at Bethsaida. One wonders if there were something special about either the number 53 or 153 in connection with the city Bethsaida. It is easy to imagine how "100" could have been added or omitted in the passing of the traditions. Thus it is appropriate to explore further possible connections of a Bethsaida location with this account.

---

33. Raymond E. Brown, *The Gospel According to John*, The Anchor Bible (Garden City, N.Y.: Doubleday, 1970) 2:1074–6.

Chapter 6

Houses of Fishermen and Others

Josephus tells us that during his travels through the Galilee during the Jewish revolt of 67 C.E., the Roman Cestius Gallus remarked about his high impression of the architecture of Galilean houses (Josephus, *War* 2.503-4). The common limestone and, in the Golan area, basalt made attractive and durable houses. The Gospels frequently speak of the daily life that takes place in the setting of such houses. For example, the Q saying of Jesus speaks of people gathered for eating and drinking in the courtyard, others at work on the roof, women busy grinding meal, and others in bed sleeping (Luke 17:22-36). A glimpse of this setting can be seen from the Hellenistic and Roman houses uncovered at Bethsaida.

The Simple House

Most people lived in a relatively simple house consisting of only one or two rooms with a small courtyard in front.[1] According to the Mishna, the smallest size for a building designated a house was four cubits by six cubits or about six feet by nine feet.[2] However, most houses were certainly much larger. According to Hirschfeld's survey of simple houses, the size could range from 180 square feet to 2,500 square feet.[3] Certainly this is the case at Bethsaida. An example of a simple house from Bethsaida can be seen from the plan presented on the following page:

---

1. A most helpful resource for understanding the architecture of first-century housing is Yizhar Hirschfeld, *The Palestinian Dwelling in the Roman-Byzantine Periods* (Jerusalem: Israel Exploration Society, 1995).
2. Baba Bathra 6:4.
3. Hirschfeld, *The Palestinian Dwelling in the Roman-Byzantine Periods*, 100.

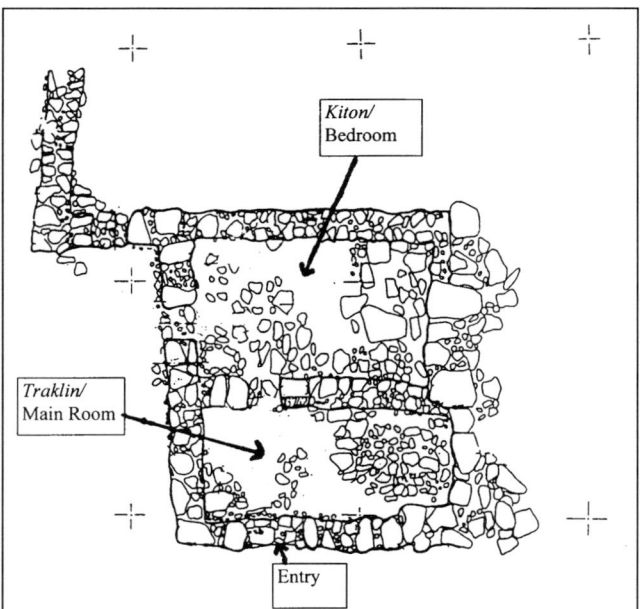

The Simple House

This two-room house opened to a small courtyard area which was probably shared with a number of other dwellings. It probably would have been joined to a street by narrow alleyways.[4] Unfortunately, as is often the case in excavations, later disturbances have made the complete picture of this house unclear.

This particular house is basically a square structure measuring about 21 feet by 21 feet. Because the walls are nearly two feet thick, this leaves a living space of only about 255 square feet. The house, with the entry to the west, has two main rooms. The main room was called the *traklin* which derived from the Latin *triclinium* for the dining room with three couches for reclining. Here is the area where family members sat together and where meals were taken. They usually sat on the floor around a small raised platform. Often the floors were of beaten earth though in this particular house the flooring was of stone. Matting on the floors provided a smooth surface. Dim lighting was provided by oil lamps or streams of natural light from the outside. Thus the unusual effort by the woman who swept her house in search of the lost coin (Luke 15:8-10).

---

4. S. Safrai, "Home and Family Life," *The Jewish People in the First Century* (Philadelphia: Fortress Press, 1976) 2:728–92.

A doorway in the east wall of the *traklin* led to the slightly smaller *kiton* or bedroom deriving from the Greek κοῖτον. The residents often slept side by side on straw mattresses unrolled on the floor. Beds were also used although this was often a sign of luxury. This is demonstrated from the midrash: "The poor man sits and complains, saying, 'How am I different from so-and-so, yet he sleeps in his bed and I sleep on the ground.'"[5]

The thick basalt stone walls of the Golan were strong enough to support a second story, although there is no evidence that this was the case in this particular house. The flat roof was probably made of large timbers, preferably cedar (Isa 9:9), covered with reeds and clay. It was possible to break through this kind of material as is demonstrated by the story of the paralytic let down to Jesus from the roof (Mark 2:4). This type of roof required regular maintenance. A midrash calls attention to prepare for the winter rains: "The first rain that falls instructs the people to collect their fruit and to plaster their roofs."[6] The householder would need to patch holes and then roll the roof with a stone roller, several of which have turned up at Bethsaida. The rooftop would be used for numerous domestic activities in the warm summer months and also served for storage and drying fruits and vegetables. Peter is described as going to the rooftop for his prayers (Acts 10:9) and it was also considered a good place for study.

Courtyard of "Fisherman's house"

5. Midrash Rabbah Leviticus 34:16.
6. Sifrei on Deuteronomy 42. See also Midrash Rabbah Leviticus 35:12.

Courtyard Style Houses

The excavations at Bethsaida have uncovered two excellent examples of courtyard style houses. This type of house includes a courtyard which is often surrounded by the various rooms of the house and a stone wall which separates it from the street and creates a large private space for the family's domestic activities in a comfortable outdoor setting. This likely denotes a higher class status since in a town like Bethsaida it provided a larger living space. According to Hirschfeld's survey, courtyard style houses range in size from 720 square feet to 10,000 square feet with a mean of 2,880 square feet.

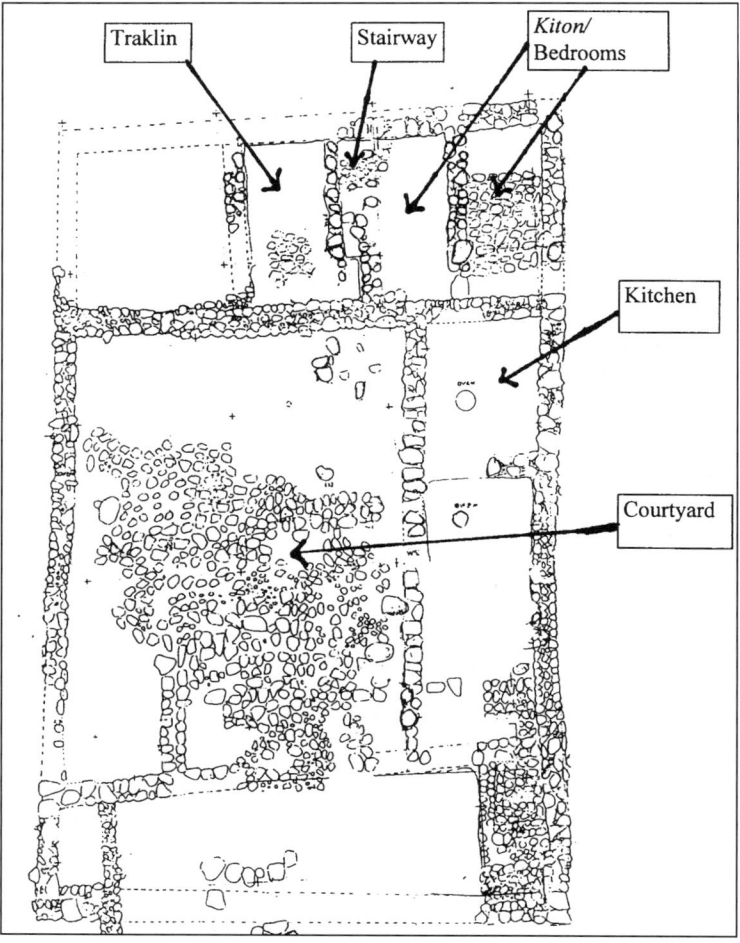

"The Fisherman's House"

In area B, a courtyard style house was called "the fisherman's house" because various fishing equipment was found in the courtyard.[7] The assumption is that the large spacious courtyard provides ample space for business activities such as repair of nets and sails and storage of equipment. Yet the large size of this house likely does not point to the lifestyle of a common fisherman. The dimensions are 54 feet by 81 feet providing a total area of over 4,300 square feet. The courtyard itself, paved with small stones, comprises about one third of this space. Unfortunately, the house has been severely damaged so that only a single course of stones stand on the west side (the northwest corner is completely destroyed) while the best preserved part of the wall on the east side stands about three feet tall.

Possible Reconstruction of Courtyard House

One of the best preserved rooms is a large kitchen on the east side where two ovens were found. There was also an abundance of shards of cooking ware including one intact Hellenistic cooking pot. Three of the four smaller rooms on the north side of the house have been excavated and because of their size, one would guess that those on the northeast were bedrooms. The double wall in the center of these four rooms may indicate

7. Rami Arav, "Bethsaida Excavations: Preliminary Report, 1987–93," *Bethsaida* (1995) 22–3, 27.

70 *Bethsaida: Home of the Apostles*

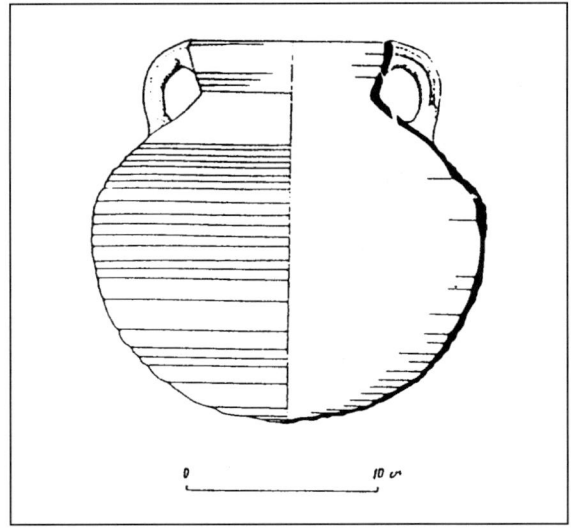

Hellenistic Cooking Pot

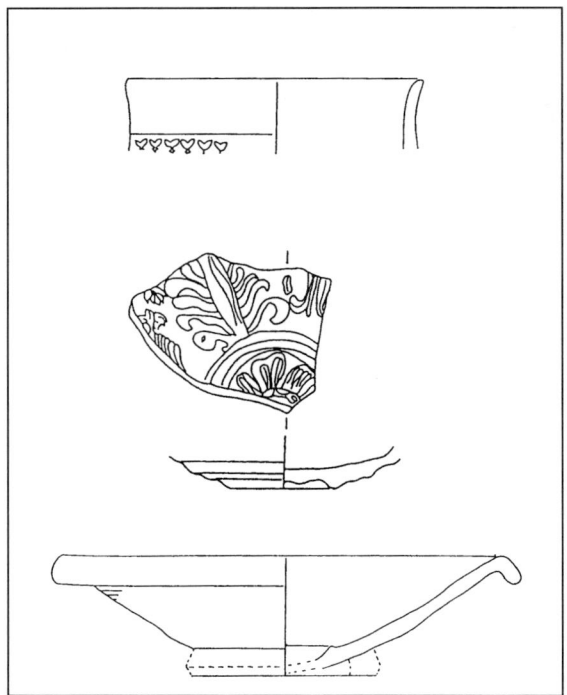

Hellenistic Fine Ware

a stairway to an upper story or the roof. The high quality of life is indicated by the discovery of 156 shards of imported Roman fineware which includes fishplates and finely decorated pieces of Roman Eastern Terra Sigillata pottery.[8] The fact that half of the pieces of this fineware were found in the courtyard area demonstrates that daily life centered around the courtyard. The highest concentration of fineware in the various rooms occurs in the third room from the east on the north side of the house. This may point to the use of this room as the *traklin*, while meals were moved outside to the western part of the courtyard in warmer weather.

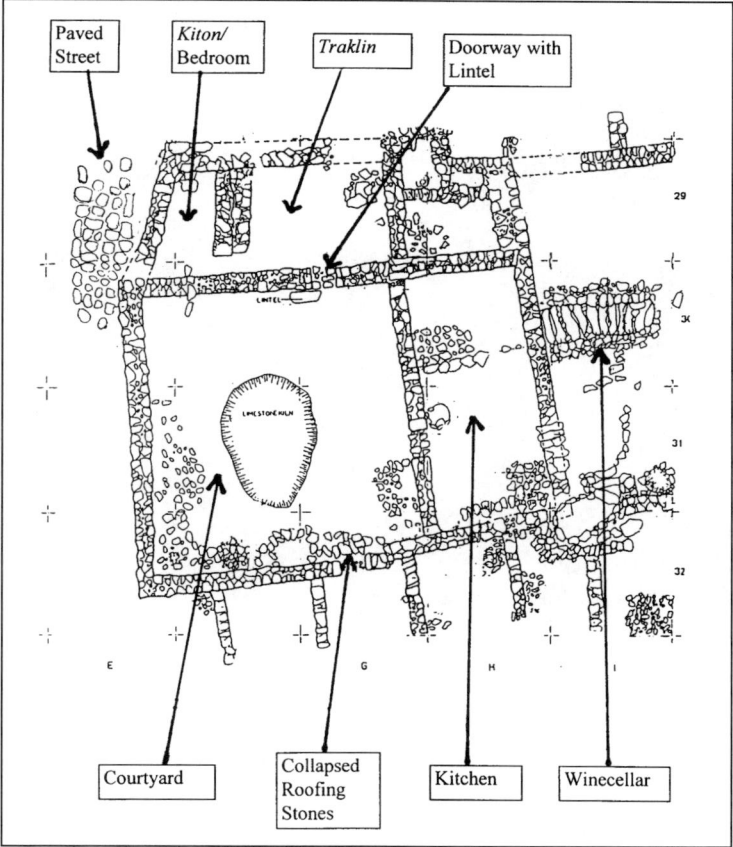

The *"Winemaker's"* House

8. Sandra Fortner, "Hellenistic and Roman Fineware from Bethsaida," *Bethsaida* (1995) 99–126. Distribution patterns were presented in a paper delivered at the 1995 international meeting of the Society of Biblical Literature in Budapest, Hungary.

A second courtyard house from area C of Bethsaida has been called "the winemaker's house."[9] A narrow north-south street passes just to the west of the courtyard. The complex covers an area of about 2,700 square feet measuring about 50 feet by 54 feet. About half of this is made up by the large 36 feet by 38 feet courtyard on the southwest part of the house. Later structures, perhaps shops, were added outside the courtyard to the south. A well-preserved spacious (13 feet by 34 feet) kitchen is on the east side of the house with walls of fine masonry standing about four and a half feet high. Among finds in the kitchen were an oven, a number of grinding stones of various sizes, and much kitchen ware. Along the southern wall were found six or seven complete broken vessels suggesting the presence of a shelf. Three rooms along the north of the house included a larger (18 feet by 14 feet) room in the center which perhaps served as the *traklin*.

Street Passing by "Winemaker's" House

There are several unusual features about this house. Outside the house on the east was uncovered an undisturbed wine cellar with four complete Hellenistic jars and one cooking pot. The cellar was covered with ten basalt slabs, each about four feet long and over a foot in width. The use of basalt slabs for roofing is common in the Hauran although it also occurs in the Talmudic village at Qatzrin. Similar slabs of basalt were found collapsed along the southern part of the kitchen suggesting that this type of corbeling roofing was employed here as well. Likewise a destruction layer of basalt slabs in the southeast part of the courtyard may have covered the

9. Rami Arav, "Bethsaida Excavations: Preliminary Report, 1987–93," 29–34.

eastern part of the courtyard. These would have been supported by the two-foot-thick kitchen wall and most likely a row of pillars in the courtyard. Possibly these were made of limestone since a medieval limestone kiln in the center of the courtyard was used to make lime fertilizer for the fields from such limestone fragments.

Wine cellar with complete jars

This courtyard house also included three nicely made doorways. The main entry on the south is preserved only to a height of two feet. A second doorway to the rooms on the north occurs directly across the courtyard from this entry way. A finely worked lintel rests where it fell just inside that doorway. The finest preserved doorway occurs in the east wall of the courtyard into the kitchen. The threshold of this four-foot-wide doorway is preserved and long iron nails indicate that the doorway had a wooden frame. In excavating the floor in the southeast corner of the kitchen, a Roman doorkey key was discovered. This is the type of key described in Rabbinic literature as a *knee* or *elbow* key because there is a bend in the shaft. When the key is inserted into the keyhole, the bend makes it possible for the part with the teeth to reach around the bolt and engage the tumbler enabling the bolt to be pulled back out of the socket of the door jamb.[10] The ring on the key enabled the householder to carry it conveniently. Thus a Rabbinic ruling is made that "A woman shall not go out in public [on the Sabbath] with a key which is on her finger. If she does go out, it binds her to make a guilt offering."[11]

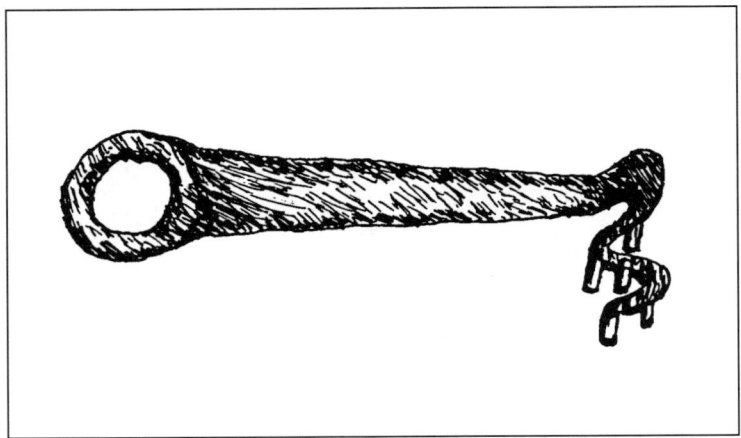

Roman Key

The inhabitants of this house also displayed a rather comfortable style of life. There were also numerous examples of imported fineware as well as Rhodian amphorae. The prize find, however, was a gold earring which uses both granulation and filigree techniques and depicts an unidentified animal. The inhabitants were clearly influenced by Hellenistic culture and made use of a strigilis as was common in the Greek gymnasium. There were also a few items of fishing equipment including a hook and anchors. However, there were also tools of other trades including three iron sickles of the type used in the grape harvest. This fits well with the presence of the wine cellar attached to the house.

The excavation of these houses points to a comfortable lifestyle in first-century Bethsaida. The type of life that centered in this context can be illustrated to some degree by the reconstruction of houses in the Talmudic village in nearby Qatzrin. One expects that future excavation at Bethsaida will continue to shed more light on first-century daily life.

---

10. Yigal Yadin, *Bar Kochba* (London: Weidenfeld & Nicholson, 1971) 194–200.
11. Tosefta Shabbath 4:11.

Houses of Fishermen and Others 75

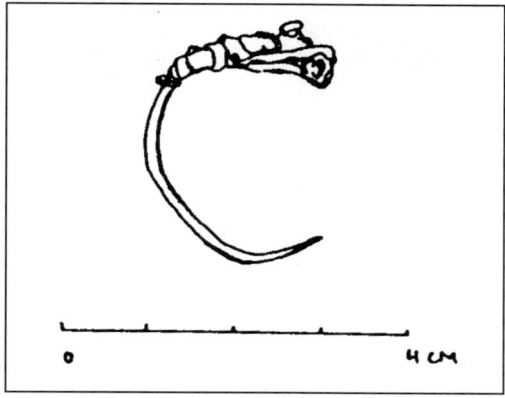

Gold Earring

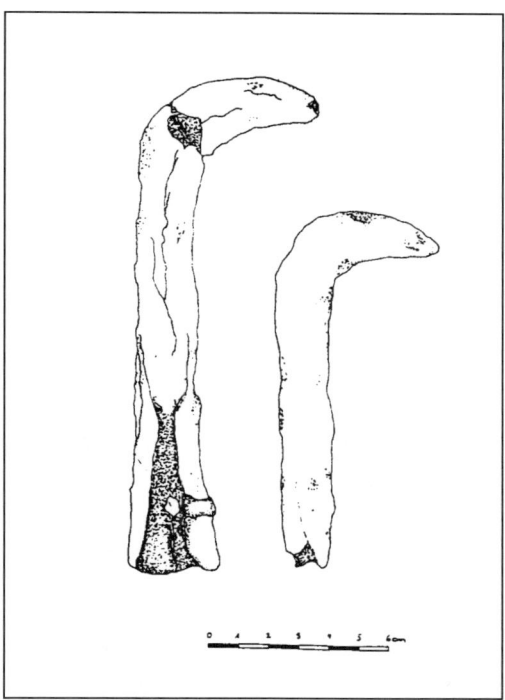

Iron Sickles

Chapter 7

Philip as Ruler

The city of Bethsaida was situated within the Tetrarchy of Philip, the son of Herod. The historical framework for the gospel presented by Luke 3:1-2 designates his rule comprising the region of Iturea and Trachonitis. According to Josephus, this includes the territories of Gaulanitis, Batanea, Trachonitis, Paneas, and Iturea (Josephus, *Ant.* 17.189; *War* 2.168). Roughly this is the area northeast of the Sea of Galilee with the upper Jordan as its western border. Today it corresponds to the Golan Heights[1] and territory extending to the east. The only two cities of this region mentioned in the New Testament are Caesarea Philippi in the north and Bethsaida in the south. The miracle of the Gadarene/Gerasene demoniac was probably located on the eastern coast of the lake, today designated as Kursi (Mark 5:1-20). Later in the reports of the Jewish revolt, Josephus also mentions the cities of Gamla and Seleucia.

This territory did not have a long history of Jewish occupation and was incorporated under the Hasmonean rule through the conquests of Alexander Jannaeus in 83–81 B.C.E. (Josephus, *Ant.* 13.393-397) about one century before the time of the Gospels. In 23–20 B.C.E., Augustus granted Herod the Great allotments which included the Golan as well as Paneas and Iturea to the north. He then settled Jews from Babylon under the

---

1. The Golan Heights today has an area of about four hundred square miles extending about thirty-three miles in a north-south direction and between ten to fifteen miles in an east-west direction. Its average elevation is 2,700 feet above sea level, sloping down to the area around Bethsaida which is below sea level even though it is on a small mound. The Sea of Galilee itself is 895 feet below sea level. The Golan or Gaulanitis was at the heart of Philip's territory although the name does not occur in the New Testament. The other territories extended his rule to the east. The name Golan actually derives from a city (Deut 4:43; Josh 20:8) today to the east of the actual Golan territory.

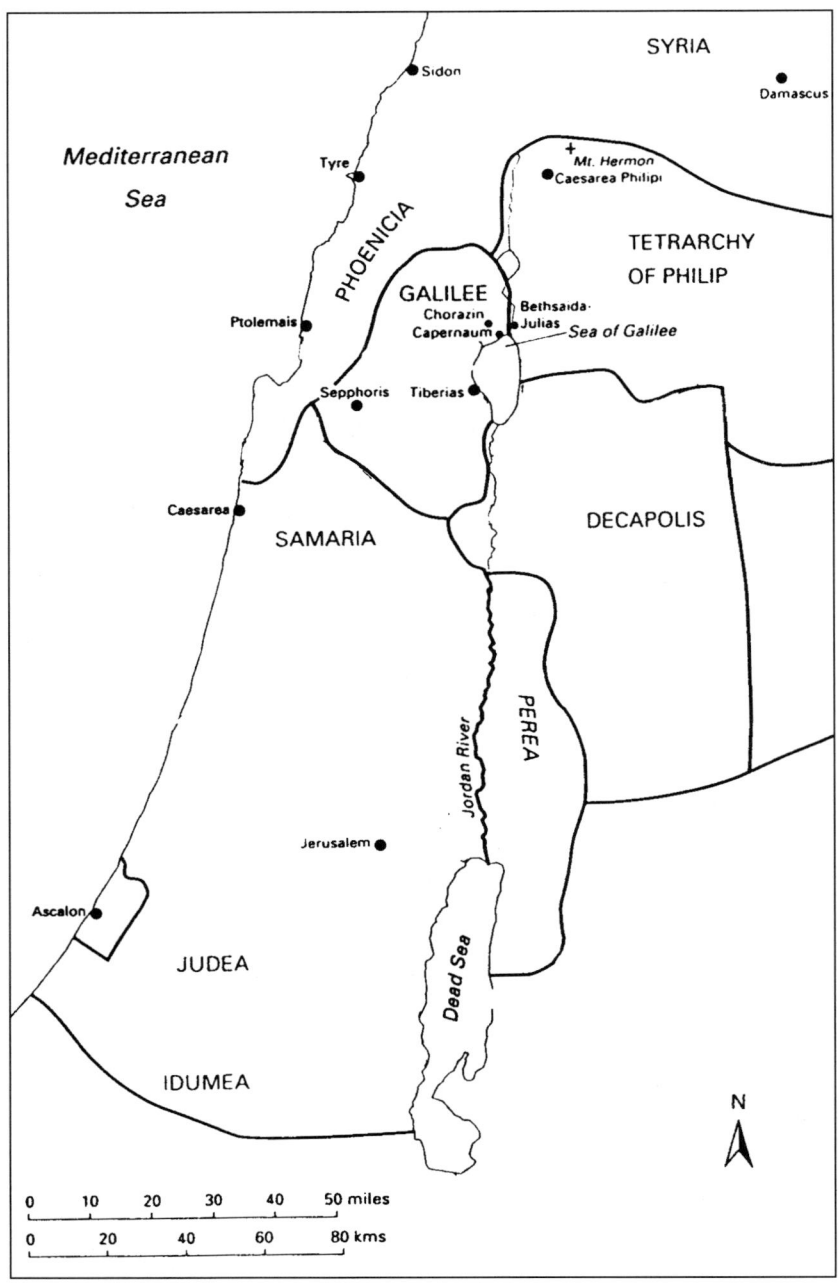

The Territory of Philip

leadership of a certain Zamaris (Josephus, *Ant.* 17.23-29) and Idumeans (Josephus, *Ant.* 16.285) to bring some sense of order to an area with a reputation for lawlessness.

Overview of Philip's Life

As the child of Herod and Cleopatra of Jerusalem, Philip was one of his few children to outlive or, more appropriately, to survive Herod during his later years of paranoia and terror.[2] Philip was probably born around 22 B.C.E. in the same year as his half brother[3] Archelaus and several years before Antipas.[4] He apparently had one full brother named *Herod* (Josephus, *Ant.* 17.21) although there may be some confusion with another son of King Herod by Mariamme 2 (Josephus, *Ant.* 17:14). Philip was sent to Rome, probably around the age of twelve years, where he was educated with the imperial family until the age of seventeen (Josephus, *Ant.* 17.80-2; *War* 1.603), as was common for the children of client kings. As in the case of his elder brothers, Philip's education may have been under the direction of the well-known orator C. Asinius Pollio (Josephus, *Ant.* 15.342-3).[5] At the death of Herod in 4 B.C.E., his kingdom was divided among three sons who were given the title "tetrarch": Archelaus in Judea; Antipas in Galilee and Perea; and Philip in the Golan.[6] While Archelaus was deposed after a decade and replaced with Roman procurators in Judea, both Antipas and Philip completed long tenures in office continuing to rule until after the death of Jesus. Philip died in 34 C.E. and Antipas was eventually deposed in 39 C.E.

Philip's Reputation as Ruler

The tetrarchy of Philip was the poorest of the three in economic resources. Josephus reports that Philip received one hundred talents annual income from his tetrarchy while Archelaus received four hundred talents and Antipas two hundred talents (Josephus, *War* 2.95). This is confirmed

---

2. Emil Schürer, *The History of the Jewish People in the Age of Jesus Christ*, rev. ed., G. Vermes and F. Millar (Edinburgh: T & T Clark, 1973) 1:336–40.

3. On one occasion Josephus erroneously states that Philip was a full brother of Archelaus. Josephus, *Ant.* 17.189.

4. Harold W. Hoehner, *Herod Antipas* (Cambridge: Cambridge University Press, 1972) 12.

5. This figure had served as consul of Rome in 40 B.C.E. and is mentioned in the dedication of Virgil's *Fourth Eclogue*.

6. Herod's will was changed several times. However, the final will designated three brothers as heirs, which was made official only after ratification by Augustus. Josephus, *Ant.*17.188, 224; *War* 1.672; 2.20.

The language of this inscription dating to 29/30 C.E.—"Our Lord Philip"—denotes a very positive attitude toward a relatively distant ruler. Presumably Philip's territory had a smaller population than the two hundred thousand inhabitants of Galilee[9]—perhaps only half the size.

Philip's Marriage

Apparently Philip remained a bachelor throughout the majority of his years. The gospel texts mention him, although in a problematical way, in connection with the story of the death of John the Baptist. According to Mark and Matthew, John had been arrested because of his criticism of Antipas' marriage to Herodias in 26 C.E. (Josephus, *Ant.* 18.109-10). This was especially offensive to John because Herodias, the daughter of Aristobulus, was already married to Antipas' brother. According to Mark and Matthew, Herodias' first husband is identified as Philip (Mark 6:17; Matt 14:3). In a number of manuscripts, however, the reference to Philip is omitted. Likewise Luke, who seems to have inside information about the family of Herod, significantly drops the name of Philip and only states that Herodias was married to Antipas' brother (Luke 3:19). This corresponds to the report of Josephus that Herodias had been married to a son of Herod the Great and Mariamme 2 who was also named Herod (Josephus, *Ant.* 17.14; 18.109; *War* 1.557). The evidence is overwhelming that Philip had not been married to Herodias. Subsequently, however, he married Salome, the daughter of Herodias who danced for the Baptist's head (Josephus, *Ant.* 18.106, 136-7),[10] and together they lived out the remaining years of Philip's life in Bethsaida. Philip died childless (Josephus, *Ant.* 18.106-8).

Relationship of Philip with Roman Procurators

On the whole, Philip and his brother Antipas appear to have had good relationships as they governed adjoining territories for such a long time. On the other hand, Philip showed some reservation about the rule of procurators in Judea. This can be established by looking at the coin mint-

---

9. Hoehner, *Herod Antipas*, 52–3. Josephus, *War* 3.43, gives a population for Galilee as three million inhabitants which would equate to four thousand persons per square mile. Hoehner estimates the population of Galilee to be about 266 persons per square mile or 25,000 for each of four major cities and five hundred for each of two hundred villages.

10. Salome was probably born between the years 10 and 15 C.E. since her mother Herodias was born before her brother Agrippa in 10 B.C.E. The Gospels refer to her as κοράσιον (Mark 6:22, 28; Matt 14:11) placing her at marriageable age.

ing patterns of both Philip and Antipas.[11] The following chart shows the year of each of Philip's eight mintings and also connected historical events:

Year	Coins of Philip	Event	Coins of Antipas
4 B.C.E.		Philip and Antipas begin reign	
1 C.E.	1st issue	Caesarea Philippi celebrated	
6 C.E.		Coponius, procurator, issues coins	
8 C.E.	2nd issue	Reaction to taxation	
9 C.E.		Ambibulus, procurator	
12 C.E.	3rd issue	Annius Rufus, procurator	
15 C.E.	4th issue	Valerius Gratus, procurator	
20 C.E.		City of Tiberias founded	1st issue
26 C.E.	5th issue	Pontius Pilate, procurator	
29 C.E.	6th issue	1st Pilate coins	2nd issue
30 C.E.	7th issue	2nd Pilate coins	3rd issue
31 C.E.		3rd Pilate coins	
33 C.E.	8th issue		4th issue
34 C.E.		Death of Philip	
39 C.E.		Antipas deposed	5th issue

It is significant that Philip issued the coins of his second, third, fourth, and fifth mintings shortly after new procurators came into office. Following the deposing of Archelaus and the arrival of the procurators to govern Judea, the great census took place for the purpose of taxation and Coponius issued coins. Shortly thereafter, Philip issued his own coinage. In the years 12 C.E. and 15 C.E., immediately upon arrival of new procurators Annius Rufus and Valerius Gratus, Philip again issued coins as a way of establishing his rights as a Jewish ruler. With Gratus ruling for eleven years, there was a long interval in which Philip did not put out new coins. With the arrival of Pontius Pilate in 26 C.E., the mintings of Philip resumed.

The ten-year rule of Pontius Pilate (26–36 C.E.) brought about a flurry of minting activity. During his tenure, Philip issued a total of eleven different coins in four different years. During the previous twenty-eight years, he had issued only two coins per year in four different years, for a total of eight. In addition, Antipas joined Philip in issuing coins in 29, 30, and 33 C.E. This all came about in reaction to Pilate's own minting practice in which he deliberately flooded the market with small bronze coins in the

---

11. Fred Strickert, "The Coins of Philip," *Bethsaida* (1995) 165–89. See also Strickert, "Coins as Historical Documents," Rami Arav and John Rousseau, *Jesus and His World: An Archaeological and Cultural Dictionary* (Minneapolis: Fortress Press, 1995).

years 29, 30, and 31 C.E. Leading Israeli numismatist Y. Meshorer notes that Philip and Antipas cooperated in this effort in order to "emphasize their legitimate rights as Jewish rulers."[12] Pilate was so successful that many of these small coins continue to be uncovered in excavations throughout the Galilee as well as in Pilate's own Judea. Interestingly, no Pilate coins have shown up at Bethsaida.

Philip's Leadership against Pontius Pilate

There is one particular occasion when Philip and Antipas were called upon to join forces against Pilate. This came about in response to a series of actions by Pilate which managed to offend the Jewish leadership of Jerusalem. Josephus describes how, on one occasion, Pilate ordered the troops to make their winter quarters in Jerusalem bearing the Roman standards with the image of the emperor (Josephus, *Ant.* 18.55-62), in violation of Jewish laws about images. Later he built an aqueduct, which he then chose to fund by taking money from the temple treasury (Josephus, *War* 2.167-77). Finally, he decided to display in the Herodian palace some golden shields with dedications to the emperor. Philo records this event as follows:

> One of his lieutenants was Pilate, who was appointed to govern Judea. He, not so much to honor Tiberius as to annoy the multitude, dedicated in Herod's palace in the holy city some shields coated with gold. They had no image work traced on them nor anything else forbidden by the law apart from the barest inscription stating two facts, the name of the person who made the dedication and of him in whose honor it was made (Philo, *Embassy to Gaius* 38.299).

When the Jerusalem leadership protested to no avail, Philo states that they called upon Philip and Antipas to intervene:

> But when the multitude understood the matter which had by now become a subject of common talk, having put at their head the king's four sons, who in dignity and good fortune were not inferior to a king, and his other descendants and the persons of authority in their own body, they appealed to Pilate to redress the infringement of their traditions caused by the shields and not to disturb the customs which throughout all the preceding ages had been safeguarded without disturbance by kings and by emperors (Philo, *Embassy* 38.300).

This intervention by Philip and Antipas was successful in bringing a resolution to the problem. Philo completes the account by describing a letter of reprimand sent by the Emperor Tiberius to Pilate:

---

12. Ya'akov Meshorer, *Ancient Jewish Coinage* (Dix Hills, N.Y.: Amphora Books, 1982) 2:38, 180.

> For at once without even postponing it to the morrow he [Tiberius] wrote to Pilate with a host of reproaches and rebukes for his audacious violation of precedent and bade him at once take down the shields and have them transferred from the capital to Caesarea on the coast surnamed Augustus after your great-grandfather, to be set up in the temple of Augustus, and so they were (Philo, *Embassy* 38.305).

This episode likely took place shortly before the crucifixion so that at the trial of Jesus the opposition to Jesus, apparently aware of the reprimand of Pilate, cried out, "If you release this man, you are no friend of the emperor" (John 19:12). The cooperation between Pilate and Herod Antipas at the trial of Jesus helped to smooth things over between the two. After reporting on Jesus' hearing before Antipas, Luke notes, "That same day Herod and Pilate became friends with each other; before this they had been enemies" (Luke 23:12).

There is no indication that Philip and Pilate were reconciled. The fact is that both continued their own self-promotion by an increased frequency in coin mintage. One particular coin is of special interest. Months following Jesus' death, on April 7, 30 C.E., Philip issued a coin which appears to be nothing less than propaganda against Pilate. If my interpretation is correct, this coin even depicts the same shields removed from Jerusalem and displayed in the temple of Augustus. On this coin bearing the images of both Augustus and his wife Livia, Philip followed his usual practice of depicting a tetrastyle temple on the reverse.[13] It is generally assumed that this

Philip Coin—30 C.E.: Augustus and Livia

---

13. Meshorer, *Ancient Jewish Coinage*, coin type 6, vol. 2, 245. This coin is dated to 30 C.E. on the basis of weights and measurements, symbolism, and inscriptions. See Strickert, "The Coins of Philip," 173–81. Jacob Maltiel-Gerstenfeld, *260 Years of Ancient Jewish Coins* (Tel Aviv: Kol Printing Services Ltd., 1982) 143, 148.

temple represents the temple of Augustus at Caesarea Philippi (Paneas) which Herod the Great constructed shortly after the visit of Augustus to Palestine (Josephus, *Ant.* 15.363; *War* 1.404). On this particular coin, the round object in the center of the temple has taken the place where the dates are usually inscribed on Philip's coins. In fact, the two center columns have been positioned further to the sides to call attention to the round object. This symbol has perplexed scholars and a number of interpretations are possible.[14] However, one must assume that this symbol was identifiable by the general public of Bethsaida and nearby towns and that its significance was timely since it had occurred on none of Philip's previous coins. We therefore conclude that Philip made use of this symbolism on the coins of 30 C.E. to remind his subjects of his triumph over Pilate.

Evidence of Judaism within Philip's Territory

It is not totally clear what was the extent of Judaism within the territory of Philip. Josephus characterizes it as having "a mixed population of Jews and Syrians" (Josephus, *War* 3.57). As to the degree of devotion to Judaism, there is some uncertainty. Those in Iturea conquered by Aristobulus 1 in 105–104 B.C.E. were incorporated through forced circumcision (Josephus, *Ant.* 13.318-319). By implication it appears that those conquered under Alexander Jannaeus in 83–81 B.C.E. also were expected to adopt the national customs of the Jews (Josephus, *Ant.* 13:397). One would assume in those cases a less stringent attitude. On the other hand, the Jewish settlers from Babylon during Herod's rule were "devoted to the ancestral customs of the Jews" (Josephus, *Ant.* 17.26).

This kind of attitude of devotion seems to have been in force at Gamla where excavators discovered what is perhaps the oldest synagogue.[15] A nearby mikveh, or ritual bath, corresponds to Jewish legal prescriptions. Even the city planning with houses joined close together and connected by alleyways enclosed by gates resembles regulations set forth in Talmudic law. Bethsaida also certainly included a Jewish community. The Bethsaida disciples clearly had strong Jewish roots. Coin evidence of the first century B.C.E. shows use almost entirely of Hasmonean coins while in previous centuries the community was dominated by a coin market from Tyre

---

14. Hendin suggests that it must be the Greek letter theta. David Hendin, *Guide to Biblical Coins* (New York: Amphora Books, 1987) 70. Meshorer, *Ancient Jewish Coinage*, 2:46, refers to it as "an enigmatic round shape, which was perhaps a decoration on the entrance door." Maltiel-Gerstenfeld, 143, calls it a "shield."

15. Shemarya Gutman, "Gamla: The Masada of the North," *BAR* 5 (Jan./Feb. 1979) 12–25.

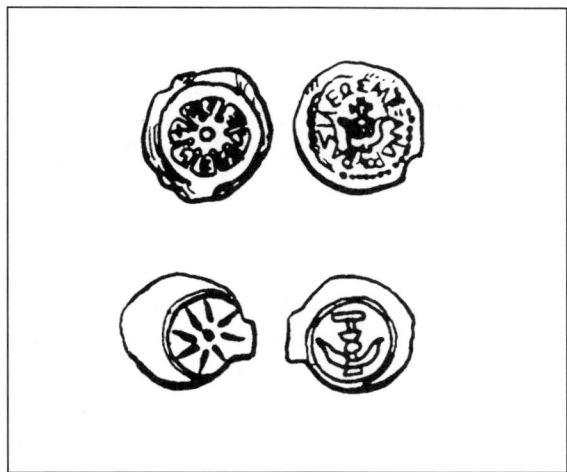

Hasmonean Coins

and other distant cities. Yet the Roman phase of excavation has yet to produce solid evidence of pious Jewish practice. There is yet no synagogue, no mikveh, no stone vessels marking purity concerns. The Judaism practiced here was certainly not dominant.

Philip's Tolerance of Greco-Roman Religion

The shields episode depicts Philip as a defender of Judaism and its customs. However, Philip's position on Jewish law and custom as it was put into practice in Jerusalem did not apply also to his territory. Philip displays an attitude of toleration. The very coin which called to mind the shields incident ironically depicted human images and a pagan temple. In fact, every coin minted by Philip includes human images: Augustus, Tiberius, Livia and his own. The image of Philip, therefore, is the only contemporary depiction of any Jewish character in the Bible. Before him, the Hasmoneans, Herod the Great, Archelaus, Antipas, and even the procurators avoided using human images on their coins. Evidently Philip considered his territory to fall under a different standard of Jewish legal interpretation from Jerusalem, Judea, and Galilee.

Philip simply followed the custom of his territory. This is evidenced by his first coin in 1 C.E. which, by depicting images of Augustus and himself (see illustration, page 80), imitated the coin minted by Zenodorus in 27 B.C.E. with depictions of Octavian and Zenodorus.[16] He was also

---

16. A. Kindler, "A Coin of Herod Philip—the Earliest Portrait of a Herodian Ruler," *IEJ* 21 (1971) 162.

demonstrating his continued loyalty to Augustus and Livia, who assisted in his Roman education and were responsible for his appointment as Tetrarch. This was further made evident through the renaming of Paneas and Bethsaida, the two major cities of his territory, to honor the imperial family: Caesarea Philippi and Julias. As we shall see later, it also led to the promotion of the imperial cult in Philip's territory.

Philip and the Jesus Movement

Philip's attitude of toleration appears to have benefited the Jesus movement as well. Following the chronology of the Synoptics—which is shaped by Mark—the first part of Jesus' ministry is concentrated in the Galilee, the territory of Philip's brother Antipas (Mark 1:14-6:13). At a certain point in his Galilean ministry, Herod Antipas began to perceive Jesus as a threat and to fear that he was John the Baptist raised from the dead (Mark 6:14-16). To emphasize the implications of this threat, Mark at this point recounts the episode of the violent death of John the Baptist (Mark 6:17-29). When Jesus received word of Antipas' growing hostility, Jesus departed from Galilee by boat for "a lonely place"—probably the less populace region near Bethsaida—where he would reflect on this turn of events (Mark 6:30-32). The Matthean version is even more dramatic since it omits the report of the disciples' return and directly links Jesus' decision to cross the sea to the report about Antipas' growing hostility toward Jesus (Matt 14:13). The attempt of Jesus to seek solitude is thwarted by the crowds who follow on foot. Jesus reacts in compassion which leads him to feed the multitude (Mark 6:33-44) and to follow them back to Galilee after a night alone on a nearby mountain (Mark 6:45-52).

Yet from this point on, Jesus moves in (Mark 6:53-7:23 and 7:31-8:12) and out of Galilee (Mark 7:24-30) and soon ends up at Bethsaida once again where he heals a blind man (Mark 8:13-26). Jesus sojourns for some time in the Golan, providing the setting for two critical episodes: the confession of Peter near Caesarea Philippi (Mark 8:27-9:1) and the transfiguration near Mount Hermon (Mark 9:2-13). There is no subsequent restoration of a Galilean ministry, only a short stop passing through in secret (Mark 9:30-31). This sojourn in the Golan—the territory of Philip—allowed Jesus opportunity to reflect on his ministry and to set his face toward Jerusalem (Mark 10:1) and his inevitable arrest and death (Mark 11-15).

Nowhere do we have a report about Philip's attitude toward Jesus as we do about Antipas. However, a close analysis of Jesus' itinerary does suggest at least that Jesus felt more comfortable in Philip's territory during the latter stages of his ministry. This also fits the general tolerant spirit portrayed by Philip. The arrest and execution of Jesus apparently did nothing to mend the antagonistic relationship between Philip and Pilate, as it did in the case of Antipas. As we saw above, coin evidence points to a continued suspicion of Pilate by Philip. This may have created a more open climate for the establishment of the early Christian community in Bethsaida—a topic to which we will return in a later chapter.

The Death of Philip

Philip's career as tetrarch began with the establishment of the city of Caesarea Philippi in the northern part of his territory. That city would serve as his capital. Later Philip's attention was redirected to the southern regions where he undertook a building campaign and founded a second city, Bethsaida-Julias. That city apparently became a favorite residence for Philip and there he died in the year 34 C.E. Josephus reports on his death:

> Now it was at this time that Philip, Herod's son, died in the twentieth year of Tiberius' reign and after 37 years of his own rule over Trachonitis and Gaulanitis. . . . He died in Julias. His body was carried to the tomb that he himself had erected before he died and there was a costly funeral (Josephus, *Ant.* 18.4-6, 106-8).

Remains of this tomb which Philip had constructed at Bethsaida-Julias have continued to elude the modern explorers and excavators of Bethsaida. Nevertheless, the older Bedouins who once frequented the lower Golan recall the traditional stories which led to their choice of et-Tell as a burial ground—it had been established because it had been the burial place of a very important man from many centuries ago.[17]

Philip's Successor: Agrippa 1

Josephus reports that the territory of Philip including the city of Bethsaida was handed over to Agrippa 1[18] (Josephus, *Ant.* 18.237). Agrippa 1, the son of Aristobulus and Bernice was born around 10 B.C.E. and, like other Herodians, was educated in Rome (Josephus, *Ant.* 18.143). His mother was a close friend of Antonia, widow of Tiberius' brother Drusus. He therefore was raised along with (ὁμοτροφίας) the future emperor Claudius and Tiberius' own son Drusus (Josephus, *Ant.* 18.143, 146, 165). Leaving Rome in 23 C.E., Agrippa 1 spent some time in debt before he

---

17. These Bedouins now inhabit the village of Tuba in northern Galilee. Interviews have been recorded on videotape.
18. Daniel R. Schwartz, *Agrippa I: The Last King of Judaea* (Tübingen: J.C.B. Mohr, 1994).

began his political career as supervisor of markets in the city of Tiberias (Josephus, *Ant.* 18.143-9).

Upon Philip's death, however, Agrippa did not immediately receive his territory. Tiberius first placed the territory of Philip under the authority of Syria while funds were placed in a trust fund, probably to pay off Agrippa's debts. He then returned to Rome befriending Caligula until Tiberius' death in 37 C.E. when Agrippa returned to Palestine to make his rule secure. Subsequently Antipas was deposed (39 C.E.), and Agrippa's territory began to expand so that the Golan was combined once again with the Galilee and Judea in the kingdom of Agrippa (41–44 C.E.). It was Agrippa who undertook one of the first persecutions of the early Christians in Jerusalem in the year 44 C.E., putting to death the apostle James and imprisoning for a time Simon Peter (Acts 12:1-19). Shortly thereafter Agrippa died while making a public appearance in Caesarea (Josephus, *Ant.* 19.343-52). According to the Acts of the Apostles, he was struck down by an angel and eaten by worms (Acts 12:20-23).

Since Agrippa's son was still a minor, the territory was again placed under the control of Syria until 53 C.E. when Agrippa 2 began to rule. Recent excavations at Caesarea Philippi have uncovered an elaborate palatial complex apparently constructed by Agrippa 2.[19] For the remainder of the first century, Bethsaida was under his control (Josephus, *Ant.* 20.138; *War* 2.573). Several coins of Agrippa 2, minted across the lake at Tiberias, have been discovered at Bethsaida. During the Jewish revolt in 67 C.E. when Agrippa lost control of the Galilee, he retreated to the Golan where he set up a government in exile. The Bethsaida area became important for him in his strategy to regain control of the Galilee. It was at this time that Agrippa's forces under the command of Sulla camped near Bethsaida to cut off the supply routes of his opponents. Had the Galilean forces under Josephus been successful against Sulla, Agrippa's hold on the Golan would have been weakened. However, with the defeat of the Galilean forces, Agrippa secured his hold on the Golan and began to retake Galilee. Eventually, this led to the fall of Jerusalem. Agrippa 2 returned to Rome, befriending the emperors, and secured his rule over Bethsaida and the Golan until his death at the end of the first century.

---

19. John F. Wilson and Vassilios Tzaferis, "Banias Dig Reveals King's Palace," *BAR* 24 (Jan./Feb. 1998) 54–61, 85.

Chapter 8
The Founding of Bethsaida-Julias

On September 22 in the year 30 C.E., Philip officially founded Bethsaida-Julias. This marks the most important day in the history of this seaside city and most likely was a day of gala celebration. This is an especially significant event because it comes at the heart of the New Testament era. With the death of Jesus dated to April 7, 30 C.E., there can be no doubt that the transformation of this city had an impact on Jesus and the disciples.[1]

The Reports of Josephus

The founding of this city is reported twice by Josephus. In both cases, he reports together on the two cities founded by Philip. In *The Antiquities of the Jewish People* he writes:

> Philip for his part made improvements at Paneas, which is situated at the headwaters of the Jordan, and called it Caesarea; he further granted to the village Bethsaida on the Sea of Galilee both by means of a large number of settlers, and through further expansion of strength, the rank of a city and named it after Julia, the daughter of Caesar (Josephus, *Ant.* 18.28).

This report provides four important pieces of information about Bethsaida city. First, the founding is interpreted in terms of additional settlers and extensive building projects. It is clear that this was not to be a new city built from scratch, but an expansion of an already existing settlement. This is consistent with the finds at et-Tell which show the Roman phase of building as a further development of the Hellenistic city. This counters the

---

1. Fred Strickert, "The Founding of Bethsaida-Julias: Evidence from the Coins of Philip," *Shofar: A Journal for Inter-Jewish Dialogue* 13 (1995) 40–51.

arguments of those who would like to see two separate settlements with the Hellenistic fishing village in the Beteiha plain and the Roman city on the acropolis about a mile away.[2]

Second, Josephus describes a change in status from a village (κώμη) to a city (πόλις). It is not clear, however, whether the status of *polis* included all the official rights granted with the name or whether the name was more symbolic. Third, Josephus notes that the founding included a name change from *Bethsaida* to *Julias*. This text is significant because it is the only one which combines both names Bethsaida and Julias. The biblical texts consistently use *Bethsaida* and Josephus, as also Pliny and Ptolemy, use *Julias*. Finally Josephus notes the significance of the name change stating that it was instituted to honor Julia the daughter of Augustus.

If taken at face value, this would mean that Bethsaida-Julias was founded around the year 3 B.C.E. since Philip took over his rule in 4 B.C.E. and Augustus' daughter Julia was exiled for her adulterous behavior in 2 B.C.E.[3] This would be consistent with the treatment of the founding also of Caesarea Philippi which took place shortly after Philip took over his rule. However, the decision to build two different towns simultaneously is not typical for rulers of this time. Philip's brother Antipas, for example, first built Sepphoris in Galilee, then Livia in Perea, and then Tiberias in Galilee over a period of 24 years. It is unlikely that Philip would have founded two towns at the beginning of his rule and then nothing over the next 36 years. One wonders also how the name Julias would have persisted with regard to this town in view of the scandal associated with the daughter of Augustus.

Josephus' second report about the founding of these cities offers some insight. In *Jewish War*, he writes:

> On the death of Augustus, who had directed the state for 57 years, six months, and two days, the empire of the Romans passed to Tiberius, son of Julia. On his accession, Herod Antipas and Philip continued to hold their tetrarchies and respectively founded cities: Philip built Caesarea near the sources of the Jordan in the district of Paneas, and Julias in lower Gaulanitis; Herod built Tiberias in Galilee and a city which also took the name of Julia in Perea (Josephus, *War* 2.168).

Here it is significant that the context for the description about the founding of these cities follows his report about the death of Augustus and the accession of Tiberius as Emperor, events which occurred in 14 C.E. One would expect that what follows—the founding of cities—took place after 14 C.E. In fact, the city of Tiberias in Galilee was founded by Antipas in

2. James Strange, "Bethsaida," *The Anchor Bible Dictionary*, ed. David Noel Freedman (Garden City, N.Y.: Doubleday, 1992) 1:692–3.
3. Tacitus, *Annals* 3.24.

20 C.E. and, in 15 C.E. in Perea, the name *Julia* was given to the city of Livia (formerly Betharamphtha), which had been founded only several years earlier (Josephus *Ant.* 18.27). Although Tiberius had rebuilt and founded Sepphoris around 8 C.E., this is not mentioned here. The context of this passage clearly points to events following 14 C.E.

Also it is significant that the only *Julia* mentioned here is not the daughter of Augustus, but his wife and the mother of the Emperor Tiberius. In fact, it was not until the time of Augustus' death that she was given the name *Julia*. Her given name was Livia and she had become the most powerful woman in Rome. She had married Augustus on January 17, 38 B.C.E., three days after giving birth to Drusus. Her other son by Tiberius Nero was Tiberius, who was three years old at the time of her second marriage. Previously Augustus had been married to Scribonia whose daughter Julia gave Augustus two grandsons, Gaius and Lucius, who were adopted by Augustus as heirs, but preceded him in death. Since Augustus and Livia together had no children, Tiberius was named as Augustus' heir. Through the action of the Roman Senate, Augustus was deified and, following the wishes of Augustus, Livia was officially adopted into the Julian clan. This gave her the right to use the name *Julia* as well as the title Σεβάστη (Sebaste), the Greek equivalent of Augusta.[4] This action indirectly made Tiberius a Julian and paved the way for his accession as emperor. At the same time Livia/Julia was elevated to the position of Empress Mother and, in reality, made her co-regent with her son Tiberius. This made her a person to be highly respected (and feared) in Rome and to be highly honored throughout the provinces.

As can be seen in this section from Josephus, Livia/Julia was highly respected also in Palestine. It is especially significant that Josephus himself chose to use the name *Julia*, not Livia, to designate her as mother of Tiberius. He also notes that Antipas had named a city in Perea in her honor. Since Augustus and Livia had held a special place in the lives of the Herodians, it was natural that Philip would have dedicated a city in honor of each: Caesarea Philippi in honor of Augustus and Bethsaida-Julias in honor of Livia/Julia.[5]

The Imperial Family and the Herodians

King Herod had developed a special relationship with the imperial family and was dependent on them for his position of power (Josephus, *Ant.* 15.199, 361; 16.290, 338). As noted in the previous chapter, many of

---

4. Tacitus, *Annals* 1.8.14; Dio Cassius, *Roman History* 56.32.1; 46.1; 57.12.2; Suetonius, *Augustus* 101.2.

5. The late fourth-century pseudo-Hegesippus interprets Josephus this way with the reading *Liviam Urbem*.

Herod's children and grandchildren had been sent to Rome for their education. This included first Aristobulus, Alexander, and Antipater; then Philip, Archelaus, and Antipas; later Agrippa; and finally Agrippa 2. Augustus himself took a personal interest in their studies and directly reported back to Herod upon their completion (Josephus, *Ant.* 15.342-3; 16.6, 78-86; 17.80-2; 19.360). Thus it is not surprising that Josephus uses the term ὁμοτροφίας (raised together) to describe their relationship with the children of the imperial family including future emperors Tiberius, Caligula, and Claudius (Josephus, *Ant.* 18.165).

During this time, a number of the women in Herod's family also came to Rome developing close friendships with the women of the imperial family. This included especially Herod's sister Salome and her daughter Bernice (Josephus, *Ant.* 17.10, 134-41; 18.31, 143, 156, 165; *War* 1.566, 641-3; 2.167).[6] It was Salome who became very close with Livia. When the will of Augustus was contested, it was Salome who helped facilitate the settlement which led to the tetrarchies of Archelaus, Antipas, and Philip (Josephus, *Ant.* 17.220, 321; *War* 2.15, 98). This is rather significant since Herod's will had granted Archelaus the title "king" and greater power. Yet Salome's personal animosity for Archelaus was instrumental in reducing his status.[7] In this settlement, Salome herself received the territory of Jamnia, Azotus, and Phasaelis as well as five hundred thousand pieces of silver and an annual revenue of sixty talents (Josephus, *Ant.* 17.321; *War* 2.98). When Salome died, she bequeathed her territories to Livia/Julia (Josephus, *Ant.* 18.31; *War* 2.167).

The Founding of Betharamphtha-Livia

In view of Salome's influence with Livia and her animosity towards certain members of the Herodian family, it was politically wise for both Antipas and Philip to court Livia's respect. The timing of Antipas' dedication of the city Betharamphtha-Livia is instructive. The rebuilding of this city probably began soon after the completion of Sepphoris around 8 C.E. The dedication took place certainly before 14 C.E. because Josephus reports that it was first renamed *Livia* (Josephus, *Ant.* 18.27) and then renamed *Julia* after the assession of Tiberius as emperor (Josephus, *War* 2.168). Since it was customary to coordinate the founding of cities with important dates in the lives of the emperors,[8] it is likely that Antipas chose the year 13 C.E. for its founding since that year marked the fiftieth wed-

---

6. Strabo, *Geography* 16.2.46.
7. Harold W. Hoehner, *Herod Antipas* (Cambridge: Cambridge University Press, 1972) 18–39.
8. M. Avi-Yonah, "The Foundation of Tiberias," *IEJ* 1 (1950–51) 168–9.

ding anniversary of Livia and Augustus and also her seventieth birthday.[9] The building of Betharamphtha-Livia thus took place between the years 8 and 13 C.E.

This is significant because it followed closely after Archelaus had been deposed in 6 C.E., and the Roman procurators had been established in Judea. Although Josephus explains the cause of Archelaus' downfall as a conflict with leading Jews and Samaritans (*Ant.* 17.342-4; *War* 2.111), Dio Cassius explains it in terms of accusations by Archelaus' own brothers.[10] A contemporary of these events, Strabo, suggests that the accusations were not all one-sided, but he notes that Herod's sons were not so successful in the arrangement as co-rulers, and that they "became involved in accusations."[11] The result of a hearing before Augustus in Rome is that Archelaus was banished while Antipas and Philip were allowed to continue their rule, yet not without difficulty— θεραπεία πολλῇ μόλις. It is also from this point on that the title "Herod" is associated with Antipas.[12] So he came out of this situation, not merely surviving, but also benefiting.

To what did he owe this turn of events? One would expect that Salome again had played a role through the influence of Livia. This may be deduced by the fact that it was Salome who now came to control the estate of Archelais with its abundant palm groves,[13] which she then passed on to Livia several years later in her will. In other words, Antipas was greatly indebted to Augustus via Livia via Salome who, not only helped him through this crisis, but even helped him to improve his lot. When Salome died several years later, and then Augustus, it was critical that he cultivate his favor directly with Livia. Thus he honored her with a city named *Livia* in 13 C.E., which he subsequently renamed *Julia* to celebrate her new status upon adoption into the Julian clan.

The Julia Coins of the Procurators

Antipas was not alone in courting the favor of Livia. The procurators of Judea began dedicating their coins to Julia after Augustus' death. From 15–26 C.E., Valerius Gratus issued six different coins with ΙΟΥΛΙΑ inscriptions.[14] Then in the year of Livia's death, 29 C.E., Pontius Pilate issued

---

9. Hoehner, *Herod Antipas*, 87–91.
10. Dio Cassius, *Roman History* 55.27.6.
11. Strabo, *Geography* 16.2.46.
12. Hoehner, *Herod Antipas*, 105–9.
13. Compare Josephus, *Ant.* 17.321 with 18.31 and *War* 2.67 with 2.167.
14. Ya'akov Meshorer, *Ancient Jewish Coinage* (Dix Hills, N.Y.: Amphora Books, 1982) 2:173.

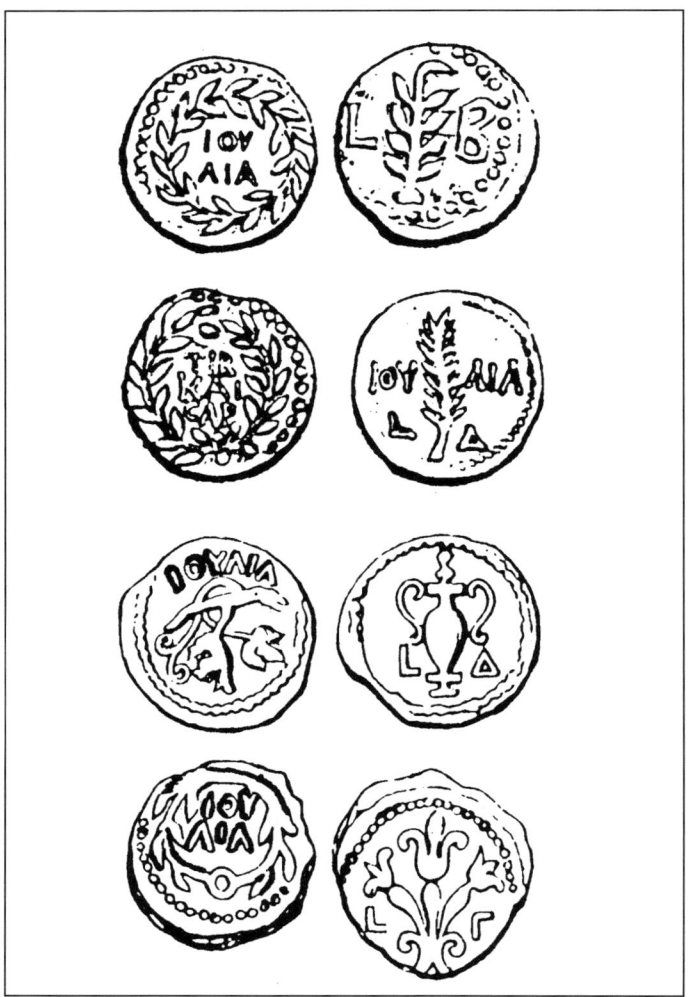

Julia Coins of Procurator Gratus—15 to 17 C.E.

a Julia coin.[15] There was no question about his allegiance. The inscriptions were ΤΙΒΕΡΙΟΥ ΚΑΙΣΑΡΟΣ and ΙΟΥΛΙΑ ΚΑΙΣΑΡΟΣ on the two sides respectively. In previous years, the procurators had employed neutral symbols on their coins showing respect for Jewish custom. Pilate, however, depicted on the obverse a *simpulum*, which was a ladle used by Roman priests to pour wine over sacrificial animals. On the reverse, he depicted three ears of grain bound by stalks.

15. Meshorer, *Ancient Jewish Coinage*, 180, 283.

Pontius Pilate Coin—29 C.E.

The use of grain symbolism here is extremely significant. Gertrude Grether notes that Livia was frequently associated with Abundantia (= ΕΥ-ΘΕΝΙΑ), the goddess of agricultural plenty or identified with Demeter in the Mystery cults.[16] Statues of her have been found in the context of the Eleusian mysteries and at cult centers in Asia Minor. On coins of Augustus from 2 B.C.E. to 14 C.E., she is often depicted seated and holding ears of grain and a scepter. Following her adoption into the Julian clan, her role is that of a goddess who plays a central role in the imperial cult, especially in the provinces. Tiberius continued the practice of depicting the image of the seated Livia on the reverse of denarii bearing his own image. Since this was used for the tribute tax it was familiar to Roman subjects even in Palestine, as the gospel accounts confirm. Thus the coin of Pilate appropriately depicts her as priestess of Augustus and the goddess of plenty.

This coin issued by Pilate is unique among the various Julia coins in that the depicted ears of grain are drooping. This occurs, of course, to commemorate the death of Livia/Julia earlier that same year. The events surrounding her death reveal a controversy concerning her relationship with her son Tiberius the Emperor. Her adoption into the Julian clan, which made possible his accession to the throne, at the same time elevated her status so that she stood in competition with him. The friction had increased to the point where he retreated from Rome and spent little time there during the last years of her life.

---

16. Gertrude Grether, "Livia and the Roman Imperial Cult," *AJP* 67 (1946) 222–52.

When she died, only a simple funeral was held for Livia/Julia and Tiberius chose not to return for it. This came about as a rebuff to her own wishes for deification as was the case with her husband Augustus some fifteen years earlier.[17] By staying away, Tiberius was able to deter any efforts toward an elaborate funeral and to avoid taking a public stand which might appear unpopular. At Tiberius' wish, the senate denied her request for deification and instructed only that Tiberius construct an arch in her honor—an order that was never carried out. The senate also declared an official period of mourning for one year. On the surface this order seems to demonstrate a high degree of respect for Livia/Julia. However, it was a carefully planned move which contrasted with the funeral of Augustus when mourning was forbidden because he had now ascended as a god.[18] In contrast, Livia/Julia was to be treated as a mere human. The Julia coin of Pilate in 29 C.E., with the drooping ears of grain, shows that this mourning was taken seriously throughout the empire. It also served as a political statement. The two drooping ears of grain could easily represent Livia and Augustus; the one erect ear, Tiberius. It was essential that Pilate cultivate his favor at a time when his position was being challenged.

The Evidence of Philip Coins

Philip issued Julia coins only in the years 30 and 33 C.E., both after her death. These coins carry on the obverse side the inscription ΙΟΥΛΙΑ ΣΕΒΑΣΤΗ, which notes both the name she received in 14 C.E. and the title as the reverent one or Augusta. This latter title had been used on other coins of

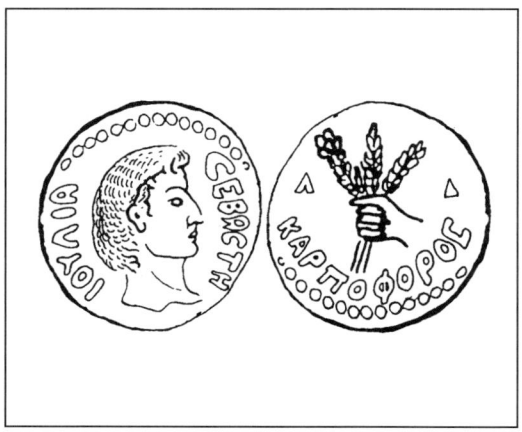

Philip Coin—30 C.E.: Image of Livia

17. Dio Cassius, *Roman History* 58.2; Suetonius, *Tiberius* 51; Tacitus, *Annals* 5.1-2.
18. Dio Cassius, *Roman History* 56.41.

the provinces, but not on the coins of the procurators. Totally unique among Palestine coinage is the depiction of Livia/Julia herself, the first woman to appear on a Jewish coin. On the reverse are depicted three ears of grain. It would seem that Philip is here responding to Pilate's coin of 29 C.E. As noted in the previous chapter, his coins follow a pattern which responds to the events surrounding the procurators in Judea. It is also significant that this is a smaller denomination of coin than Philip had previously produced, yet it corresponds to the small coins used by Pilate to flood the markets.[19]

The imagery of three ears of grain also seems to be a response to Pilate's coin. Yet there are three differences. First, the grain is not drooping, but erect. Second, they are depicted as held in a hand. Third, an inscription explains the imagery: ΚΑΡΠΟΦΟΡΟΣ (Fruitbearing). The message is that Livia-Julia, even though she was physically dead, continues to serve as benefactress for her subjects, bestowing on them an abundance of grain through her own outstretched hand.

The difference between this coin and that of Pilate is a difference between the attitudes of people about Livia/Julia in Rome itself and in the provinces. For a long time, subjects in the provinces, where ideas of divine rulers were often long accepted, had granted various divine titles to Livia/Julia. Yet in Rome deification could occur only after a ruler had died, and only in a limited number of cases. Tiberius and the senate had spoken. Livia/Julia was a mere mortal. Yet a grassroots movement continued to persist in the provinces which supported her deification and Philip was part of that movement. These efforts continued for several years until 41 C.E. when Livia's grandson, the Emperor Claudius, declared her deification.[20] It is not surprising that Philip's successor, Agrippa 1, also issued a coin in 42 C.E. which depicted the three ears of grain—a sign of honor for Livia-Julia.

Philip did more to honor Livia/Julia than just issue coins. He also founded a city Bethsaida-Julias. Although Josephus in *Antiquities* connects this city with the daughter of Augustus, in *Jewish War*, he implies a connection with Livia, wife of Augustus. The coin evidence firmly establishes this latter connection. The city of Bethsaida-Julias was founded in 30 C.E. when the Julia coin was issued. In fact, Philip issued four different coins in the year 30 C.E., unlike his pattern of issuing only two coins per mint in previous years. These four coins can be identified by the images depicted:

- Augustus and Livia
- Tiberius
- Livia-Julia
- Philip

19. Strickert, "The Coins of Philip," *Bethsaida* (1995) 171–8.
20. Suetonius, *Claudius* 11; Dio Cassius, *Roman History,* 60.

Philip Coin—30 C.E.: Image of Philip

Especially significant is the Tiberius coin, which, with the image of the emperor on the obverse and tetrastyle temple on the reverse, is identical to coins of previous mints with one exception. The inscription reads ΕΠΙ ΦΙΛΙΠΠΟΥ ΤΕΤΡΑΡΧΟΥ ΚΤΙΣ (During the rule of Philip the Tetrarch, Founder). This is the only time that those final four letters occur on a coin of Philip. The letters ΚΤΙΣ are an abbreviation for the Greek word κτίστης, meaning "founder" and, of course, implying "the founder of cities." In fact, in the passage from *Jewish War* quoted above, Josephus

KTIS Coin of Philip: Tiberius—30 C.E.

uses the same root κτίζει to describe Philip founding Caesarea Philippi and Bethsaida-Julias. The presence of this coin along with the Julia coin in the mint of 30 C.E. make absolute the conclusion that Philip founded Bethsaida-Julias in the year 30 C.E.[21]

The coin depicting both Augustus and Livia is also significant. It includes the inscription ΤΩΝ ΣΕΒΑΣΤΩΝ, which, paralleling the Julia coin, bestows upon Livia honors equal to that of Augustus. This coin makes it possible to date the founding even more precisely. Cities of client kings throughout the empire customarily celebrated the birthdays of both

Philip Coin—30 C.E.: Augustus and Livia

Augustus and Livia together in a three-day celebration in September. This began on September 22 with the recognition of Livia/Julia and it culminated on September 24 with the celebration of Augustus' birthday and the beginning of a new year. The gala celebration, which continued long after their deaths, often included sacrifices, games, and plays. In the year after Livia's death, it likely also included a special dedication ceremony adopting the name *Julias* for the newly expanded city of Bethsaida. September 22 in the year 30 C.E., therefore, marks the founding of Bethsaida-Julias.

As was noted above, the founding of cities often corresponded with the important dates in the lives of the imperial family. Since these coins were reissued in 33 C.E., it is likely that Philip had originally intended to dedicate the city in that year which would have marked the ninetieth birthday of Livia-Julias and her seventieth wedding anniversary with

---

21. Meshorer, *Ancient Jewish Coinage*, 49, suggests that this must refer to the thirtieth anniversary of the founding of Caesarea Philippi.

Augustus. However, her death in 29 C.E. prompted Philip to celebrate its founding in the year 30 C.E.

Reasons for Founding Bethsaida-Julias

It may seem unusual that Philip had waited so long—thirty-four years into his rule—before offering this demonstration of respect to Livia-Julia. His brother Antipas had dedicated a city to Livia some seventeen years earlier. There are a number of factors to consider. One may have been the expense involved in offering such improvements to a city. Philip's territories did offer less revenue than neighboring Galilee or Judea. Another factor may have been the attraction of a seaside town, which became important to Philip only after Tiberias was founded in 20 C.E.

One must also consider the political issues. There are signs that Philip had always been much less ambitious for political power than his brothers. When Archelaus and Antipas traveled to Rome in 4 B.C.E. to contest Herod's will both seeking kingship, Philip quietly stayed behind in Jerusalem to look after the affairs of government (Josephus, *Ant.* 17.219-20). Later, when Archelaus was deposed, Philip may not have been directly involved since Josephus does characterize it as a dispute between Jews and Samaritans (Josephus, *Ant.* 17.342-4) and this may be related to the fact that Archelaus and Antipas were the sons of the Samaritan Malthace. The point is that Philip may have had no real need to cultivate favor with Livia. He was simply doing his job quietly and successfully and remained popular with his subjects.

Was there some kind of change emerging in the mid-20s C.E. which began to challenge his rule? One possible source of concern for Philip may have come from Agrippa 1 who eventually did receive Philip's territory after his death in 34 C.E. Agrippa, the grandson of Livia's close friend Salome, had continued to live in Rome for thirty years after he was first taken there for his education in 5 B.C.E. He was raised with the imperial family and developed close friendships with Tiberius' son Drusus and future emperors Caligula and Claudius. Such an upbringing was designed precisely to produce future rulers.

By the year 25 C.E., Agrippa was thirty-five years old, but still did not have a kingdom. It was about this time that Agrippa's influential mother Bernice died, that he married, and that he left Rome for Judea. Although he was thwarted in his ambitions for a time by his own personal debt, Agrippa eventually emerged to succeed Philip and to secure the deposing of Antipas after numerous accusations. Philip's decision to marry for the first time at the age of over fifty years also may have been related to such political concerns since his wife Salome was Agrippa's niece. Likewise, it may be no coincidence that Antipas had recently married Agrippa's sister Herodias. Such marriage connections would make it difficult for Agrippa to seek their removal from office. Yet it was the founding of Bethsaida-Julias which guaranteed that Philip would continue his rule until his natural death in 34 C.E.

The Livia Cult

The practice of founding a city in honor of a member of the imperial family often led to more than just an honorary name change. The most complete evidence of the imperial cult comes from Asia Minor. When client kings were given permission to establish the cult, they agreed to offer worship to the emperor as well as to the goddess Roma. They would construct a temple in honor of the designated imperial family member and they would form a group of priests and officers to conduct the cult. They would also erect other structures such as a theater, amphitheater, and a stadium which would be used during the festivities taking place at the time of birthday celebrations in September.

It is not certain to what degree these practices were incorporated in Palestine. In 27 B.C.E., the same year that Octavian became Augustus, King Herod founded the city of Sebaste in Samaria with a temple dedicated to Augustus, a theater, and a stadium. In 13 B.C.E., the year of Augustus' fiftieth birthday, Herod founded Caesarea Maritima with an impressive elevated temple to Augustus, a theater, a stadium, and a hippodrome. In the case of Caesarea Philippi, the temple for Augustus was built in 20 B.C.E. although the city was not founded until the rule of Philip. In the case of cities founded by Antipas—Sepphoris-Autocrates, Betharamphtha-Julia, Tiberias—less is known.

What practices of the cult of Livia were included at Bethsaida-Julias? Josephus' comment that Bethsaida-Julias was given the status of *polis*, would seem to imply that the founding involved more than just an honorary change of name. However, evidence for typical Roman structures such as a stadium or a theater has mostly been elusive. In the summer of 1996, however, in a prominent position in the center of the mound, the foundations of a building were excavated, which has tentatively been identified as a Roman temple. The structure, oriented in an east-west direction, includes four major sections typical of Roman temples: a porch, an approaching hall *(pronaos),* the holy of holies *(naos),* and a back room *(opisthodomous).*[22] Although the structure is in a state of ruin, a segment

---

22. Rami Arav and Richard Freund, "An Incense Shovel from Bethsaida," *BAR* (Jan./Feb. 1997) 32.

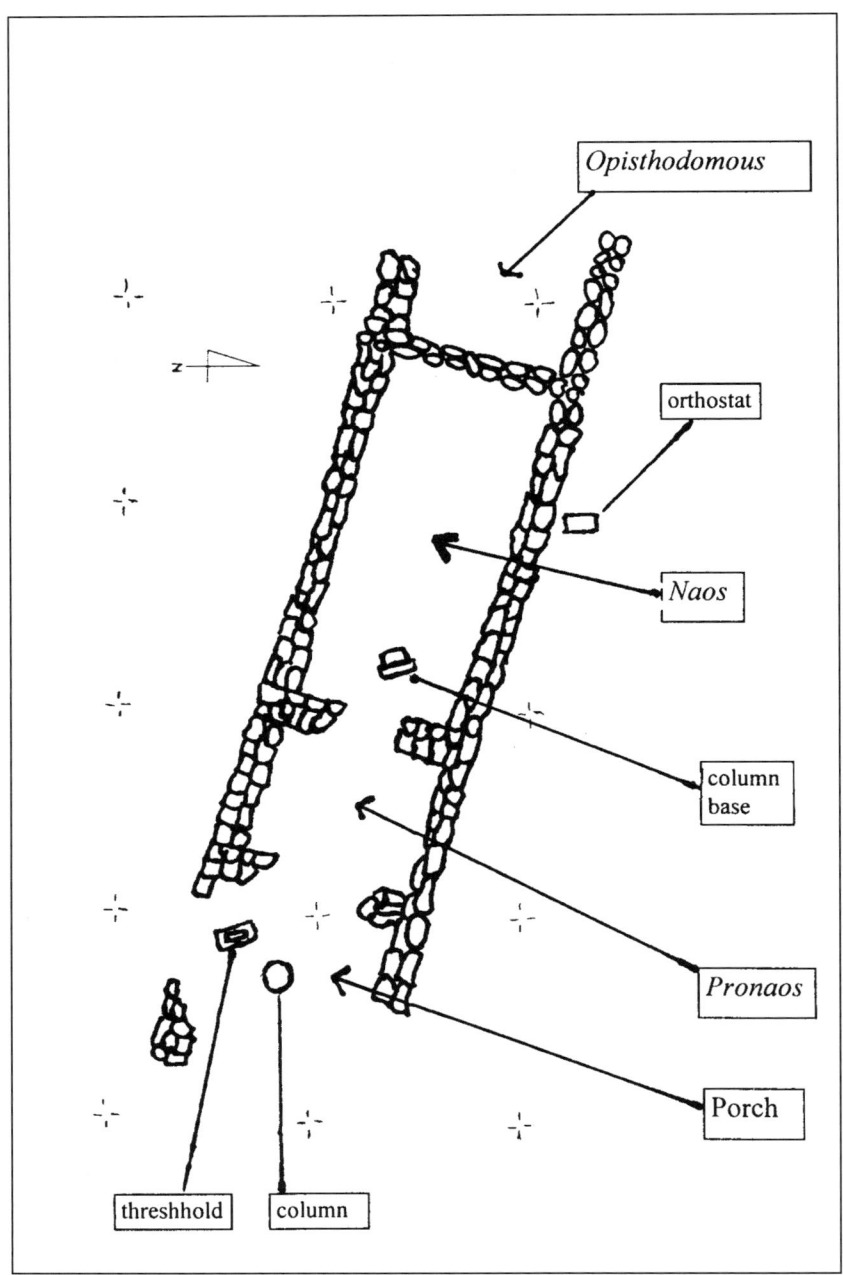

Plan of "Livia Temple"

of one column remains positioned in the exact center of the porch and several other column fragments and a column base were uncovered scattered throughout the rubble.

Incense Shovel, Livia Cult

Among the artifacts discovered in connection with the building is an eight-inch-long bronze incense shovel typical of the Roman imperial cult. The only other parallels for this were discovered in the Bar Kochba caves, which Yadin reasons must have been among booty captured from the Roman army, who had brought them from Padua where they had been manufactured.[23] The ornate find from Bethsaida, with a Corinthian-column-shaped handle and a rectangular pan engraved with concentric circles and adorned with two protruding leaves, provides a small glimpse of the splendor that once was displayed at Bethsaida. This recent discovery is reason to study further the imagery of the Philip coins. One possibility is that the unique depiction of the temple on the Augustus/Livia coin (see illustration, page 101) may reflect the Bethsaida-Julias temple, differing from the other Philip coins which depict the Caesarea Philippi temple. Thus the prominent circular object may well reflect a ritual object of the imperial cult. The discovery of the incense shovel leaves no doubt that this relatively small settlement was a place where the imperial cult was practiced and, at least for a time, played a dominant role.

There is also some evidence for the existence of statues of Livia/Julia. A small figurine, measuring ¾ inch by 1½ inch, shows the head of a female figure draped with a veil that is characteristic in depicting Livia as

---

23. Yigal Yadin, *Bar Kochba* (London: Weindenfeld and Nicolson, 1971).

Clay "Livia" Figurine

priestess of Augustus.[24] Likewise her curled hair, with traces of red, is of a style typical of statues of Livia/Julia during the rule of Tiberius. Because this figure was made in a mold with clay, the details may not be as fine as with most depictions of Livia/Julia. Yet the medium may suggest mass production.

Another clue may come from the 30 C.E. Julia coin of Philip mentioned above (see illustration, page 98). The depiction of a hand holding the three ears of grain is somewhat unusual. It may represent a portion of a large statue well known to the inhabitants of Bethsaida-Julias. Unfortunately, limestone statues may have been destroyed in more recent times as is evidenced by several limestone kilns found throughout the site. One may hope that future seasons of excavation may provide finds which may broaden our understanding of the Livia cult.

Implications for the Gospels

The name *Julias* does not occur in the Gospels. One would have expected the name *Julias* rather than *Bethsaida* in the Gospels if Josephus' comment were correct concerning the connection between Bethsaida-Julias and the daughter of Augustus because the founding would have taken place in 3 B.C.E. The founding date of September 22, 30 C.E., estab-

---

24. Rami Arav, "Bethsaida Excavations: Preliminary Report, 1987–93," *Bethsaida* (1995) 21.

lished by coin evidence, fits perfectly with literary documents. Since the crucifixion is generally dated to April 7, 30 C.E., a reference to Julias in the Gospels would have been anachronistic. The name Bethsaida is therefore quite appropriate. Likewise it is interesting that Mark uses the term κώμη (village) to designate this location (Mark 8:23) while Luke and John designate it as πόλις (city) suggesting a later perspective (Luke 9:10; John 1:44).

The period of Jesus' ministry corresponded exactly to this active time of building and expansion in Bethsaida that would have consumed a number of years' labor. It is difficult to imagine that Jesus and his disciples would have been unaffected by such activity. One must ask also whether this involvement would have been more than just the casual observations of those passing through. Jesus is identified in the Gospels as a carpenter. The term τέκτων (Mark 6:3) refers to various building activities including woodwork, building with stone, masonry, and the like and, therefore, Jesus may have been involved in general construction work connected with the building of cities.[25]

It has been suggested that Joseph the carpenter settled in Nazareth because Antipas was actively building the nearby city of Sepphoris. One can imagine with a flurry of building activity taking place at Caesarea Philippi, Sepphoris, Betharamphtha-Livia, Tiberias, and Bethsaida-Julias that construction workers found themselves migrating from town to town following the work. Is it possible that Jesus' interest in Bethsaida stems from his career as a carpenter? The Gospels offer no explanation why Jesus chose to leave Nazareth and to focus his ministry on the northern Sea of Galilee area. It may well be that Jesus originally came to this area seeking work as a carpenter. His interest in this area and its inhabitants would lead him to focus his preaching and healing ministry here after his contact with John the Baptist.

---

25. Chester C. McCown, "ὁ τέκτων," *Studies in Early Christianity*, ed. Shirley Jackson Case (London: The Century Co., 1928) 173–89; Richard A. Batey, "Is Not This the Carpenter?" *NTS* 30 (1984) 249–58.

Chapter 9

The Disciples of John the Baptist

There is an underlying assumption in the Gospels that many of Jesus' followers originally had gone out into the desert to hear the preaching of John the Baptist and had been first baptized by him. It is the Gospel of John that makes this connection between disciples of John and disciples of Jesus explicit and interestingly also makes a connection with Bethsaida.

Disciples of John Who Follow Jesus

At the beginning of the Fourth Gospel, John the Baptist is introduced as baptizing "in Bethany across the Jordan" (John 1:28). After serving in the role as pointing the way to Jesus—identifying him as the Lamb of God and describing how he witnessed the Spirit descending upon him—John sends two of his own disciples to follow Jesus (v. 37). One is later identified as Andrew, a disciple from Bethsaida (v. 40). The other is not identified. Therefore speculation has been offered concerning his identity. The two likely candidates are Philip, who is introduced by name in verse 43, and John the son of Zebedee, who goes unnamed throughout the Fourth Gospel. The authorship of the Fourth Gospel is a complex question, but many see the driving force as the one called the "beloved disciple" or "the other disciple," who is then identified as John, Zebedee's son. With the focus on the role of eyewitness testimony (John 19:35), it is natural to expect such testimony from the very beginning and continuity between the circles of John and Jesus.

Urban Context for Q Sayings about John

It is important to note that the disciples mentioned in relation to John the Baptist also have a Bethsaida connection. This is fitting in view of the series of sayings which are joined together in Q:

Jesus began to speak to the crowds about John: "What did you go out into the wilderness to look at? A reed shaken by the wind? What then did you go out to see? Someone dressed in soft robes? Look, those who put on fine clothing and live in luxury are in royal palaces" (Matt 11:7-8 = Luke 7:24-26).

The context of this particular saying is the city. Jesus is addressing crowds who have gone out into the wilderness to see and hear John and his comments contrast what they have seen with the sights in their own city. The common sight of those dressed in soft robes and living in luxury in royal palaces limits the choice of cities to those connected with Antipas and Philip: Sepphoris, Tiberias, Caesarea, Philippi, and Bethsaida.

With the flurry of new building activity including palatial structures in Bethsaida, one can imagine the soft-robed Philip more frequently gracing its streets to inspect the progress of improvements, all the while attracting crowds of people curious to get a glimpse of royalty. The choice of Bethsaida as the context for this saying is underscored by the second image used in this section, the reed blowing in the wind. Because of its location at the mouth of the Jordan River, the bottom areas below the city are made up of reed-covered marshland. Wind-blown reeds and soft-robed royalty come together at Bethsaida.

The city life likewise contains the busy market with children dancing and playing their flutes (Matt 11:16-17 = Luke 7:32) and is the gathering place for "tax-collectors and sinners" (Matt 11:19 = Luke 7:35). Bethsaida provides a fitting setting for these sayings concerning John the Baptist. In Matthew's editing of the sayings material from Q, the woe saying about Bethsaida (Matt 11:21) follows directly. In Luke, that saying comes several chapters later (Luke 10:13). They are joined in Matthew as prophetic sayings from the lips of Jesus, who now speaks in the prophetic train of John (Matt 9:11-15 = Luke 7:26-28).

It is also significant that these prophetic words are spoken in a context in which John has been arrested and now sits in prison wondering if Jesus is indeed the one who is to come. Disciples of John have come to seek an answer from Jesus. In response Jesus does not give a "yes" or "no," but rather recounts a list of the marvelous deeds that have been accomplished:

> The blind receive their sight, the lame walk, the lepers are cleansed, the deaf hear, the dead are raised, and the poor have good news brought to them (Matt 11:2-6 = Luke 7:18-23).

The woe saying against towns such as Bethsaida naturally follows since that is where Jesus has done most of his deeds of power and there has been no repentance (Matt 11:20 = Luke 10:13).

Bethany Across the Jordan

There is no question that the people who went out to see John had come from every town and village. The traditional picture is that John was baptizing primarily in the waters of the Jordan River near Jericho and not far from where the river empties into the Dead Sea. Thus John is often connected with the wilderness of Judea, denoting the area west of the Jordan from Jericho on to the south (Matt 3:1). However, there are also notations that John himself had traveled about through "all the region around the Jordan" (Luke 3:3). In the Fourth Gospel, two such locations are named: Aenon near Salim where there was abundant water (John 3:23) and Bethany across the Jordan (John 1:28). The former site apparently is located west of the Jordan, but closer to Beth Shean where there are springs of water. The location of the latter site is uncertain.

The name Bethany is familiar as the village on the eastern slopes of the Mount of Olives not far from Jerusalem (John 11:18). Yet this Bethany is identified as "across the Jordan." There are no such towns otherwise identified east of the Jordan River. Because of familiarity with the name Bethany, one might expect confusion with less familiar, but perhaps similar names. Suggestions have been made about possible confusion with the town Betharamphtha, renamed Julia by Antipas, or a site named "Bethabara" which occurs on the Madaba map east of the Jordan. This is a variant reading that occurs in a number of ancient texts beginning with Origen, yet has gained little support. Perhaps the most important clue offered by John is that Bethany is not identified as a city or village, but as a τόπος (place) (John 10:40).

The site of Bethsaida is located at et-Tell at the edge of the Beteiha plain. This plain today extends one and a half miles from et-Tell to the present northern shore of the Sea of Galilee. It begins at the Jordan River and extends three miles east along the northern part of the lake continuing with a narrow strip along the eastern shore. A connection between Beteiha and Bethany is appealing, yet there are two major concerns. First, there is uncertainty about the extent of the Beteiha plain with two thousand years of geological changes, as was noted in a previous chapter.[1] Second, it is not clear how old is the name Beteiha.

Likely "Beteiha" derives from the word "Betah" which often was used to denote a hollow, column-like receptacle for collecting rain water.[2] One

---

1. John F. Shroder, Jr., and Moshe Inbar, "Geological and Geographical Background to the Bethsaida Excavations," *Bethsaida* (1995) 74, 82–3.

2. Rami Arav, "Bethsaida Excavations: Preliminary Report, 1987–93," *Bethsaida* (1995) 3; Marcus Jastrow, *A Dictionary of the Targumim, the Talmud Babli and Yerushalmi, and the Midrashic Literature* (Philadelphia: Traditional Press, 1975) 156.

would assume that this name was connected with the plain because of its marshy character where much water collected because there empties the various rivers of the Golan: the Jordan, Meshoshim, Zawitan, Yehudiye, Sefamnun, and Daliyot. This name is thus quite appropriate for the activity of John who sought out certain locations "because water was abundant there" (John 3:23). The key to understanding the name "Bethany" in John 1:28 may be this understanding of abundant water, whether it was connected with the modern Beteiha plain or some other site where much water collected.

Another suggestion is that the name Bethany in John 1:28 is related to the region on the eastern edge of Philip's territory known as Batanea, corresponding to the Old Testament Bashan.³ This is especially appealing because it is designated in several places (Josephus, *Ant.* 8.37; LXX Num 32:32-3; Deut 3:8; 4:47) as περαν του˒ Ιορδανου (beyond the Jordan), the same expression in John 1:28. This is the area where Herod settled 3,000 Jewish immigrants from Babylon under the leadership of Zamaris (Josephus, *Ant.* 17.23-29). Josephus describes them as "devoted to the ancestral customs of the Jews," and they possibly had Essene connections.⁴ According to Epiphanius, the Nazorite and Ebionite Jewish-Christian groups were heavily populated in this area.⁵ It is, therefore, not surprising that John the Baptist would have included them in his ministry. It would also be expected that in this location John would have drawn crowds especially from Bethsaida. When one fits Batanea into the context of John 1, it is clear that Bethsaida plays a critical role—Mark Appold calls it a crossroads—linking this important area of John's ministry with that of Jesus in the Galilee.⁶ After leaving Batanea with two former disciples of John, Jesus' itinerary west to Cana in Galilee passed directly through Bethsaida where further disciples were added to the growing circle around Jesus. A Batanea ministry of John thus is closely related to the centrality of Bethsaida in the ministry of Jesus.

Late Tradition about Philip and John

Perhaps these details in the Fourth Gospel point to the existence of Baptist groups in and around Bethsaida. Although the Greek text of Jose-

---

3. Rainer Riesner, "Bethany Beyond the Jordan," *The Anchor Bible Dictionary*, ed. David Noel Freedman (Garden City, N.Y.: Doubleday, 1992) 1:703–5.

4. Bargil Pixner, "Unraveling the Copper Scroll Code: A Study on the Topography of 3 Q 15," *Revue de Qumran* 11 (1983) 323–66.

5. Epiphanius, *Haer.* 29.7; 30.2.

6. Mark Appold, "Bethsaida: Crossroads of the Galilee," paper presented to the 1995 International Meeting of the Society of Biblical Literature, Budapest, Hungary.

phus nowhere mentions contact between Philip and John the Baptist, later traditions speak of a dream which Philip had before his death in Bethsaida. In this tradition, John the Baptist came to interpret a dream where an eagle came and plucked out his eyes. The tradition states that various wise men attempted with no avail to interpret the dream, but that a convincing interpretation came through John the Baptist:

> When Philip was still reigning he dreamed that an eagle was about to pick out both his eyes. He called the wise men, but they were unable to interpret his dream, the one giving this, the other a different explanation. But that man of whom we have written before, the one who dressed in animals' hair, was cleansing the people in the Jordan, called John, arrived without being called from the desert—in fact, quite unexpectedly—and said: "Listen to the word of the Lord: The dream which you have seen foreshadows your death, for that eagle is a bird of prey and has picked out your eyes." And after he had said this, Philip died the same evening.[7]

Although Philip was considered moderate in character and was rather popular, his political concerns increased during his latter years, as we saw in the previous chapter. With the eagle a common symbol for Rome, it is not difficult to see the emerging threats of Pilate, Agrippa 1, and Tiberius following Livia's death.

There are a number of difficulties with this tradition. A serious concern is its late date since it occurs in a Rumanian version of Josephus which was dependent upon a Russian version.[8] The Slavonic version of Josephus also includes the tradition of the dream, but with significant embellishments which are clearly Christian interpolations.[9] In that version John the Baptist interprets the dream in terms of both the threat of Agrippa taking his kingdom and Antipas taking his wife Herodias and it explains these events as a result of Philip's venality. These statements clearly are inconsistent with the statements of Josephus in the Greek versions. Yet, in the Rumanian version, the only difficulty may be the comment describing Philip's subsequent death occurring that very night.[10] There is clearly a relationship between the Rumanian and Slavonic versions, the shorter version would seem to be earliest. Whether it reflects an authentic independent

---

7. "The Rumanian Josephus Fragments," Robert Eisler, *The Messiah Jesus and John the Baptist according to Flavius Josephus* (N.Y.: Dial Press, 1931) 599–600.

8. This manuscript, Codex Gaster, No. 89, also includes later traditions such as the Gospel of Nicodemus and the Acts of Pilate.

9. "The Slavonic Josephus," *Flavius Josephus*, trans. H. St J. Thackeray, (Loeb Classical Library) (Cambridge, Mass.: Heinemann's) 3:646. Eisler, *The Messiah* (1931) 229.

10. Philip's death occurred early in the year 34 C.E. while the Gospels describe John's death as preceding the death of Jesus.

tradition about Philip is impossible to know. However, it is significant in that it does assume John as being active in the territory of Philip and it does imply an openness of Philip towards John.

Jesus Returns to the Place of John's Ministry

The fourth evangelist pays one further visit to Bethany. Toward the end of Jesus' ministry as he began to face a hostile Jewish leadership, Jesus "went away again across the Jordan to the place where John had been baptizing earlier, and he remained there" (John 10:40). There Jesus meets with a measure of success. It has been suggested that this episode is paralleled in the Synoptics as Jesus left the Galilee and "went to the region of Judea and beyond the Jordan" (Mark 10:1; Matt 19:1).[11] Earlier Jesus' movement away from Galilee into the regions around Bethsaida resulted from reports that Antipas feared Jesus to be John raised from the dead (Mark 6:31; Matt 14:13). With Galilee no longer offering security to Jesus and those connected with John the Baptist, the territory of Philip apparently remained open to them. Perhaps the territory of Philip—and also the city of Bethsaida—became the center for the Baptist community following John's death. For Jesus to retreat from Galilee to the Perea beyond the Jordan, also Antipas' territory, would make no sense. More likely Jesus retreated to Batanea beyond the Jordan. Bethsaida would have served as a perfect stepping off point as Jesus made his way again to the wilderness.

---

11. Raymond E. Brown, *The Gospel According to John*, The Anchor Bible (Garden City, N.Y.: Doubleday, 1966) 1:414.

Chapter 10

The Multiplication of Loaves and Fishes

The Multiplication of Loaves and Fishes is the only miracle which occurs in all four Gospels (Mark 6:31-44; Matt 14:13-21; Luke 9:10-17; John 6:1-14). While Matthew and Luke may derive similarities from Mark, John presents an independent witness from the Markan tradition.[1] Similarities in all four versions may well denote evidence of early traditions. One is also struck by the fact that in three Gospels this miracle is followed directly by the episode of the walking on the sea (Mark 6:45-52; Matt 14:22-34; John 6:16-21).[2] This all points to the earliness of the traditions surrounding this material.

It is also significant that this material has connections to the city of Bethsaida. In Luke 9:10, the feeding takes place at Bethsaida, and, in Mark 6:45, the disciples head towards Bethsaida following the feeding. Neither Matthew nor John identify the location explicitly although both include information which support the Lucan geographical framework. It is true that such geographic references are likely additions by the evangelists. In this particular case, the contradiction suggests confusion on the part of the evangelists. For some this means that it is impossible to locate these accounts. For others, such confusion may still point to a Bethsaida connection which can only be determined by careful examination of details.[3]

---

1. The Johannine version presents enough variation to demonstrate independence from the Synoptic tradition. Raymond E. Brown, *The Gospel According to John*, The Anchor Bible (Garden City, N.Y.: Doubleday, 1966) 1:236-44. Also similarities between Matthew and Luke may be evidence of a third version. Joseph Fitzmyer, *The Gospel According to Luke*, Anchor Bible (Doubleday, 1981) 1:763.

2. Only Luke omits this miracle which is part of the great omission in which Luke avoids doublets of the feeding episode and healing of a blind man in Mark 6–8.

3. Among my Bethsaida colleagues who have written on this topic, Kuhn takes the former position while Appold and Rousseau take the latter position. I am grateful for all their helpful insights.

Texts

Matthew 14:13-21	Mark 6:31-44	Luke 9:10-17	John 6:1-14
13 Now when Jesus heard this, he withdrew from there in a boat to a deserted place by himself. But when the crowds heard it, they followed him on foot from the towns.	31 He said to them, "Come away to a deserted place all by yourselves and rest a while." For many were coming and going, and they had no leisure even to eat. 32 And they went away in the boat to a deserted place by themselves. 33 Now many saw them going and recognized them, and they hurried there on foot from all the towns and arrived ahead of them.	10b He took them with him and withdrew privately to a city called Bethsaida. 11 When the crowds found out about it, they followed him;	1 After this Jesus went to the other side of the Sea of Galilee, also called the Sea of Tiberias. 2 A large crowd kept following him, because they saw the signs that he was doing for the sick. 3 Jesus went up the mountain and sat down there with his disciples. 4 Now the Passover, the festival of the Jews, was near. 5 When he looked up and saw a large crowd coming toward him,
14 When he went ashore, he saw a great crowd; and he had compassion for them and cured their sick.	34 As he went ashore, he saw a great crowd; and he had compassion for them, because they were like sheep without a shepherd; and he began to teach them many things.	and he welcomed them, and spoke to them about the kingdom of God, and healed those who needed to be cured.	
15 When it was evening, the disciples came to him and said, "This is a deserted place, and the hour is now late; send the crowds away so that they may go into the villages and buy food for themselves."	35 When it grew late, his disciples came to him and said, "This is a deserted place, and the hour is now very late; 36 send them away so that they may go into the surrounding country and villages and buy something for themselves to eat."	12 The day was drawing to a close, and the twelve came to him and said, "Send the crowd away, so that they may go into the surrounding villages and countryside, to lodge and get provisions; for we are here in a deserted place."	Jesus said to Philip, "Where are we to buy bread for these people to eat?" 6 He said this to

The Multiplication of Loaves and Fishes

Matthew 14:13-21	Mark 6:31-44	Luke 9:10-17	John 6:1-14
			test him, for he himself knew what he was going to do.
16 Jesus said to them, "They need not go away; you give them something to eat." 17 They replied,	37 But he answered them, "You give them something to eat." They said to him, "Are we to go and buy two hundred denarii worth of bread, and give it to them to eat?" 38 And he said to them, "How many loaves have you? Go and see." When they had found out, they said,	13 But he said to them, "You give them something to eat." They said,	7 Philip answered him, "Two hundred denarii would not buy enough bread for each of them to get a little." 8 One of his disciples, Andrew, Simon Peter's brother, said to him, 9 "There is a boy here who has five barley loaves and two fish. But what are they among so many people?"
"We have nothing here but five loaves and two fish."	"Five, and two fish."	"We have no more than five loaves and two fish—unless we are to go and buy food for all these people." 14 For there were about five thousand men. And he said to his disciples,	
18 And he said, "Bring them here to me." 19 Then he ordered the crowds to sit down on the grass.	39 Then he ordered them to get all the people to sit down in groups on the green grass. 40 So they sat down in groups of hundreds and of fifties.	"Make them sit down in groups of about fifty each." 15 They did so and made them all sit down.	10 Jesus said, "Make the people sit down." Now there was a great deal of grass in the place; so they sat down, about five thousand in all. 11 Then
Taking the five loaves and the two fish, he looked up to heaven, and blessed and broke the loaves, and gave them to the disciples, and the disciples gave them to the crowds.	41 Taking the five loaves and the two fish, he looked up to heaven, and blessed and broke the loaves, and gave them to his disciples, to set before the people; and he divided the two fish among them all.	16 And taking the five loaves and the two fish, he looked up to heaven, and blessed and broke them, and gave them to the disciples to set before the crowd.	Jesus took the loaves, and when he had given thanks, he distributed them to those who were seated; so also the fish, as much as they wanted. 12 When they
20 And all ate and were filled; and they took up what was left over of the broken pieces,	42 And all ate and were filled; 43 and they took up	17 And all ate and were filled. What was left over was gathered up,	were satisfied, he told his disciples, "Gather up the fragments left over, so that nothing may be lost." 13 So they gathered them up,

118 Bethsaida: Home of the Apostles

Matthew 14:13-21	Mark 6:31-44	Luke 9:10-17	John 6:1-14
twelve baskets full.	twelve baskets full of broken pieces and of the fish.	twelve baskets of broken pieces.	and from the fragments of the five barley loaves, left by those who had eaten, they filled twelve baskets.
21 And those who ate were about five thousand men, besides women and children.	44 Those who had eaten the loaves numbered five thousand men.		
			14 When the people saw the sign that he had done, they began to say, "This is indeed the prophet who is to come into the world."

The Setting for the Miracles

Although only Luke explicitly places this miracle at Bethsaida, the other three accounts are in agreement that the location for the feeding was reached by boat. Prior to the feeding, the evangelists describe Jesus and his disciples embarking by boat and going ashore. Afterwards Jesus sends his disciples away by boat, and, after a struggle, they reach their destination where they moor the boat. Only Luke does not include references to boats at the beginning, middle, and end of this section. Significantly, the same three speak of "the other side" (Matt 14:22; Mark 6:45; John 6:1) and of "crossing over" (Matt 14:34; Mark 6:53) and "going across" (John 6:17). The place of origin is not mentioned by name, but the Synoptics imply that they began on the western shore in the territory of Antipas whose growing hostility has led to Jesus' decision to withdraw for a while. Three of the evangelists report a return to the western shore at the end of this section, with Matthew and Mark mentioning the destination as Gennesaret (Matt 14:34; Mark 6:52) and John mentioning their eventual arrival at the synagogue of Capernaum (John 6:59). John also reports that people had searched for Jesus on the following day, traveling by boat from Tiberias to the place of the feeding and then to Capernaum (John 6:23-24).

All of these accounts, therefore, are in agreement that the feeding took place on the eastern side of the Sea of Galilee, that is, the section east of the mouth of the upper Jordan. Even Luke, who does not mention boat travel at this point, implies a location on the east side since the next episode—having omitted two chapters from Mark—is the confession of Peter which takes place at Caesarea Philippi. The difficulty in Mark 6:45—going "toward Bethsaida"—does not imply a site on the western shore, but rather one further east of Bethsaida.

Another similarity between the different versions of the feeding episode is that the crowds who wish to follow Jesus travel, not by boat, but on foot. There is a slight variation in the different accounts:

> Mark 6:33—Now many saw them going and recognized them, and they *hurried there on foot* from all the towns and arrived ahead of them.
> Matt 14:13—But when the crowds heard it, they *followed him on foot* from the towns.
> Luke 9:11—When the crowds found out about it, they *followed* him.
> John 6:2—A large crowd *kept following* him.

At the end of the feeding, Jesus dismissed the crowds while he sent his disciples by boat. The site therefore is one that is accessible both by land and by boat—and within a reasonable walking distance.

The Synoptics imply that the crowds walk to the site of the feeding, that they hear Jesus' teaching, that many are healed, that they are fed, and that they return to their homes—all in a single day. The account in John speaks of healing those who were sick and reserves the report of teaching until the following day in the Capernaum synagogue. Nevertheless, they agree that this was quite an undertaking for a single day. One cannot imagine a journey of more than six to eight miles each way. A typical day's journey for the Roman army was twenty-four miles. That assumed travel by Roman roads and not cross-country over mountainous terrain in the company of people who were sick and injured. In calculating distances, one must not be misled by the modern northeast shoreline of the Sea of Galilee and the easy access by the modern road crossing into the Golan at the Aphik bridge.

When Theodosius visited the site in 530 C.E., he reported the distance from Capernaum to Bethsaida as six miles. This distance implies travel by the Roman road which went from Capernaum to Chorazin and then east to Bethsaida. With the rugged ancient coast line, this is a likely course for those described as traveling on foot in the feeding miracle. It involved a steady climb from the plains around Capernaum up to Chorazin, a steep descent down to the Jordan River, and then another climb up from the Jordan. Therefore, with those on foot coming from the place of Jesus' departure (Capernaum) as well as from towns along the way, one cannot imagine a destination too much further east of Bethsaida. Bargil Pixner has suggested Tell Khader on the east side of the lake for a feeding miracle, yet it is difficult to imagine the additional three to four miles travel on a single day.[4]

---

4. Bargil Pixner, "The Miracle Church of Tabgha on the Sea of Galilee," *BA* 48 (Dec. 1985) 199.

Hills, Much Grass, and a Deserted Place

The accounts also give a number of other details concerning the location. Although the site was near the sea, it was also hilly. In Mark and Matthew, Jesus ascends a nearby hill at the end of the feeding (Mark 6:46; Matt 14:23). In John, however, Jesus climbs a hill at the beginning, and the crowds ascend to him (John 6:3). Later, after coming down with the crowds, he ascends the hill once again (John 6:15). Another detail is that the place was grassy where the people sat (Matt 14:19). John notes that there was "a great deal of grass" (John 6:10) and Mark notes that it was green grass (Mark 6:39). Since the entire lake is surrounded by hills, the detail about grass helps to limit the possible sites, yet it is still somewhat ambiguous.

The other significant detail is that the site is described in the Synoptics as "a deserted place" or "a lonely place," depending upon the translation. There is no question that this expression is to be emphasized since it occurs as often as three times in one account (Mark 6:31, 32, 35; Matt 14:13, 15; Luke 9:12). The term ἔρημος can be translated as desert, but because of the reference to grass, it probably denotes only a place with sparse population. Still there are farms and villages nearby. In view of the connections between John the Baptist, the desert, and Bethany beyond the Jordan, there may be some intended link to the area east of Bethsaida, yet the Fourth Gospel itself does not include the desert focus in the feeding episode. Rather, it comes in the discussion which takes place on the following day (John 6:49).

The question is raised whether Jesus originally intended to withdraw as far as the desert area of Batanea—which will be the case later on (Mark 10:1 = John 10:40)—yet compassion for the crowds drew him back to Galilee for a time. Although the later gospel accounts refer to the crowds following Jesus to the site of the feeding, the earlier Markan account suggests that they knew of Jesus' intended destination from the beginning (Mark 6:33). Jesus' words, "Come away to a deserted place" (Mark 6:31) thus imply that the term ἡ ἔρημος denotes a well-known place. The crowds are aware of Jesus' destination and set out to meet him there. Whether or not Jesus actually reached his intended destination, he and the crowds do come together in a place described as "deserted" and he spends the day in teaching and healing (Mark 6:35).

The Location of the Roman Road

Our earlier discussion concerning the roads near Bethsaida (pages 36–41) is helpful for understanding the feeding miracle. Especially significant is the east-west route which connected Bethsaida with Chorazin

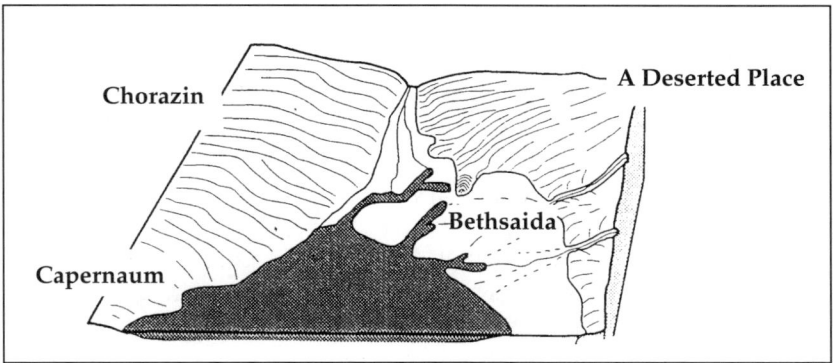

The Feeding Episode: A Possible Route

to the west and Gamla to the east. As noted, there is significant evidence that this road did not pass through Bethsaida itself, but rather followed a course about a mile to the north.

If one assumes a Bethsaida locale for the feeding miracle, a likely place of encounter between Jesus, who arrived by boat, and the crowds who arrived by land, was not at Bethsaida itself nor a site near the shore, but a location north of the town, perhaps near the crossroads a mile in distance. The travel of Jesus and the disciples thus included the crossing by boat, docking at the harbor of Bethsaida, making their way through the city, and hiking by foot from Bethsaida northward. This would realistically point to the possibility of the two groups beginning to come together at this junction. It would also explain Mark's notation that Jesus already saw the large crowd as he was getting out of the boat. The high ridge on the western side of the Jordan—the location of the Roman road—offers a prevailing view from et-Tell. The topography thus makes possible continued visual contact between the two groups.

This also helps to explain Jesus' reluctance to send the crowds into Bethsaida for food. For those on foot, Bethsaida was not on their itinerary and would lead to a detour and a delay of several additional hours. By feeding the crowds and directly sending them on their way, they could reasonably reach their homes that same night.

Luke's Reference to Bethsaida

This picture is apparently complicated because Luke directs Jesus and his disciples to a city named Bethsaida. Technically it was not yet a πόλις (city), since this episode predates Bethsaida's founding on September 22, 30 C.E. As some manuscripts note, it should properly be designated a κώμη (village). Nevertheless, with extensive building activity going on, Bethsaida likely had a population of at least 5,000–10,000.[5] Some would, therefore, be inclined to discredit the historical value of Luke's report. However, with Luke's own reference to a deserted place (Luke 9:12) and his mention of farms and villages, it does not appear that he intended the city of Bethsaida itself as the location for the feeding, but rather the region nearby. The Lukan account need not be considered at odds with the other evangelists.

A location for the feeding a short distance northeast of Bethsaida is fitting in view of the details mentioned above. When one considers a location outside of Galilee, yet within walking distance and with a harbor nearby, the grassy hills of the Golan provide an appropriate setting for the feeding miracle. Because the hillsides are covered with basalt stone, there is nonetheless an abundance of grass. Yet the population was quite sparse and could easily be designated as ἔρημος.

The meal of bread and fish, although common all around the lake, is especially fitting for a location near Bethsaida. As a fishing town, one would naturally expect the presence of fish. Although the Synoptic accounts use the general term ἰχθυς for fish, John uses ὀψάριον which denotes the dried fish, possibly an important export product of Bethsaida. One of the important Hellenistic discoveries at Bethsaida is an oval structure, built with massive boulders, measuring twenty-one feet by seventeen feet.[6] This is likely a granary used to collect wheat harvested from the Golan region.

Other than Jesus and his disciples, the characters in this miracle story are not identified in the Synoptic accounts. John, however, includes a discussion between Jesus and Philip concerning the difficulty of feeding such a large crowd. Another disciple, Andrew, locates the boy with the loaves and fish. This is quite appropriate because these are Bethsaida disciples. By identifying Andrew as Simon's brother and repeating the name of Philip three times, John reminds the reader of his introduction which linked the three disciples together and established their origins at Bethsaida (John 1:40).

The Significance of the Feeding Miracle

The feeding of 5,000 is described as an act of compassion that Jesus has for people who have found themselves in physical need, because their spiritual hunger has led them to leave their homes in search of spiritual

---

5. On the basis of limited excavations, it is not yet possible to estimate accurately the population of Bethsaida. Hoehner, *Herod Antipas* (Cambridge: Cambridge University Press, 1972) 52, estimates an average population of 25,000 for cities in Galilee and 10,000 for cities in Perea.

6. Rami Arav, "Bethsaida Excavations: Preliminary Report, 1987–93," *Bethsaida* (1995) 16.

food. Following an afternoon of spiritual nourishment—teaching and healing—Jesus then provides the physical nourishment necessary for their long walk home. As is the case with numerous miracles, there is also a deeper symbolic or theological meaning. John alludes to this by calling the miracle a sign and by following it with a long interpretive sermon.

First, one sees this as the gathering of a spiritual army.[7] On Jesus' previous trip to the eastern shore, he healed a demonic possessed by spirits named "Legion"—a clear reference to the occupying forces of the Roman army (Mark 5:1-20). The political significance of the feeding miracle is suggested by the context since the preceding episode describes Antipas' execution of John and his growing hostility toward Jesus. The retreat to the desert, in the first century, was typical for rebel movements. In the feeding miracle, the number 5,000 is thus typical of the size of a Roman legion stationed in Palestine. It also corresponds to the number of Galilean troops assembled by Josephus and Jeremiah at Bethsaida-Julias during the 67 C.E. revolt (Josephus, *Life* 398–406). As they eat, they are divided into groups of fifty, similar to the Roman cohort. Just as the Roman army often played a role in selecting new emperors, so those who are fed seek to make Jesus their king (John 6:15). Supported by this spiritual army, Jesus thus returns to Galilee where he continues his ministry unafraid of Antipas' threats.

A second image is that the feeding points to a reenactment of Israel's desert experience under the leadership of Moses. They have crossed the sea just as the Israelites crossed the Red Sea. They are now located in the desert, where they are fed as Moses provided manna from heaven (John 6:26-35). Subsequently, they will cross over into the promised land. Related to this is the connection with the Christian communal meal. John notes that it is Passover time, a detail that is supported by Mark's reference to the green grass in the spring of the year. Jesus' actions in preparing the food have a liturgical ring: Jesus took the loaves . . . "he looked up to heaven, and blessed and broke the loaves, and gave them . . ." (Mark 6:41). Superior to this food, is the nourishment that comes in his flesh and blood (John 6:47-51).

A third image comes from our new knowledge about Bethsaida-Julias. The Julia coins (see illustration, page 98) in fact depict ears of barley and designate her gift to the community in terms of an abundance of produce. The inscription reads καρπόφορος (fruit-bearing). In Livia's role as the goddess Demeter in the imperial cult, she guarantees that abundance for

---

7. John J. Rousseau, "The Impact of the Bethsaida Finds on our Knowledge of the Historical Jesus." Paper presented to the Historical Jesus Section, SBL, 1995. H. Montefiore, "Revolt in the Desert," *New Testament Studies* (1957–8) 135–49.

her community. Interestingly, John notes that the bread was made from barley. The spring context points to the beginning of the dry season when the land becomes a desert and people wonder if the earth will ever produce again. In that desert atmosphere, Jesus also feeds the crowds. Not only do they eat, but they are full and have baskets left over. This feeding portrays Jesus as a provider superior to Livia/Julia.

Walking on the Water

The feeding episode is followed in three Gospels with the account of walking on the water. Central to the impact of this miracle is the fact that the western shore of Galilee is not readily accessible from the site of the feeding miracle. This certainly could be the case from any location on the eastern shore, but it is also the case with Bethsaida, as recent geological research has noted. The disciples have departed by boat—the only available boat according to John 6:22. The crowds have departed on foot, possibly by way of the Chorazin road. Jesus has stayed behind for a quiet evening alone in prayer on the hillside.

The disciples' arrival is hindered by the typical strong winds coming from the west. Jesus then began to make his way back to the western shore on foot. Yet Jesus does not travel by the longer Chorazin route, but makes his way by the sea—ἐπὶ τῆς θαλάσσης (Mark 6:48; John 6:19). The preposition ἔπι with the genitive can denote walking "beside the sea" or "on the sea." One can try to figure this out logistically in a number of ways as Jesus struggles along a rugged coast line or perhaps following a sandbar or dry land next to an estuary. Mark's comment that he "was going to pass them by" (Mark 6:48) suggests that Jesus' intention was merely to reach the same destination on the western shore. Yet as he sees the disciples in trouble, he comes to them on the water bringing calm in the midst of storm and courage in the midst of doubt. They arrived at Gennesaret and Jesus began anew his ministry in the Galilee.

Chapter 11

The Healing of the Blind Man

Mark 8:22-26 presents the story of the healing of a blind man at Bethsaida. In this account, Jesus crosses the sea by boat with his disciples and arrives at the town of Bethsaida. As Jesus is passing through, a blind man is brought to him for healing. Jesus leads him outside of the town where he heals the man by spitting on his eyes. The man receives only partial sight and says that what he sees is like trees walking. After Jesus laid his hands upon his eyes, the man then was able to see. Jesus then sent him home instructing him not to return to Bethsaida.

The Text: Mark 8:22-26

> 22 They came to Bethsaida. Some people brought a blind man to him and begged him to touch him. 23 He took the blind man by the hand and led him out of the village; and when he had put saliva on his eyes and laid his hands on him, he asked him, "Can you see anything?" 24 And the man looked up and said, "I can see people, but they look like trees, walking." 25 Then Jesus laid his hands on his eyes again; and he looked intently and his sight was restored, and he saw everything clearly. 26 Then he sent him away to his home, saying, "Do not even go into the village."

The Uniqueness of the Markan Account

Interestingly, this is one of the few episodes from Mark which is not repeated elsewhere. Because it is attested in only one source, some might question its authenticity. However, there are several issues which explain its uniqueness. First, one must consider that this episode includes material which can be considered offensive and embarrassing. Jesus heals by spitting in the man's eyes. In two other episodes, the evangelists mention

Jesus spitting in the healing process. In John 9:6, Jesus spat on the ground making a mud plaster which was applied to the eyes. In Mark 7:33, Jesus spat and touched the man's tongue. Yet here Jesus spat directly on the eyes. The New Revised Standard Version perhaps tames the language a bit stating that Jesus "put saliva on his eyes." It demonstrates that people are concerned with "offensive" language. This episode also presents the only healing of Jesus which does not bring about complete success on the first attempt. This can be an embarrassment which seems at odds with the common image of Jesus who brings healing simply through speaking a word. In a similar way the statement about Nazareth in Mark 6:5 that "he could do no deed of power there" was changed in Matthew 13:58 to read "he did not do many deeds of power there, because of their unbelief." One should therefore not be surprised that later evangelists omitted this story. In fact, this is a strong argument for authenticity since the early Church would likely not have created an episode with such problematic details.

A second issue has to do with duplication. There are several miracle stories which describe the healing of blind men. All three Synoptics include the account of blind Bartimaeus at Jericho (Mark 10:46-52; Matt 20:29-34; Luke 18:35-43). Matthew alone includes the episode of two blind men in Galilee (Matt 9:27-31) and John alone includes the episode of the man born blind in Jerusalem (John 9:1-7).[1] In the Q episode of the healing of a dumb demonic, Matthew also includes the element of blindness (Matt 12:22) while Luke does not (Luke 11:14). Matthew, therefore, has three other episodes about healing the blind, which may account for this omission. In the case of Luke, the healing at Bethsaida is part of a longer section known as the "Great Omission" including the material from Mark 6:45 to 8:26. Several explanations have been offered including the possibility that there was an earlier shorter manuscript of Mark; that Luke skipped from one mention of Bethsaida to the next; or that Luke wanted to avoid a section with several doublets.[2] Even though this episode occurs only in Mark, there is good reason to consider it an authentic historical event.[3]

The Context in Mark

The episode of the Bethsaida blind man fits well with other geographical information in Mark 8. In verse 10, Jesus and his disciples are

---

1. For similarities between the Markan miracle and the Johannine healing of a blind man, see Thomas L. Brodie, *The Quest for the Origin of John's Gospel: A Source-Oriented Approach* (N.Y.: Oxford University Press, 1993) 48–66.

2. Joseph A. Fitzmyer, *The Gospel According to Luke*, Anchor Bible (Garden City, N.Y.: Doubleday, 1981) 1:770.

3. E. S. Johnson, "Mark viii 22-26: The Blind Man from Bethsaida," *NTS* 25 (1979) 370–83.

in the district of Dalmanutha, which is the area around Magdala on the western shore of the lake. In verse 13, they get into a boat to cross to *the other side* of the lake. In verse 22, they arrive at Bethsaida where the healing takes place. Following the healing they move further north to Caesarea Philippi where Peter offers his confession. The natural stopping-off place between the western shore of the lake and Caesarea Philippi is Bethsaida.

This episode is also appropriately located because of several theological themes in Mark. During the boat trip across the sea, the disciples remember that they had forgotten to bring bread for the journey (Mark 8:14-21). The following discussion then centers around the two feeding miracles, one which took place on the shore behind them (Mark 8:1-10) and the other near Bethsaida before them (Mark 6:30-44). The reminder about the baskets of bread left over perhaps carries a special symbolic meaning since the number of baskets is designated as twelve and seven. Usually these numbers are said to designate the Jewish world and the Gentile world respectively. The connection then with the western and northeastern shores is significant. The former is representative of Judaism and the latter is representative of the Gentile world.

This is especially significant in view of the final episode taking place on the western side. While Jesus is still at Dalmanutha, Pharisees—as representatives of traditional Judaism—come asking Jesus to perform a miracle to demonstrate that God approves of his work (Mark 8:11-13). Jesus soundly rejects their request:

> Why does this generation ask for a sign?
> Truly, I tell you, no sign will be given to this generation (Mark 8:12).

Rather, Jesus immediately got into the boat and crossed over to Bethsaida. In view of this rejection of the Pharisee's request for a sign, it is especially significant that Jesus heals a blind man as soon as he sets foot on the northeastern shore. The difference to be sure is one of motive. These acts of power are not accomplished for curiosity sake, but to meet genuine human need. As in the case of his previous Bethsaida miracle, the feeding of the five thousand, Jesus acts out of compassion, not to give proof of his identity. The fact that it takes place at Bethsaida points ahead to the future of the church in Gentile areas.

The irony of this particular miracle is that the healing of the blind was considered one of the expected messianic signs. Thus Jesus began his inaugural sermon at Nazareth by quoting Isaiah concerning the recovery of sight to the blind (Luke 3:18). In response to the question of John the Baptist in prison, Jesus instructs his followers, "Go and tell John what you hear and see: the blind receive their sight . . ." (Matt 11:4-5 = Luke 7:22).

The episode of the Bethsaida healing thus is a perfect lead-in to the Caesarea Philippi confession of Peter: "You are the Messiah" (Mark 8:29). Yet just as Jesus denied such a demonstration of proof for the Pharisees, so even in the Bethsaida miracle it is critical to note that healing takes place only outside the town and away from the crowds.

The healing of blindness thus has a deeper spiritual level. In the boat on the way to Bethsaida, Jesus notes the disciples' lack of understanding:

> Why are you talking about having no bread? Do you still not perceive or understand? Are your hearts hardened? Do you have eyes, and fail to see? (Mark 8:17-18).

The theme of the disciples' lack of understanding, which has prevailed since the beginning, comes into focus at this critical juncture of the gospel.

It has often been noted that the Gospel according to Mark is structured around three major sections:

1. The Galilean Ministry (Mark 1:14–8:30).
2. The Road to Jerusalem (Mark 8:31–10:52).
3. Death and Resurrection in Jerusalem (Mark 11:1–16:8).

Within this structure Mark has carefully positioned two healing miracles: the Bethsaida blind man at the end of section one (Mark 8:22-26) and blind Bartimaeus of Jericho at the end of section two (Mark 10:46-52). In both cases, the preceding episode highlights the disciples' lack of insight and understanding (Mark 8:14-21 and 10:35-45). The final section of the Gospel, it has been said, then leads to the third healing miracle. The disciples once again show lack of understanding in deserting Jesus at the crucifixion, but they will finally overcome their blindness when they *see* the resurrected Jesus in Galilee (Mark 16:7). The episode of the Bethsaida blind man—although omitted by later evangelists—plays a crucial role in the organization of the earliest gospel. The reader can only move from one section to the next when eyes are opened. It is therefore appropriate in the Bethsaida episode that healing is not altogether successful at first. True insight and understanding comes about only in stages. Therefore, the idea of sight is reinforced by the repetition and variation of words about seeing. In Greek this includes not only βλέπω, but compounds such as ἀναβλέπω, διάβλεπω, and ἐμβλέπω, as well as ὁράω. The Markan account deals with more than physical sight.

The Bethsaida Context

One expects to find a blind man waiting for Jesus in a town like Bethsaida. In the ancient world the blind were often forbidden from the acceptable circles of society and joined with the lepers and lame as outcasts.

Blindness was apparently rather common resulting from latent trachoma, a chronic contagious conjunctivitis cause by chlamydia.[4] Congenital blindness was also often related to various disorders which occur readily among societies struggling with economic and political oppression—as was typical in first-century Palestine. Interestingly, another report of healing a blind man includes the discussion of the commonly held belief of a connection between blindness and the sin of parents (John 9:2).

Thus the blind were often stigmatized by their disease and forced to live as beggars gathering near cities. In the story of blind Bartimaeus, he is found begging along the main road outside the city of Jericho (Mark 10:46). As the major population center in the southern Golan, Bethsaida likely also had a large number of blind beggars. It is not surprising that at the end of the episode Jesus makes a distinction between the man's home and the town of Bethsaida:

> Then he sent him away to his home, saying "Do not even go into the village." (Mark 8:26).

He was apparently from one of the surrounding villages and came to Bethsaida to beg.

Mark does not state exactly where Jesus encountered the blind man. Like most travelers, Jesus likely arrived at the harbor, climbed to the top of et-Tell, made his way through the main part of the town, and continued along the main road leading north in the direction of Caesarea Philippi. One would guess that one gathering place for beggars was the harbor area, below the actual city. There they would meet the many travelers arriving by boat. Jesus, however, took his hand and led him out of the city and away from the crowds—perhaps along the road leading north towards the east-west crossroads.

Technique of Healing

In most accounts of Jesus' healing, there is not a whole lot of detail given concerning the actual technique used to bring about healing. Most often the focus is on the spoken word. Jesus simply speaks and healing immediately follows. In several cases the actual words of Jesus, *Ephrata* or *Talitha Kumi* ("be opened" or "little girl arise"), were preserved in Aramaic by the early Church. In others, healing is related to the touch of Jesus. He takes a person's hand or lays hands upon their head. Healing even occurs when a woman touches Jesus' garment.

---

4. This section is highly dependent upon the work of my colleague John Rousseau, "The Healing of a Blind Man of Bethsaida," *Bethsaida* (1995) 257–66.

On a few occasions, healing involves the use of physical intermediaries. In the healing of the blind man recorded in John 9, Jesus applied clay to the man's eyes after forming the clay when he spit on the ground. Then Jesus follows with a command for washing. In the case of the Bethsaida blind man, Jesus spat on the eyes and placed his hands over the man's eyes.

The actions of Jesus in this miracle resemble those of many healers in the Hellenistic world. They are thus appropriate for the multicultural setting of Bethsaida. A number of parallels come from the various temples related to Asclepios, the god of healing. When the blind Alcetas of Halice visited the shrine at Epidaurus, the god of healing appeared to him and ran his fingers over his eyes. When his eyes opened, he first began to see the trees of the temple precincts.[5] Aristophanes describes a healing which took place in the temple of Asclepios at Piraeus. During the night a priest, who appears with mortar, pestle, and a box, mixes a plaster of vinegar and hot spices and applies them to the eyes of the patient. A number of healed patients also describe how snakes appeared at night and licked the eyes.[6]

The use of saliva was also common, because it offered a ready fluid, but perhaps also because of the saline and enzyme content which might help draw out infection. The emperor Vespasian is reported to have restored sight to a blind follower of Serapis by moistening his eyes and cheeks.[7] Pliny the Elder reports on the effect of saliva: "The best of all safeguards against serpents is the saliva of a fasting human being."[8] Saliva was frequently used to treat boils, leprous sores, and eye diseases.[9] The use of saliva by Jesus at Bethsaida to bring healing to a blind man is therefore consistent to the practice of healing in the Greco-Roman world and is especially appropriate for a town like Bethsaida.

---

5. Mark Appold, "The Mighty Works of Bethsaida: Witness of the New Testament and Related Traditions," *Bethsaida* (1995) 235.

6. Aristophanes, *Plutus*. Howard Clark Kee, *Miracles in the Early Christian World* (New Haven: Yale University Press, 1983) 81. Rousseau, "The Healing of a Blind Man of Bethsaida," 263.

7. Tacitus, *Histories* 4.81; Suetonius, *Vespasian* 7; Dio Cassius, *Roman History* 65.271.

8. Pliny, *Natural History* 30.

9. Howard Clark Kee, *Medicine, Miracle and Magic in the New Testament Times* (Cambridge: Cambridge University Press, 1986) 104.

Chapter 12

Woe Saying against Bethsaida

It has often been suggested that Jesus focused his ministry on an area known as the "evangelical triangle." This designation is associated with an area linked between the three towns of Bethsaida, Chorazin, and Capernaum near the northern part of the Sea of Galilee. It is in this area that Jesus taught the crowds and performed most of his miracles. Nevertheless, Matthew and Luke preserve a saying of Jesus in which he berates these communities for their lack of faith. The towns of Jesus' day are compared with ancient cities with a reputation for evil deeds. Just as those ancient cities were destroyed, so also the three cities of Jesus' day are condemned.[1]

The Q Saying

The woe saying of Jesus has been preserved by two evangelists: Matthew and Luke. It therefore fits the criteria for the sayings collection known as Q. A comparison of the two versions of the saying is as follows:

Matthew 11:20-24	*Luke 10:13-15*
20 Then he began to reproach the cities in which most of his deeds of power had been done, because they did not	

---

[1]. This chapter is dependent in part on conversations, papers, and three published articles by my Bethsaida colleagues: Mark Appold, "The Mighty Works of Bethsaida: Witness of the New Testament and Related Traditions," *Bethsaida* (1995) 229–42; Heinz-Wolfgang Kuhn, "Bethsaida in the Gospels: The Feeding Story in Luke 9 and the Q Saying in Luke 10," *Bethsaida* (1995) 243–56; Kuhn and Rami Arav, "Bethsaida Excavations: Historical and Archaeological Approaches," *The Future of Early Christianity*, ed. Birger A. Pearson (Minneapolis: Fortress Press, 1991) 77–107.

132   *Bethsaida: Home of the Apostles*

Matthew 11:20-24	*Luke 10:13-15*
repent. 21 "Woe to you, Chorazin! Woe to you, Bethsaida! For if the deeds of power done in you had been done in Tyre and Sidon, they would have repented long ago in sackcloth and ashes. 22 But I tell you, on the day of judgment it will be more tolerable for Tyre and Sidon than for you. 23 And you, Capernaum, will you be exalted to heaven? No, you will be brought down to Hades. For if the deeds of power done in you had been done in Sodom, it would have remained until this day. 24 But I tell you that on the day of judgment it will be more tolerable for the land of Sodom than for you."	13 "Woe to you, Chorazin! Woe to you, Bethsaida! For if the deeds of power done in you had been done in Tyre and Sidon, they would have repented long ago, sitting in sackcloth and ashes. 14 But at the judgment it will be more tolerable for Tyre and Sidon than for you. 15 And you, Capernaum, will you be exalted to heaven? No, you will be brought down to Hades."

In the central part of this saying, the two versions of this saying show a high degree of verbal agreement with only slight variations in the Greek text: Matthew uses ἐγένοντο while Luke has ἐγενήθησαν. Luke has the single additional word "sitting" in verse 13. Otherwise these portions are identical. Since there is no parallel in Mark, it is most certain that Matthew and Luke have drawn upon a common source known as the sayings collection Q. Yet there are some significant differences. Matthew is the longer version including an introduction which notes that most of Jesus' miracles were, in fact, carried out in these towns. Matthew also includes a final comparison of Capernaum with the Old Testament city of Sodom.

There is good reason to believe that the shorter Lukan version reflects the earlier Q version of the saying. The introductory material in Matthew provides no additional material that could not have been derived from the saying itself. The material concerning Sodom which comes at the end parallels another saying of Jesus concerning the rejection by various unnamed towns of Jesus' disciples. They are to shake the dust off their feet because:

> Truly I tell you, it will be more tolerable for the land of Sodom and Gomorrah on the day of judgment than for that town (Matt 10:15).

The same saying occurs in Luke 10:12 just prior to the Bethsaida woe saying. One could perhaps argue that Luke has omitted the final section from Q to avoid repetition. However, for Luke who has an appreciation for parallel structure, such an omission seems unlikely.[2] The introductory πλὴν

---

2. John Kloppenborg, *Q Parallels: Synopsis, Critical Notes, and Concordance* (Sonoma, Calif.: Poleridge, 1988) 74.

λέγω ὑμῖν in Matthew 11:24a betrays his hand since it is identical to verse 22a. The plural pronoun, however, is inconsistent with the use of the singular in the rest of verses 23–24 and with the context. Likewise, the final section includes the typically Matthean μέχρι τῆς ἥμερον (Matt 10:15; 27:8; 28:15). The expression "land of Sodom" (v. 24) using γη with a genitive plural is characteristic of Matthew (Matt 2:6, 20, 21; 4:15; 10:15). Presently, Luke mentions three contemporary cities and two ancient cities while Matthew mentions three each. It is more likely that Matthew has added material to create an appearance of parallelism. Nevertheless the parallelism is somewhat lacking since there is no reference to repentance as in the first part. Just as Luke is closest in preserving the sayings of Q in general, so in the case of this particular saying it is likely that the Q version is represented by Luke.

The matter of Q has also become quite complicated with recent research focusing on several strands of materials. In this light, the present prophetic saying is something of an intrusion into an earlier level of wisdom material and therefore may belong to a second edition of Q known as Q-2.[3] Nevertheless, it shows the marks of an originally independent saying that was only later joined with other such sayings.

The Question of Authenticity

There is considerable debate whether this saying was actually spoken by Jesus or whether it represents the words of the spirit-led community of the early Church. The recently published *The Five Gospels: The Search for the Authentic Words of Jesus* of the Jesus Seminar concludes that this saying was not in character with the preaching of Jesus and that it likely stemmed from early Christian prophets in frustration over a lack of acceptance of their message.[4] Among my colleagues at Bethsaida, Mark Appold is in general agreement with this view while Heinz-Wolfgang Kuhn argues that it was actually spoken by Jesus.

It is significant that both Matthew and Luke place this saying in the context of mission activity of Jesus' followers. Matthew 10 reports Jesus' commissioning of the twelve who are sent out into neighboring towns and villages. This is followed in chapter 11 by the question of the imprisoned John the Baptist, a section of sayings about the followers of John, and then

---

3. Burton Mack, *The Lost Gospel of Q* (San Francisco: Harper and Row, 1993) 36; Helmut Koester, *Ancient Christian Gospels* (Philadelphia: Trinity Press, 1992) 140; John Kloppenborg, *The Formation of Q* (Philadelphia: Fortress Press, 1987) 195–6.

4. Robert W. Funk, Roy W. Hoover, and the Jesus Seminar, *The Five Gospels: The Search for the Authentic Words of Jesus* (N.Y.: Polebridge Press, 1993).

the Bethsaida woe saying. Luke 10 reports Jesus sending out the seventy. The saying follows directly after the advice concerning their response to towns who are not receptive. The contexts, of course, are the creation of the evangelists. Yet they are appropriate since the saying does speak about Jesus' mighty works as if they are already accomplished events. The saying thus gives the impression of presenting the point of view of the early Church looking back on the ministry of Jesus.[5]

At the same time, one could argue that it would be surprising for the early Church to focus entirely on one phase of Jesus' ministry, his miracles, at the expense of his teaching ministry. Yet this is the case in this particular saying. These towns are condemned because they have seen his mighty acts and have not believed. Yet not a word is said about his teaching activity in these same areas. This is ironic in one sense because the sayings collection emphasizes the teaching of Jesus and includes only a few references to miracles. However, current study on the Fourth Gospel calls attention to early interest in the signs of Jesus and an early signs collection which does focus on that aspect of his ministry. One cannot exclude a connection between this particular saying and the signs tradition.

Another critical issue concerns the actual situation of these particular towns. What do we know about them both in terms of Jesus' ministry and in the history of the early Church? Rudolf Bultmann argued that this saying could not be authentic because it assumed a later situation when preaching in Capernaum ended in failure.[6] The Synoptic picture is exactly the opposite. Capernaum is described as the center of Jesus' activity and this ministry meets with amazing success so that crowds of people are always surrounding Jesus. Unfortunately, the Acts of the Apostles and the canonical epistles are silent with regard to further developments in Capernaum, as also Bethsaida and Chorazin. Yet archaeological work since the time of Bultmann suggests a picture of a continuation of Jesus' ministry by the early Church in Capernaum and no evidence of any interruption in this community.

Capernaum, of course, is not the only town mentioned in this saying. In fact, a case can be made that it plays only a secondary role. The actual saying focuses primarily on a parallelism between the two ancient cities of Tyre and Sidon and cities contemporary to Jesus: Chorazin and Bethsaida. Since sayings against Tyre and Sidon were typical in the Old Tes-

---

5. David A. Catchpole, *The Quest for Q* (Edinburgh: T. and T. Clark, 1993) 172.

6. Rudolf Bultmann, *The History of the Synoptic Tradition* (Oxford: Blackwell, 1968) 112. Bultmann gives three arguments against authenticity: (1) the saying describes Jesus' activity as already completed; (2) it assumes the failure of preaching in Capernaum; and (3) it would be difficult for Jesus to imagine Capernaum as exalted because of his preaching activity.

tament prophets (Isa 23; Jer 47:4; Ezek 26-28; Joel 4:4-8), their inclusion here adds to the dynamic of early Christian prophets. Thus a connection with cities of Jesus' day was natural. Because of the similarity in sound between *Sidon* and *Tzaidan* (Bethsaida), the role of this city predominates the saying. Also striking is the fact that Bethsaida is paralleled with Chorazin, since Bethsaida is usually linked by its connections across the sea. Chorazin and Bethsaida were linked by Roman road, one city to the west of the Jordan in Galilee and the other to the east of the Jordan in the Golan. The saying may not derive then from the experience of fishermen apostles, but from those later itinerant preachers with sandals on feet and staff in hand walking from town to town—and speaking the word of the risen Jesus.[7]

With Bethsaida and Chorazin linked together, there is even a contrast with Capernaum on the sea. The two former sites are cities set on a hill.[8]

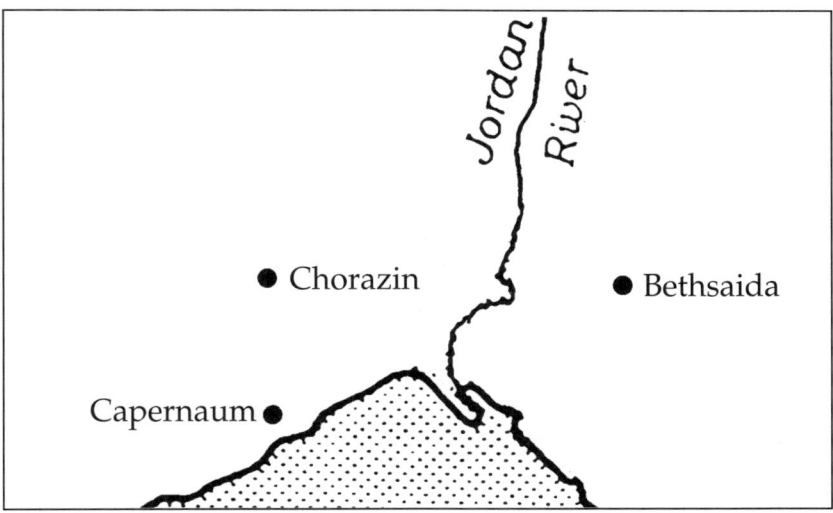

The Evangelical Triangle

With their lights shining at night, they cannot be hid and therefore have a grandeur about them. Capernaum, in contrast, sits below next to the sea. Thus the significance of Jesus' words, "Will you be exalted to heaven?" Capernaum is condemned, not to tumble with mountains into the sea, but to sink to Hades with the earth opening up around it. Implicit here is a

---

7. Gerd Theissen, *Social Reality and the Early Christians* (Minneapolis: Fortress Press, 1992) 37–59.
8. Although Bethsaida was located near the sea, it was situated on a mound rising ninety feet above the level of the Sea of Galilee.

comparison with the prophetic condemnation of Babylon in Isaiah 14:13-14. However, Capernaum is treated only briefly. Later, Matthew has drawn another connection with the destruction of Sodom by the side of the Dead Sea and thus expanded the saying.

This saying points to a flurry of activity not reported in depth by the New Testament writers. It is a reminder that the evangelists have reported only one small part of that story and that archaeology may be the only means available to capture even a glimpse of that total picture. This is underscored by the mention of Chorazin. Absolutely nothing is reported about the ministry of Jesus in this first-century town, apart from this saying. Here it is said that Jesus worked miracles, but not a single story survives. In this case even archaeological excavations have not been able to take us back further than a third-century site. So the picture is only partial. In the case of Bethsaida, we are much better off. We do have a number of episodes in the Gospels to supplement and expand on the Q saying and we now have archaeological evidence. Yet one would be mistaken to think that Jesus' ministry in Bethsaida, as also in the other cities, was limited to these few reports. This saying points to an extensive ministry by Jesus and its continuation in the early days of the Church.

Where He Performed Most of his Miracles

Matthew includes an introduction to the woe saying from Q in which he states that Jesus had performed most of his miracles in the area of this evangelical triangle bounded by Chorazin, Bethsaida, and Capernaum (Matt 11:20). The version of this saying in the second-century Jewish-Christian Gospel of the Nazareans gave the number of miracles performed in Bethsaida as fifty-three.[9] In previous chapters, we have already given attention to three miracles connected with Bethsaida: the feeding of the five thousand; the walking on water; and the healing of the blind man.

Is there evidence for other miracle traditions to be connected with Bethsaida? One episode that fits the context of Bethsaida is the story of the miraculous catch of fish in connection with the risen Jesus' appearance to seven disciples (John 21). Like many miracles, the story itself does not indicate specifically the location. The context of the story is that the disciples have gone back to their former lives, careers, and homes. Under the leadership of Peter they return to the Sea of Galilee and a night of fishing. It is natural to assume that Peter would choose to return to his home, Bethsaida. There are also parallels with the episode of the feeding of the five thousand since Jesus then offers them a meal of bread and fish. Even the language is similar: "He took the bread, and gave it to them" (John 21:13).

---

9. Kurt Aland, ed., *Synopsis Quattuor Evangeliorum* (Stuttgart: Württembergische Bibelanstalt, 1963) 153.

Finally, there may be a connection between the number of fish 153 and the tradition of 53 Bethsaida miracles. It is common in textual transmission for a number like 100 to be added or omitted to a text. These clues suggest a Bethsaida context for this miracle.

One other miracle which has been connected with Bethsaida is the healing of the lame man lying beside a pool of water where there were five porches (John 5:1-18). Archaeological evidence has pointed to the existence of such a pool at St. Anne's Church near Stephen's Gate in Jerusalem. There is also evidence from a later healing cult that this had traditionally been a site where healings took place. The Jerusalem location is fitting since a subsequent discussion in the Temple concerns the issue of healing on the Sabbath. From Josephus we learn that the northeast quarter of the city near the Temple was named *Bezetha* (Josephus, *War* 2.15). From the Dead Sea scrolls we learn about a pool named *Bet 'Esdatayin* (plural) on an eastern hill in Jerusalem.[10] However, the manuscript evidence for neither of these names is very good in John 5:2. The name *Bethesda* is attested only by the fifth-century codices Alexandrinus and C. The name *Bethzatha* is attested by the fourth-century codex Sinaiticus and *Belzetha* by Manuscript D. The strongest manuscript evidence points to the name *Bethsaida*, attested in P66 from around 200 C.E. and the important third-century P75 and the fourth-century Codex Vaticanus among others.

Thus the translators of the Vulgate and King James Version included *Bethsaida* as well. One could perhaps argue for a Bethsaida locale for this miracle based on the complexity of issues concerning an early Jerusalem ministry of Jesus and the presence of a Synoptic parallel for this miracle in Galilee (Mark 2:1-12). However, John's knowledge about Bethsaida (John 1:44; 12:22) would argue against the possibility of such an error. Because of the witness to the site in both ancient literature and archaeology,[11] it is generally assumed that the name of the pool associated with this miracle was *Bethzatha*.[12] Apparently the less familiar name would have been replaced by later scribes with the more familiar *Bethsaida*. There is even more reason to expect such a change if Bethsaida had gained such a reputation associated with the miracles of Jesus.

---

10. 3 Q15 xi 12-13. J. T. Milik, *Discoveries in the Judean Desert III* (Naperville, Ill.: Allenson, 1962) 271.

11. Remains of the pool have been uncovered near the Church of St. Anne. There was located a pool divided by a bedrock causeway (thus the Qumran plural notation) so that five porches stood upon it, one on each side and one on the causeway. Yigael Yadin, *Jerusalem Revealed* (Jerusalem: Israel Exploration Society, 1976).

12. Raymond E. Brown, *The Gospel According to John*, The Anchor Bible (Garden City, N.Y.: Doubleday, 1966) 1:206–7.

The Gospels do present some evidence for the miracle tradition at Bethsaida. By nature of the gospel materials, one can only expect that a small segment of the Jesus tradition has been passed down. In the case of Chorazin, there is none. However, in the case of Bethsaida there is ample evidence of miracle tradition.

Chapter 13
Early Christian Community in Bethsaida

In May 1994, a cross was discovered inscribed on one of the thousands of shards of pottery excavated at Bethsaida. Is this a Christian cross? Was it made by a member of the early Christian Church in Bethsaida? One does not expect to find remains left behind by Jesus and the crowds listening to his teaching. Yet the issue of his followers in the postresurrection Church is another matter. It is not uncommon to find evidence of early Christianity throughout the whole Mediterranean world. Can this also be the case for Bethsaida? The discovery of this cross thus raises the question about the early Christian community in Bethsaida. Did it exist? What can we know about it?

The Acts of the Apostles and Early Christian Letters

The New Testament nowhere explicitly mentions the existence of a Christian community in Bethsaida. For that matter, none of the other communities connected with the ministry of Jesus—with the exception of Jerusalem—is mentioned by name. This should not be surprising since the picture of the early Church preserved in the canonical writings is predominated by the mission activity of Paul. The communities that Paul mentions are scattered throughout the Mediterranean area. The focus of Luke in The Acts of the Apostles—influenced by the Pauline picture—likewise moves throughout these Mediterranean cities.

The picture of Pauline Christianity assumes the existence also of a Palestinian Christian community. When Paul reports in Jerusalem concerning the success of his missionary endeavors in Gentile regions, James replies, "There are thousands of Jews who have become believers" (Acts 21:20). One can pick up on later references to Jewish Christian communities which imply some kind of early activity. For example, Eusebius mentions relatives of Jesus living in Galilee at the end of the first century.[1] Likewise, Jerome notes that the Jewish Christians referred to Hillel as unholy, a play on words made possible by the distinctive Galilean pronunciation of the first letter of his name.[2] However, the impression given by Acts is that these Christians are concentrated in the area around Jerusalem.

Here one has to understand the theological focus of Luke who wants to portray the spread of Christianity from Jerusalem to Rome. Thus the risen Jesus even instructs the disciples not to part from the city of Jerusalem. The first seven chapters are restricted entirely to the episodes about the church in that locale. Then the movement is gradually expanded into the Judean coastal regions, Samaria, Phoenicia, and Syria until the Mediterranean journeys of Paul are taken up. It is ironic that by the end of Acts, Christian communities have been planted in areas totally surrounding the Galilee and the Golan. They are in Damascus, Sidon, Antioch, and Caesarea, but the Galilee is mentioned only once in passing (Acts 9:31). In a summary statement, it is mentioned that the church in Galilee, along with Judea and Samaria, experienced a time of peace and growth following the conversion of Paul. Paul, likewise, who has been entrusted the ministry to the uncircumcised (Gal 2:7), asserts his independence from the Palestinian church as well as the leadership of the apostles and thus minimizes his attention of this segment of Christianity. At the same time, the Acts of the Apostles does suggest an even more complex picture by describing Gentile Christianity emerging, not only among the Pauline communities, but even in Palestine (Acts 10). The picture of the growth of Christianity from Acts and the letters of Paul is anything but complete.

Inferences from the Gospels

The four Gospels present the ministry of Jesus and are not intended to include historical reporting about the early Church. Yet since the Gospels were not put into writing until forty years later, they too must be treated like an archaeological tell with careful attention to various layers and strata.[3] The stories of Jesus offer helpful clues which can fill in gaps about early Church history.

1. Eusebius, *Ecclesiastical History* 1.7.13. See also Justin Martyr, *Dialogue* 38; Tosefta. Hullin 22; Kohelet Rabbah 1.24; 2 Baruch 41.3; 83.8. Albert I. Baumgarten, "Literary Evidence for Jewish Christianity in the Galilee," *The Galilee in Late Antiquity*, ed. Lee I. Levine (Cambridge: Harvard University Press, 1992) 39–50; L. E. Elliott-Binns, *Galilean Christianity* (Chicago: Alec R. Allenson, Inc., 1956).

2. Jerome, *Commentary on Isaiah* 8.14.

3. Howard Clark Kee, "Early Christianity in the Galilee: Reassessing the Evidence from the Gospels," *The Galilee in Late Antiquity*, 3–22.

For example, the resurrection appearance stories are a helpful corrective to the Jerusalem-centered picture of Acts. The disciples were told to go to Galilee where they were to see Jesus (Mark 16:7). They returned to the same place where they had encountered Jesus before—the Sea of Galilee—and he appeared to them there (John 21). They met on a Galilean hillside and they were sent out from there into all the world (Matt 28:16-20). The picture assumes a continuation between the communities where Jesus found followers and the communities of the early Church—which is only logical. It assumes a concentration in these same areas and then movement outward.

As we saw in the previous chapter, there are sayings in the Gospels that present a perspective of the Church looking back on the completed ministry of Jesus. Thus the sayings collection Q assumes knowledge of Christian communities in Bethsaida, Chorazin, and Capernaum (Matt 11:20-24 = Luke 10:13-15). In a similar way, the emphasis in Mark on a Capernaum-centered ministry probably implies some knowledge by that evangelist of a community there in the mid-first century.

The Fourth Gospel: Philip and Andrew, Leaders in Bethsaida

Surprisingly, it may be the Fourth Gospel, the last to be written, which provides a more detailed picture of an early Christian community—specifically that of Bethsaida.[4] The identification of this city as the home of several disciples likely is included because the community there continued to recognize and preserve their contribution. It is important to pay attention to the order in which the disciples are identified: "Now Philip was from Bethsaida, the city of Andrew and Peter" (John 1:44). That Peter is mentioned last reflects less his prominence in the stories of Jesus than his later absence from Bethsaida in view of his leadership position in the Jerusalem church (Gal 2:9; Acts 1-12). On the other hand, Philip, who is barely mentioned in the Synoptics, is now the prominent disciple from Bethsaida. He is mentioned no less than four times in the Fourth Gospel, three times in connection with Andrew, but his name always occurs first (John 1:44; 6:5; 12:20; 14:8). The inner circle of Peter, James, and John in the Synoptics is replaced by a special role assigned to Philip and Andrew.

---

4. Mark Appold, "The Mighty Works of Bethsaida: Witness of the New Testament and Related Traditions," *Bethsaida* (1995) 239; Karl Kundsin, *Topologische Überlieferungsstoffe im Johannes Evangelium* (Göttingen: Vandenhoeck and Ruprecht, 1925); Klaus Wengst, *Bedrängte Gemeinde und verherrlichter Christus* (Neukirchen-Vluyn: Neukirchener, 1983).

Bethsaida and Early Christian Communal Meals

The place of these two disciples in the episode of the multiplication of loaves and fishes (John 6:1-15) sheds light on that special role. The fact that this is the one miracle occurring in all four Gospels points to its early date. In the Fourth Gospel alone, Jesus questions Philip about what to do in this difficult situation and Andrew brings to Jesus the young lad with loaves of bread and fish. There is no question that their roles are not essential to the story since the Synoptics do not name them. It would seem that their role is not as historical characters in the miracle event, but as liturgical leaders of the community reenactment of that event.

In order to understand this, one must see the connection between the feeding of the five thousand and the miraculous catch of fishes in John 21. Both miracles have the same theme: Jesus provides for his followers in abundance. Both have a link to the Sea of Galilee, and quite possibly a setting near Bethsaida. The situation of the latter miracle is that the disciples have returned to their homes following the death of Jesus. Peter, the Bethsaida fisherman, has invited six others for a night fishing on the sea. Five of the seven disciples are named. The two nameless disciples may well be the obvious pair who need no naming, Philip and Andrew (John 21:2). What happens in the miracle is clear: after a night of failure, they meet success; out nothing, they find abundance. The disciples then join Jesus on the shore for a meal of bread and fish; they recognize Jesus; and they are commissioned for their tasks.

In the same way that the Jerusalem communities commemorated Jesus' Last Supper with a regular gathering of bread and wine, it is not difficult to see how the Bethsaida community might offer a varied form of commemoration sharing bread and fish. Early Christian art in fact depicts this variation in Lord's Supper representations. Thus the feeding of the five thousand is told in John as a liturgical meal.[5] The reader in fact is told that it is the time of Passover. The words of Jesus call forth a response from the people; a young boy delivers a basket of loaves and fish; Jesus offers a eucharistic blessing; "when he had given thanks" (John 6:11); the disciples distribute the food; and the people on the grass eat their fill. Later, the Eucharistic Prayer of *Didache* 9:4 reflects a connection with the feeding episode and especially notes the element of gathering the fragments. The eucharistic understanding is underscored later when the crowds refer to "the place where they had eaten the bread after the Lord had given thanks" (John 6:23). That they remembered, not just the action,

---

5. Raymond E. Brown, *The Gospel According to John*, The Anchor Bible (Garden City, N.Y.: Doubleday, 1966) 1:247–9.

but also the place is also significant. In summary, these texts point to an early Christian community that gathers under the leadership of Philip and Andrew at Bethsaida, the place where the risen Jesus revealed himself through mighty deeds, and where he continued to reveal himself through the sharing of a liturgical meal of bread and fish.

Bethsaida and the Gentile Mission

An interesting aspect of this early Christian community is that it likely was among the first places where Gentiles and Jews came together in fellowship. In another Johannine text, Philip and Andrew play a leadership role when "Greeks" come to them wishing "to see Jesus" (John 12:20). The context is Jerusalem at the time of Passover shortly before Jesus' death. Their presence in Jerusalem is somewhat unusual because non-Jews were not allowed to participate in the Passover meal (Exod 12:48; Josephus, *War* 6.422-7). From a literary point of view, their presence is likewise unusual because they are not mentioned again. It has been said that their place in this episode is more symbolic than historical—that the author is pointing ahead to the upcoming Gentile mission.[6] This is underlined further by including Philip and Andrew as intermediaries—disciples with Greek names—and by reminding the reader that they are from Bethsaida, a detail which had already been mentioned in John 1:44. The Passover context may well point to an inclusive sharing of the meal at Bethsaida.

The Greeks wish "to see Jesus." A number of commentaries have suggested that they simply want to "visit him and make his acquaintance" or "to have an interview with" him. Yet the verb for seeing—ἰδεῖν—may suggest rather a desire for true insight and understanding which takes place only through an experience with the resurrected Jesus and in the breaking of the bread. The element of recognition is central to the communal meal. This is illustrated well by the Emmaus disciple episode in Luke where the disciples' eyes are opened at the point when Jesus breaks bread. In the seaside resurrection appearance episode, the disciples at first "did not know—ᾔδεισαν—that it was Jesus" (John 21:4), but when they shared in the meal "they saw—εἰδότες—that it was the Lord" (John 21:12). The difference between these two statements is underscored not just by the shift in title from "Jesus" to "Lord," but also in the verbs used.[7] The same thing occurs in the feeding of the five thousand, when the people acknowledge Jesus as the coming prophet when they "saw—

---

6. Ernst Haenchen, *John*, Hermeneia Series (Philadelphia: Fortress, 1984) 2:96. Brown, *The Gospel According to John*, 2:466.

7. Brown, *The Gospel According to John*, 1:502.

ἰδόντες—the sign that he had done" (John 6:14). Earlier they had followed because they "saw—ἐθεώρουν—the signs that he was doing" (John 6:2). The difference in verbs suggests that they had moved from simple physical sight or contemplative wonder to true understanding in the sharing of the meal. There is a clear connection with the request of the Greeks.

The Passover context calls attention to their role as outsiders who can observe, but not share the meal. Yet, on the previous Passover (John 6:4), Jesus had broken tradition remaining behind at the sea to share a meal with five thousand—presumably without restrictions. Their opportunity for truly seeing rests in their association with Jesus and in the sharing of the meal of his followers, represented specifically by Philip and Andrew. The general picture has been that the Gentile mission was the contribution of Paul. That this is not totally accurate is made clear by the Cornelius episode in Acts 10 and by descriptions of the Antioch mission in Acts 11:19-21. On the basis of these Johannine texts, one can presume that the Gentile mission began quite early in Bethsaida, a community with "mixed population." It is especially interesting that Bethsaida was situated on the road from Jerusalem to Damascus, where Paul received his calling to be missionary to the Gentiles. Yet Paul's reputation for persecuting the church had already become quite well known. The statement in Acts 9:31 about the church in Galilee achieving peace can only make sense if the Galilee region previously had suffered persecutions under Paul. Acts 26:11 also mentions Paul's persecuting activity in other "foreign cities." It is reasonable to think that a community like Bethsaida may have been included.

Bethsaida, Early Christianity, and the Livia Cult

The episode of Greeks wishing to see Jesus also includes a significant saying of Jesus which sheds light on the interaction of the early Christian community with the practice of the Livia cult in Bethsaida-Julias. In response to the announcement of the Greek's request, Jesus speaks,

> Very truly, I tell you, unless a grain of wheat falls into the earth and dies, it remains just a single grain; but if it dies, it bears much fruit (John 12:24).

This saying has many characteristics which point to its earliness in the sayings tradition. In fact, it is one of only four sayings in John which is printed in color (designating a degree of authenticity) in the new *The Five Gospels* of the Jesus Seminar.[8] Its closest parallel is from Paul:

---

8. *The Five Gospels: The Search for the Authentic Words of Jesus*, new trans. Robert W. Funk, Roy W. Hoover, and the Jesus Seminar (N.Y.: Polebridge Press, 1993) 441–2.

What you sow does not come to life unless it dies. And as for what you sow, you do not sow the body that is to be, but a bare seed, perhaps of wheat or of some other grain (1 Cor 15:36-37).

Surprisingly, there is no parallel in the Synoptic Gospels, although the parables of the mustard seed and the sower provide similar images as well as similarity in form and expression. The major difference is that the grain does not represent the word or the kingdom, but a person whose death is inevitable and necessary.[9]

In some ways this theme is similar to that of the mystery cults where the annual cycle of death and rebirth was dramatized with an ear of grain. Most popular were the mysteries of Eleusis where Demeter (= Ceres) traveled to the underworld to bring back her daughter Kore so that the earth could bring forth corn. The cult played an important role in the realm of fertility, but also made individual application with issues of immorality. Nevertheless, such a parallel is inadequate because the theme of rebirth in this cycle is presented as automatic while the saying in John 12:24 emphasizes the risk of losing one's life and facing a death which is permanent and real.

Since this saying is placed in the context of the request from Greeks and since two Bethsaida disciples are involved, it is appropriate to look for a parallel in the cult of Livia. As was mentioned in chapter 8, Livia was often associated with Demeter, the goddess of grain and of plenty. Thus the coin issued in 30 C.E. to honor her as Livia/Julia made use of appropriate imagery with a hand holding three erect ears of barley and an inscription reading ΚΑΡΠΟΦΟΡΟΣ—"bearing fruit."[10] Herod Philip has depicted Livia/Julia as the benefactress of the newly founded city of Bethsaida-Julias who, through proper attention to the practices of the Livia cult, will continue to bestow an abundance of blessings upon its people.

The other critical factor is that Herod Philip's coin was issued in the year following Livia/Julia's death in 29 C.E. When one compares this particular coin with two other coins—one issued by Pontius Pilate and the other issued by Agrippa 1—its significance really comes to light. The coin of Pilate also depicts the three ears of grain, but two are drooping and denote the mourning connected with Livia/Julia's death. The situation was that her death was observed as final and real. In spite of her wishes to be deified like her husband Augustus, Tiberius with the backing of the Roman Senate declared her mortality and proscribed only the respectful

---

9. Brown, *The Gospel According to John*, 1:472.
10. Fred Strickert, "The Coins of Philip," *Bethsaida* (1995) 165–89.

recognition of an ordinary human. In contrast, the coin of Agrippa 1 issued in 42 C.E. came soon after the emperor Claudius, his own friend from childhood and Livia's grandson, declared her deification. It had taken twelve years after her death, but this recognition was complete. Thus the coin of Agrippa 1 depicts the three ears of grain as erect.

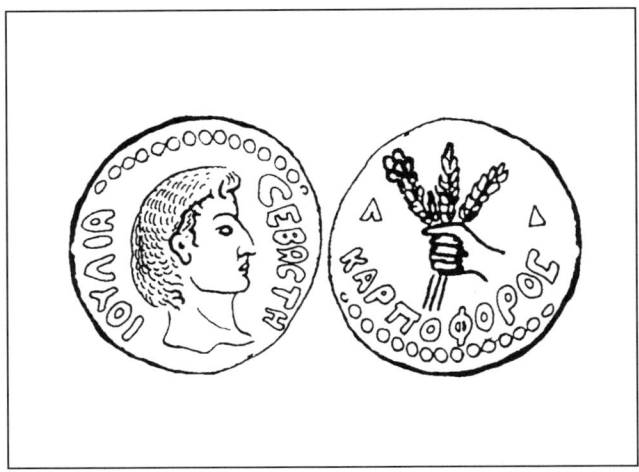

Philip Coin: Julia—30 C.E.

Pontius Pilate Coin—30 C.E.

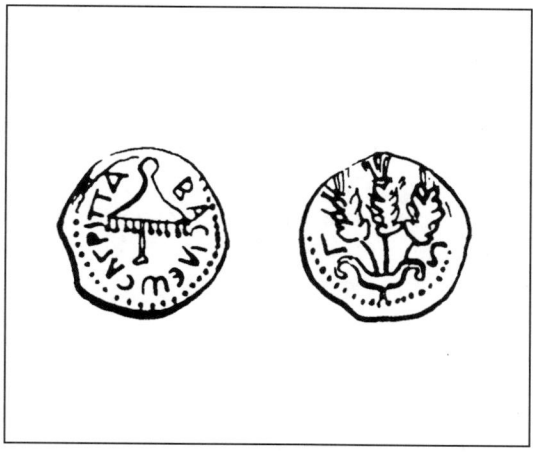

Agrippa 1 Coin—42/43 C.E.

There is no question that the issue of Livia's role following her death was debated and that it was a grassroots movement in the provinces which prepared the way for Claudius' action. Philip's Livia-Julia coin minted in both 30 and 33 C.E. demonstrates that this concern was very much alive at the time of Jesus' death on April 7, 30 C.E., and during the earliest stages of the Christian Church. The renaming of Bethsaida to Julias demonstrates that the debate was centered in the town Bethsaida.

The saying of Jesus in John 12:24 must be understood against this background. With Livia's death in 29 C.E., the grain had fallen to the ground and died. Unlike the way this motif was handled in the Demeter myth and the mystery religions, there was no automatic rebirth and no guarantees for the success of the grass roots movement of which Herod Philip was a part. Livia's death had all the appearance of being final and permanent. Yet the grain fallen to the earth would produce much fruit. The Johannine expression πολὺν καρπὸν φέρει (it bears much fruit) is a remarkable reflection of the words on Philip's coin καρπόφορος. Philip thus was expressing the view that Livia, even through death, would remain as benefactress of the Bethsaida-Julias community.

There are a number of good reasons to accept this saying as authentic.[11] These include similarities in form and imagery with the Synoptic parables, the role of coin allusions in Jesus' teaching,[12] the timeliness of this theme

---

11. C. H. Dodd, *Historical Tradition in the Fourth Gospel* (Cambridge: Cambridge University Press, 1963) 366–9.

12. Livia's image was depicted on the reverse of denarii portraying the image of Tiberius.

during the week of Passover in 30 C.E., and the actual verbal similarity of the saying with the coin inscription. However, even if one denies the authenticity of this saying, it surely must have emerged very early in the sayings tradition in the setting of the community at Bethsaida. It is especially appropriate as a statement about the superiority of Jesus as the benefactor for the Christian community as it encounters the popularity of the Livia cult. It points to a very early date when the Christians experienced and confessed the resurrected Jesus, at a time when the status of Livia was still uncertain. This would fit best the time between 30 and 41 C.E.

As we suggested earlier, the report of a resurrection appearance on the sea in John 21 may well reflect the origins of the community's experience that Jesus was in fact alive. Under the leadership of Philip and Andrew, this confession of the risen Jesus became a reality for the whole community in its sharing of a commemorative meal of bread and fish. This confession remembered also the miraculous activity of Jesus within the community, especially the feeding of a multitude and the miraculous catch of fish. In this way the dying, rising Jesus was benefactor of the community bringing forth much fruit. The request of Greeks to see Jesus, therefore, may well represent the success of the early Christian movement at Bethsaida-Julias among former adherents of the cult of Livia.

How this success was affected by the deification of Livia by Claudius in 41 C.E. is uncertain. The coin with three ears of grain issued by Agrippa 1 in 42 C.E. suggests that her cult was still active. It is interesting that shortly thereafter, Agrippa 1 began a persecution of early Christians. Our only report, Acts 12, situates the persecution in Jerusalem and notes that James, the son of Zebedee, was killed by the sword and that Peter had been arrested with the intent of being executed. Peter's miraculous rescue from prison and departure from Jerusalem to "another place" brings to an end Luke's report of this incident. Whether or not this persecution affected other communities such as Bethsaida is unclear, but the reader of Luke can justifiably be skeptical in limiting the scope of such reports to the Jerusalem church. Interestingly, the two disciples mentioned in the persecution, James and Peter, both have connections to the northern Sea of Galilee area. It is possible that Philip and Andrew were affected as well.

The sudden death of Agrippa 1 at Caesarea in 44 C.E. is reported by both Luke (Acts 12:20-23) and Josephus (Josephus, *Ant.* 19.343-52). This was interpreted as the will of God because Agrippa 1 had assumed acclamations as if a god himself. The following year, Palestine was struck by a severe famine which lasted for several years. Both Luke (Acts 11:27-29) and Josephus (Josephus, *Ant.* 20.51-53) speak of the effect of the famine on Jerusalem. Other reports suggest that its effect also reached as far north as Syria.[13] One must wonder what was the effect on the Livia cult in view of this series of events leading up to the famine: the deification of Livia in 41 C.E., the grain coin of Agrippa in 42 C.E., and the death of Agrippa in 44 C.E. She had failed in her role as ΚΑΡΠΟΦΟΡΟΣ, the provider of an abundance of grains. On the other hand, Josephus reports that a new benefactress had come upon the scene. Jerusalem was saved by the intervention of Queen Helena who purchased grain in Egypt and Cyprus and as a result, she received appropriate honors. In contrast, the book of Acts emphasizes the continued role of the risen Jesus whose spirit moved both the prophet Agabus to predict this crisis and the community of believers in Antioch to provide aid for the Jerusalem church.

The events which took place between 41 and 47 C.E. in Palestine point to a difficult situation for the Christian community at Bethsaida and a struggle perhaps for identity in relation to the Livia cult. Such a setting may well be reflected by the woe saying against the city of Bethsaida, as well as Chorazin and Capernaum (Matt 11:20-24 = Luke 10:13-15) as other early Christian prophets felt frustration over a lack of repentance. This may even be directly related to the message of the prophet Agabus who had gone down to Antioch from Jerusalem (Acts 11:27). The focus on the mighty deeds of Jesus in that Q saying fits well the suggested picture at Bethsaida which placed an undue emphasis on the role of Jesus as benefactor at the expense of neglecting the other part of the message which spoke of the grain falling to the earth and dying.

An Early Christian Cross

One would not expect to find remains of churches or particular Christian structures from first-century Bethsaida. Nor would one expect to find epigraphs or artistic representations. However, several pottery etchings may add to our knowledge of that community. Foremost among these is the etching of a cross.

The cross pottery found at Bethsaida in 1994 comes from a destruction layer in a Roman-era courtyard style house (see illustration, page 71). The somewhat rough and imperfect cross inscription measures 4¼ inches by 5½ inches although the top portion has broken off. It is composed of a circle in the center with four extended arms each made up of two connected parallel lines. The "circle" in the center is imperfect with a 1.65 inch horizontal diameter contrasting a 1.42 inch vertical diameter. Yet all three complete arms extend 2.12 inches from the center. Fainter lines continue another 1.30 inches from the lower arm which alter the appearance from a "Greek cross"—all

---

13. Orosius, *History* 7.6.12.

150 *Bethsaida: Home of the Apostles*

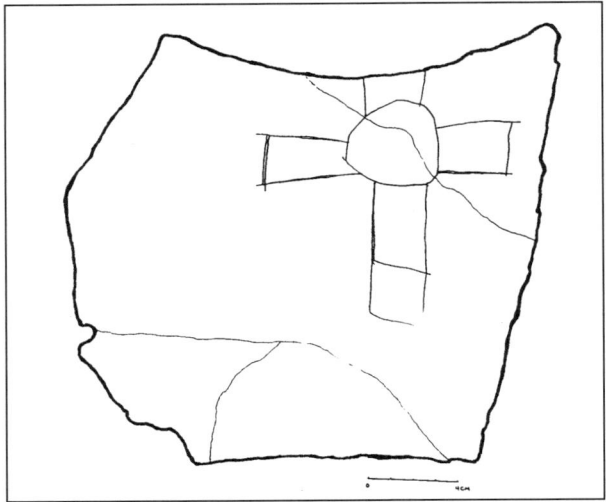

"Cross" Pottery

arms equidistant—to a "Roman cross"—horizontal arms intersecting the vertical at a distance of one third from the top. Therefore the cross presents some sort of sophistication and planning in spite of its crude appearance.

Unfortunately, the pottery vessel on which the cross-figure was found is incomplete. Only eleven shards have been retrieved. Five can be pieced together, but others, including a rim and broken handle, do not provide a continuous line for reconstruction. The largest shard measures fifteen by six inches, and the rim fragment points to an opening of over five inches. It does appear to be a large vessel such as an amphora or a storage vessel probably from the Roman period. Petrographic analysis found no basalt fragments in the clay, so it was likely brought to Bethsaida from another location. The components suggest that it was made in western Galilee.[14] The figure was not part of the original design of the vessel, but was etched after firing, possibly by the owner of the vessel at Bethsaida.

The composition of this fragment finds its closest parallel with storage jars like those found in the wine cellar in the same courtyard style house. These jars are all Hellenistic and date to 100 B.C.E. to 70 C.E.[15] Along with

---

14. The clay was composed of marly (containing calcium carbonate) and also includes terra rosa (a mixture containing iron) mudballs for thinning the clay. It was fired at a very hot temperature, 1,000 degrees C. Petrographic analysis was carried out by Dr. Yuval Goren of the Israel Antiquities Authority in Jerusalem.

15. Paul W. Lapp, *Palestinian Ceramic Chronology: 200 B.C.–A.D. 70* (New Haven, 1961), Type 11, 149–52.

Early Christian Community in Bethsaida   151

"Cross" Pottery

one complete Hellenistic cooking pot dating to the first century C.E., this provides a sealed locus for the destruction of the house and supports a first-century date for the cross. This is consistent with pottery and coin evidence discovered throughout the courtyard style house as also in the immediate location in which the cross pottery was found among destruction from a collapsed wall and doorway.

In drawing significance from such an artistic representation, one must refrain from any kind of absolutism or certainty. There is no inscription which identifies it as Christian, and it is certainly possible that it was intended as a decorative design without religious symbolism, or that it may be linked with similar symbolism from other cultures such as the ankh or swastika (ancient symbols of life and good fortune). One must also consider that the cross symbol was not that common in Christian visual art before the time of Constantine.[16] Among cross-shaped figures which are discussed for this period there is the cross-shaped bare spot on a wall of Herculaneum prior to the eruption of Vesuvius in 79 C.E.; the second-century anti-Christian graffiti from the Palatine section of Rome of a crucified human with an ass's head; cross markings on ossuaries from early Palestine—which may represent the Tau mark from Ezekiel 9:3-8; cross-figures within other symbols such as anchors and masts of ships; and

---

16. Graydon F. Snyder, *Ante-Pacem: Archaeological Evidence of Church Life Before Constantine* (Mercer University Press, 1985) 27; Jack T. Sanders, *Schismatics, Sectarians, Dissidents, Deviants: The First One Hundred Years of Jewish-Christian Relations* (Valley Forge, Pa.: Trinity Press, 1993) 31–9; Jack Finegan, *The Archaeology of the New Testament* (Princeton, 1969) 220–60.

crosses represented by the emphasis on certain letters in Christian epigraphs and documents. In this era when Christianity was trying to gain respect from the Roman government, it is understandable that a symbol which carried such a negative connotation would have been avoided. Nevertheless early Christian writers did not shy away from speaking about the cross in the most positive terms. The possibility for early crosses need not be totally unexpected.

The design of the Bethsaida fragment is unparalleled in pre-Constantine figures. Yet it does seem appropriate for the emphases discussed earlier in this chapter. The key to interpreting this cross is the presence of arms extending out in four directions from a central circle. The circle thus denotes wholeness and unity and the arms denote diversity. The diversity is fitting for a multicultural center where the imperial cult and Judaism were practiced as well as Christianity; where disciples had Greek names; and where Greeks sought to see Jesus. The wholeness and oneness could even point to the common loaf in a commemorative meal. This same focus on unity and diversity is linked with crucifixion in the John 12:24 saying of Jesus so that the death of a single grain produces diverse fruit.

Why this symbol was etched on this piece of pottery is not certain. However, the large size points to its use to store wine, grain, or other produce. Here there is an interesting parallel. Tau marks (shaped like a simple cross) were found on storage jars at Masada which Yigal Yadin interpreted as representing the "Truma"—the heave offering or the priests' portion (Exod 29:27).[17] It would not be too difficult to imagine the Bethsaida cross marking as serving a similar liturgical purpose.

Evidence of Christianity at Bethsaida may perhaps also be derived from a pottery marking on a jar handle depicting an anchor. The anchor as a symbol was used already on Jewish coins. However, in this particular case, a horizontal line is much more prominent than on Jewish symbols. The anchor was in use early as a Christian symbol of hope (Heb 6:19) and, beginning in the second century, it was not unusual that the upper portion was emphasized in such a way as to suggest a cross. The pottery from Bethsaida gives this appearance. Because of the role of fishing at Bethsaida, it is likely that the anchor was used as a commercial symbol, but at the same time may have also carried a religious meaning.

In spite of the silence in the Book of Acts in and Paul's writings concerning the early Christian community at Bethsaida, the Gospels themselves—especially John—offer numerous clues concerning an active community. Recent archaeological work is beginning to confirm its existence.

17. Yigal Yadin, *Masada* (New York: Random House, 1966) 96.

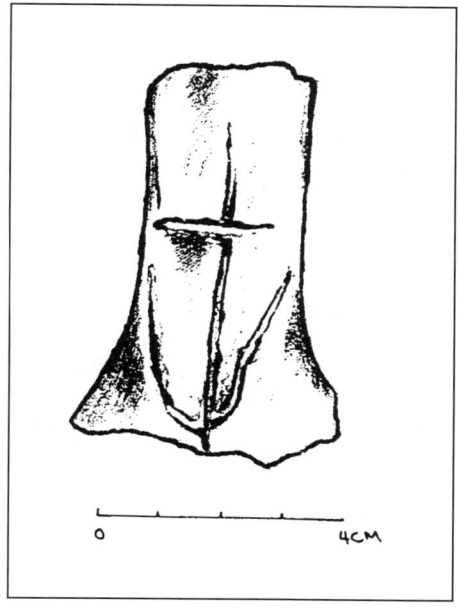

Anchor Handle

Chapter 14
The Gathering of Sayings of Jesus

In recent years there has been a lot of attention given to the sayings of Jesus. This includes primarily study of the sayings collection known as Q, which was used by Matthew and Luke, and also careful analysis of the Gospel of Thomas collection of 114 sayings discovered at Nag Hammadi, Egypt in 1945. This work has been popularized by the Jesus Seminar which undertook the careful examination of each individual saying and published findings in *The Five Gospels: The Search for the Authentic Words of Jesus*.[1]

Philip and the Sayings Tradition

The early Christian community at Bethsaida-Julias provides a possible context for the gathering of sayings about Jesus. The Apostle Philip is an appropriate character to bring about the gathering process. Bishop Papias of Hierapolis in the early second century placed Andrew and Philip, along with Peter, at the beginning of the collectors of these sayings:

> If, then anyone came who had been a follower of the elders, I inquired into the sayings of the elders—what Andrew said, or what Peter said, or what Philip, or Thomas, or James, or John, or Matthew, or any of the other disciples of the Lord said.

The first three names are those mentioned in John 1:44—"Now Philip was from Bethsaida, the city of Andrew and Peter." While the names of Thomas and Matthew are most often mentioned in connection with the sayings tradition, Philip plays no less a prominent role.

---

1. *The Five Gospels: The Search for the Authentic Words of Jesus*, new trans. Robert W. Funk, Roy W. Hoover, and the Jesus Seminar (N.Y.: Polebridge Press, 1993).

The role of Philip is highlighted in the Nag Hammadi document *Pistis Sophia* as he is introduced as "the writer of all the words which Jesus spoke and of all that he did."[2] The following words are then addressed particularly to Philip:

> Hear, Philip, you blessed one, that I may speak with you, for you and Thomas and Matthew are they to whom the charge is given by the first mystery, to write down all the things which I shall say and do . . ."Through two and three witnesses shall everything be established"; the three witnesses are Philip and Thomas and Matthew.[3]

Philip is placed alongside the two best-known gatherers of sayings. Thomas is well known today because of The Gospel of Thomas and Matthew is identified in Papias as the one who wrote "the sayings of Jesus in the Hebrew language for each one to interpret as he could." It is not surprising, then, that the Nag Hammadi Library also includes a Gospel of Philip. In later tradition, Philip was in fact remembered for his role in preserving the sayings of Jesus.

This also is made clear in the Fourth Gospel. In addition to the three occasions when Philip and Andrew are mentioned together (John 1:44; 6:6-8; 12:21-22), Philip's name occurs by itself in the farewell discourse in John 14. There Philip is depicted in the role of gathering the sayings of Jesus as he makes the following request:

> Lord, show us the Father, and we will be satisfied (John 14:8).

Jesus responds:

> The words that I say to you I do not speak on my own; but the Father who dwells in me does his works (John 14:10).

A little later as the discussion progresses, Jesus speaks directly to the sayings collection process:

> I have said these things to you while I am still with you. But the Advocate, the Holy Spirit, whom the Father will send in my name, will teach you everything, and remind you of all that I have said to you (John 14:25-26).

Here are addressed two central components of the sayings gathering process. First, is that of remembering. Although the disciples have not always understood the significance of Jesus' teaching and actions at the time they happened, the function of the Holy Spirit is to remind them and help them to understand their significance (John 2:22; 12:16). Second, the

---

2. Edgar Hennecke, *New Testament Apocrypha*, ed. Wilhelm Schneemelcher (Philadelphia: The Westminster Press, 1963) 1:272.
3. Ibid.

Holy Spirit functions as a teacher so that, as the community continues to speak and to apply itself to new situations and contexts, the words of Jesus are being spoken through them.

Philip is very much involved in the Fourth Gospel in the sayings gathering process. Since remembering is key to that process, the author has called attention to Philip at critical junctures throughout the gospel—chapters 1, 6, 12, and 14—where he serves as witness to the words of Jesus.

A Nucleus of Sayings: The Fourth Gospel

In the previous chapter, we discussed the saying of Jesus in John 12:24 about the necessity of the seed falling to the ground and dying in order to produce much fruit. That saying is set in a literary context of a response to Greeks who consult the Bethsaida disciples Philip and Andrew and it fits the historical context of the encounter of early Christianity with the Livia cult. Here we can isolate a single saying to a rather narrow context: the city of Bethsaida-Julias between the years 30 and 44 C.E. Is it possible also to build upon this single saying and to hypothesize an expansion into an early sayings collection?

The place to begin is with the larger context of the grain saying, where two other sayings of Jesus immediately follow. These two sayings read:

> Those who love their life lose it, and those who hate their life in this world will keep it for eternal life. Whoever serves me must follow me, and where I am, there will my servant be also. Whoever serves me, the Father will honor (John 12:25-26).

This unit is especially significant because verse 25, like the dying grain saying in verse 24, is printed in gray in *The Five Gospels*, which denotes a reflection of the actual teaching of Jesus. Although the Fourth Gospel is removed from the historical Jesus by some six or seven decades, it is generally assumed that these three sayings originate in a pre-Johannine source.[4] Schnackenburg has identified these three sayings as "a unit, firmly rooted in the tradition and catechesis of the primitive church."[5] What stands out the most about the latter two sayings is that parallels occur in Mark 8:34-35, but in reverse order. These sayings occur in the context of the confession of Simon Peter which is linked geographically to the area of Caesarea Philippi, just north of Bethsaida. That episode is

---

4. Raymond E. Brown, *The Gospel According to John*, The Anchor Bible (Garden City, N.Y.: Doubleday, 1966) 1:471–4; Ernst Haenchen, *John,* Hermeneia Series (Philadelphia: Fortress, 1984) 2:97.

5. Rudolf Schnackenburg, *The Gospel According to St. John* (N.Y.: The Seabury Press, 1980) 2:384.

preceded in Mark 8 by the second feeding miracle and the healing of the blind man at Bethsaida.[6] Even though it is a major revision from Mark, Luke 9 places the confession of Peter and the sayings about losing one's life and being a servant directly after the Bethsaida feeding of the five thousand episode. Further study is needed to explore in depth the relation of these three sayings to an early Bethsaida sayings source.

At this point, however, we can make three observations. First, it is significant that the theme of the necessity of the death and resurrection of Jesus is at the heart of these sayings. This stands in contrast to recent studies which portray Jesus as a Cynic teacher for a community where death and resurrection was not at the core of its teaching.[7] At Bethsaida, however, one expects that the controversy over the death and deification of Livia led to critical reflection concerning the death and resurrection of Jesus—something supported by the discovery of the early cross pottery. Second, these sayings are linked to the concept of martyrdom, not only to the result of bearing much fruit, but also with the model of discipleship. This suggests a context of conflict possibly with the Livia cult and perhaps in association with the persecutions carried out under Agrippa in 44 C.E. Third, it points to a possible connection with Q, the Synoptic sayings source, since the second saying has parallels in Q (Matt 10:37 = Luke 14:26 and Matt 10:39 = Luke 17:33).

Bethsaida and Q

In recent years it has often been proposed that the sayings collection Q originated in an urban Galilean setting in the mid-first century. Sepphoris has often been put forward as a possible setting. However, there is even more reason to consider Bethsaida as such a candidate. Although it is clear that Q originates in a Galilean setting, the only place names included are the three towns on the northern edge of the Sea of Galilee, namely Chorazin, Capernaum, and Bethsaida. This saying of woe, discussed in an earlier chapter, reflects the frustration of early Christian prophets over difficult times that developed at midcentury.

The woe saying also calls attention to the role of signs—their effect in Jesus' lifetime as well as in the early Church. Especially important for Bethsaida is the sign of the multiplication of loaves and fishes and, as was proposed, a commemorative meal. This does not occur in the Q tradition.

---

6. See Thomas L. Brodie, *The Quest for the Origin of John's Gospel: A Source-Oriented Approach* (N.Y.: Oxford University Press, 1993) 48–66.

7. John Dominic Crossan, *Jesus: A Revolutionary Biography* (San Francisco: Harper Collins, 1994); Burton L. Mack, *The Lost Gospel: The Book of Q and Christian Origins* (San Francisco: Harper Collins, 1993).

However, the parable of the mustard seed conveys a similar message: that one sown seed brings forth an abundance. While the Markan and Thomas versions closely reflect the authentic words of Jesus, the Q version (Luke 13:18-19) turns the parable into an allegory based on Daniel 4 and Ezekiel 17. The seed emerges into a large tree which provides shelter and sustenance for Gentiles. This theme is reflected also in the parable of the great supper (Matt 22:1-14 = Luke 14:15-25), where outsiders are welcome at the meal. This is expressed clearly also in the saying about the messianic banquet:

> Then people will come from east and west, from north and south, and will eat in the kingdom of God (Matt 8:11 = Luke 13:29).

These sayings fit well into the context of a community where Gentiles are welcomed to the sharing of a common meal—such as has been suggested for Bethsaida.

The Synoptic sayings source also calls attention to the dining practices of Jesus in contrast to the ascetic life of John the Baptist (Luke 7:33-34) and it includes a number of sayings which are addressed to people who have gone out to the desert to hear and to see John. They have left behind the city with its market place (Luke 7:32) and finely dressed persons and royal luxury (Luke 7:24-26)—something quite appropriate to Bethsaida. It is the fourth evangelist who has identified the continuity between the followers of John and the community of Jesus by identifying two of Jesus' disciples as former disciples of John (John 1:35-37). One is explicitly identified as Andrew (John 1:40); the other is not named, but may have been Philip (John 1:43) or John. Therefore, it is not surprising that Q also preserves a series of sayings of John the Baptist (Luke 3:7-9; 16-17; 7:18-23). A possible connection of Bethsaida with the Baptist is one further link to the Q tradition and will hopefully stimulate further exploration of the sayings of Jesus with reference to the city of Bethsaida.

Chapter 15

The Destruction of Bethsaida

The city of Bethsaida reached its height of glory in the early and mid-first century. However, it soon came to an end. Already in the Q saying of woe against the cities in Jesus' ministry, one finds a hint that Bethsaida was on the road to destruction. In order to determine the details of the end of biblical Bethsaida, one must join forces with both archaeological and literary sources. Coin and pottery finds, along with the analysis of patterns of structures, can help supplement the scant literary information to reach an understanding of Bethsaida's fate.

Evidence from Archaeology

The first ten seasons of excavations at et-Tell have yielded evidence which consistently points to the end of Bethsaida's history shortly after the New Testament period. Although a city existed on this site from the Bronze Age through Iron Age, Hellenistic, and early Roman periods, there is no sign of occupation in subsequent periods. Early Roman structures are consistently found directly below the surface. This includes the two complete courtyard style houses, referred to as the "fisherman's house" and the "winemaker's house;" a whole complex of houses adjacent to a first-century street; and various other Hellenistic structures scattered over the excavated parts of the tell. Following this period, there are no signs of later building and a portion of the site subsequently was used as a cemetery.

Coin evidence is often very helpful because it provides evidence with precise dating. At Bethsaida, about 250 coins were discovered during the 1988–96 seasons of excavation. The following listing of coin distribution of these finds can be helpful for analysis:

Number	Period	Dates
3	Persian	Pre-3rd Century
28	Ptolemaic	285–221 B.C.E.
67	Seleucid	221–139 B.C.E.
18	Hasmonean	136–63 B.C.E.
15	Herodian Period	39 B.C.E.–96 C.E.
	6-city coins	
	1-Herod —pre 4 B.C.E.	
	1-Archelaus—4 B.C.E. to 6 C.E.	
	3-Philip —29–30 C.E.	
	1-Antipas —33 C.E.	
	1-Agrippa 1 —42–43 C.E.	
	2-Agrippa 2—53 / 84 C.E.	
6	Roman	96–180 C.E.
	3 Trajan — 99 C.E.	
	1 Trajan — 108 C.E.	
	1 Antonius Pius/1 Marcus Aurelius —	138–180 C.E.
12	Roman Provincial	218–260 C.E.
2	Late Roman	307–337 C.E.
3	Byzantine	565–578 C.E.
29	Islamic	7th–17th century
	(20-Mamluk —13th–14th cents. C.E.)	
52	Ottoman	18th–19th century
15	Modern or effaced	

At first glance, this coin data would appear to be less than totally conclusive. Although the largest number of coins at et-Tell come from the biblical period and are concentrated between the third century B.C.E. and the first century C.E., there continue to be a few coins from later periods. However, a few patterns emerge. The regular appearance of coins continues through the rule of Trajan at the beginning of the second century and then there is, without a doubt, a significant drop in coin finds. After a four-hundred-year period (285 B.C.E.–108 C.E.) in which 132 coins were found, only nineteen coins turn up in the four hundred and fifty years of Late Roman and Byzantine periods (117–614 C.E.). These coins do not necessarily point to occupation. In fact, none of them was discovered in the context of the residential sections on the northern half of the tell. Rather, they were all found among the ruins of debris from the public buildings to the south, perhaps left by visitors or scavengers of a fallen city. A century-long gap (117–235 C.E.), which yielded only two coins, is especially significant in establishing that the site had been deserted.

Pottery evidence establishes a similar pattern. Throughout the Hellenistic and early Roman periods, there are extensive finds including a good number of whole vessels. These include various Hellenistic cooking pots, jugs, bowls, and jars, as well as Rhodian Amphorae and imported fineware. Other than a single shard here and there, pottery from the later periods is virtually nonexistent. Certainly there is no evidence for the types of vessels necessary for daily life.

One might expect to find a destruction layer—with extensive ashes and burnt material—to explain the sudden end of occupation around the end of the first century. This is clearly the case following an eighth-century B.C.E. conflagration apparently at the hands of the Assyrians. However, other than isolated patches of ashes, no extensive pattern of burning can be established. The same can be said for weapons of destruction. A couple of Roman arrowheads and one spearhead have turned up, along with numerous round stones which could well have served as ballistas. These do not occur in sufficient numbers to establish a pattern. They certainly do not resemble the picture presented at Gamla where there was a major battle in the Jewish revolt of 67 C.E.

However, the excavation of the "winemaker's" courtyard style house in area C proved very interesting. Roofing stones were discovered collapsed in the southwest corner of the courtyard. A lintel was positioned on ground level just inside the north courtyard doorway. Several of the walls also had a twisted appearance. Along the south wall of the kitchen were found numerous shattered, but complete, cooking vessels stacked on top of each other suggesting the collapse of shelving. This evidence points to a violent type of destruction. The discovery of a Roman key on the kitchen floor near the broken cooking vessels suggests that the occupants had to flee suddenly, unable to lock up their house for a possible return. This house did have one undisturbed section, a wine cellar on the east side, where the roofing stones remained in place—leaving a sealed locus. The pottery there was entirely Hellenistic including a complete Hellenistic everted rim cooking pot (first century C.E.) and four complete Hellenistic jars, Lapp type 11 (100 B.C.E.–70 C.E.).[1] This establishes a date for the destruction of the house around the end of the first century.

A similar picture of destruction is evident in other sections of the tell. In the recently excavated Roman temple, one east-west wall is tilted drastically to the south and several massive building stones have shifted from their original positions. There appears to have been no attempt to reconstruct the damaged walls. Instead, the picture is one of abandonment.

---

1. Paul W. Lapp, *Palestinian Ceramic Chronology: 200 B.C.–A.D. 70* (New Haven, 1961) 149–52.

164   *Bethsaida: Home of the Apostles*

Josephus and the Evidence of War

In the year 67 C.E., Josephus reports a battle which took place near Bethsaida which could possibly account for the end of the city's occupation (Josephus, *Life* 398–406).[2] This battle occurred when King Agrippa 2 sent troops to cut off the supply network between Galilee and Gamla. The troops under the command of Sulla were thus stationed over half a mile to the north of Bethsaida-Julias. The Galilean forces then arrived to do battle with two thousand men under the command of Jeremiah and three thousand men under the command of Josephus himself. There is, therefore, no reason to question the reliability of this report since Josephus himself was directly involved. His description perfectly fits the topography with the battle taking place on the level ground between et-Tell and the Jordan River and troops hiding in the ravine to the west. Josephus even describes with pride the success of the Galilean troops until his own horse stumbled in the soft marshes so that he broke his wrist and had to be removed to Capernaum. From that point on, Josephus' demoralized troops were no match for Sulla.

In spite of this clear report of a battle fought near Bethsaida-Julias, one must be careful not to make assumptions about the city itself. Nowhere is it mentioned that Bethsaida-Julias was destroyed, let alone that the battle was even extended to the city. It is also striking that Josephus' *Jewish War* does not include a parallel account. Apparently Bethsaida-Julias itself was not considered strategic to the plans of the Galileans. Interestingly, it is not mentioned as one of the cities fortified with walls (Josephus, *War* 2.573–574; *Life* 187). The purpose for the battle is to open up the supply routes to Gamla, not to control the city itself. The reason the report is mentioned in *Life* is to demonstrate Josephus' leadership as well as his dedication which led to injury in battle. On the other hand, one must consider the possibility that the inhabitants of Bethsaida-Julias were sympathetic to the side of Agrippa 2 and were not part of the rebel camp. The city did have a history of positive relations with the Herodians and also Rome. In the case of Gamla to the east, it is reported that rebel forces had gained control (Josephus, *Life* 37) and that Agrippa responded by laying siege to the city for seven months (Josephus, *War* 4.4–10). In the case of two other fortified cities of the Golan, Seleucia and Sogane surrendered without a fight (Josephus, *War* 4.4). One is struck by the absence of such reports about Bethsaida-Julias. Were Bethsaida-Julias in fact in rebel hands, it is difficult to imagine Sulla allowing himself to be drawn into

---

2. John T. Greene, "Bethsaida-Julias in Roman and Jewish Military Strategies, 66–73 C.E.," *Bethsaida* (1995) 203–27.

battle in the confined and vulnerable position between the city on the hill and the Jordan River. The evidence then about a destruction of Bethsaida-Julias in the Jewish revolt of 67 C.E. is inconclusive at best.

Certainly, the city did not go out of existence at this time. Pliny the Elder writes in the year 77 C.E. about Julias as still one of the major cities on the Sea of Galilee.[3] The presence of a coin of Domitian (84 C.E.) and four Trajan coins (97–117 C.E.) in the context of a single domestic building points to the continued occupation of the city.

The Bar Kochba Revolt

A second Jewish revolt against the Romans took place under the leadership of Bar Kochba from 132–5 C.E. The devastation was dramatic:

> Fifty of their most important outposts and nine hundred and eighty-five of their most famous villages were razed to the ground. Five hundred and eighty thousand men were slain in the various raids and battles, and the number of those that perished by famine, disease and fire was past finding out. Thus the whole of Judea was made desolate.[4]

Although the date of this revolt corresponds with the abandonment of et-Tell, there is no evidence that it extended further than Judea. In fact, this revolt did have a significant impact in the area around Bethsaida-Julias in that a large number of Judeans subsequently migrated to the Golan area so that it became heavily populated in the second to the fifth centuries. Since strategically located cities are typically rebuilt after battles, the abandonment of et-Tell is all the more puzzling. The cause of warfare is thus inadequate to explain the end of Bethsaida-Julias.

Earthquakes

The possibility of an earthquake as the cause of destruction for Bethsaida is quite high since the Jordan Rift is a major fault line. According to a recently published catalogue of earthquakes in Israel, major earthquakes are listed in 115, 130, 306, and 363 C.E. as well as others later.[5] The major earthquake in 363 C.E. destroyed 21 urban centers and the Temple restoration project initiated by Julian in 361 C.E. Eusebius, in fact, noted the fourth-century destruction at Chorazin as the fulfillment of Jesus' words

---

3. Pliny, *Natural History* 5.15.71.
4. Dio Cassius, *Roman History* 69.14. 1–2.
5. D.H.K. Amiran, E. Arieh, and T. Turcotte, "Earthquakes in Israel and Adjacent Areas: Macroseismic Observations since 100 BCE," *Israel Exploration Journal* 44 (3–4) (1994) 260–305.

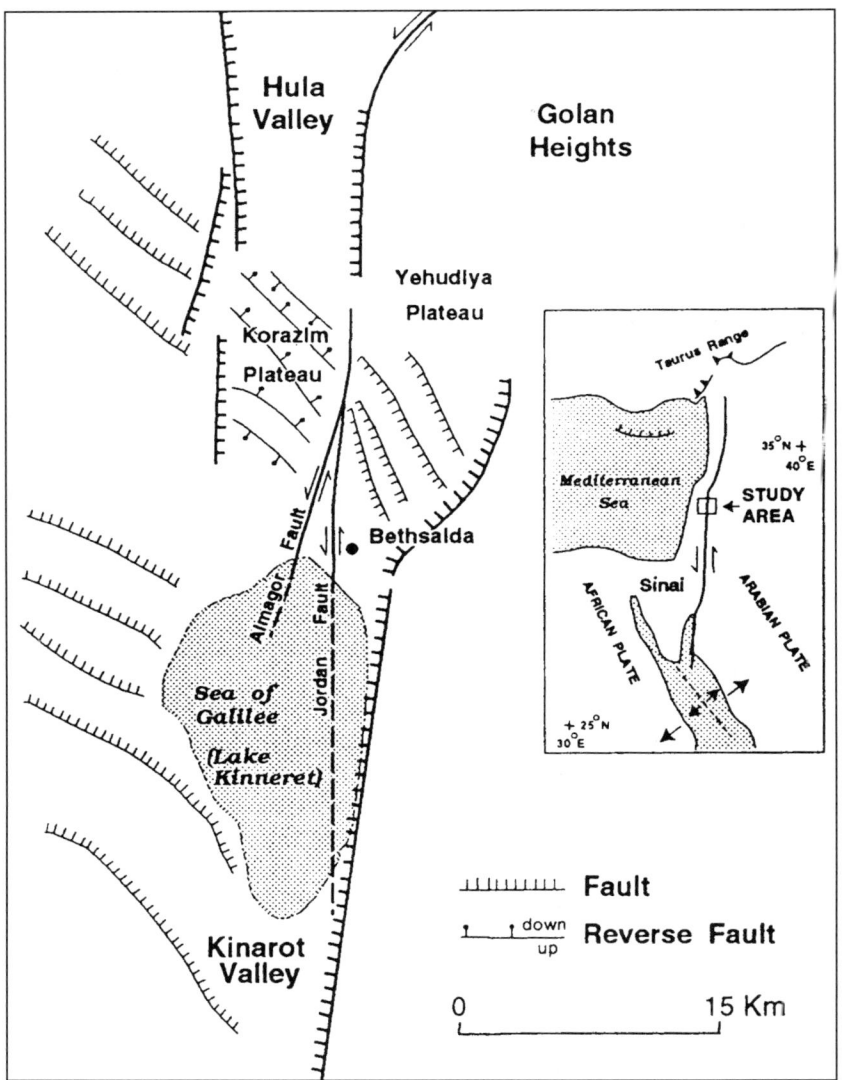

Fault System: Jordan Rift Valley

of woe in Matthew 11:20–24. Yet Bethsaida was not mentioned in that regard, perhaps suggesting that it had already gone out of existence.

The evidence of twisted walls throughout the site and particularly of the fallen roofing stones and collapsed shelving in the "Winemaker's House" in Area C is quite fitting for earthquake destruction. The pottery and coin finds—especially with four Trajan coins—point to the 115 C.E. earthquake as the most likely. This earthquake caused extensive damage in Antioch and was recorded in detail by Dio Cassius because Trajan was in the city at the time and barely escaped with his life. The scene is described in vivid detail:

> While the emperor was tarrying in Antioch a terrible earthquake occurred; Many cities suffered injury, but Antioch was the most unfortunate of all. Since Trajan was passing the winter there and many soldiers and many civilians had flocked thither from all sides . . . there was no nation or people that went unscathed; and thus in Antioch the whole world under Roman sway suffered disaster. There had been many thunderstorms and portentous winds, but no one would ever have expected so many evils to result from them. First there came, on a sudden, a great bellowing roar, and this was followed by a tremendous quaking. The whole earth was upheaved, and buildings leaped into the air; some were carried aloft only to collapse and be broken in pieces, while others were tossed this way and that as if by the surge of the sea, and overturned, and the wreckage spread out over a great extent even of the open country. The crash of grinding and breaking timbers together with tiles and stones was most frightful. . . .As for the people, many even who were outside the houses were hurt, being snatched up and tossed violently about and then dashed to the earth as if falling from a cliff; some were maimed and others were killed. Even trees in some cases leaped into the air, roots and all.[6]

This earthquake appears to have been quite extensive with evidence even of a tidal wave hitting Yavneh on the south coast and evidence of structural damage at sites as scattered as Caesarea, Jerash, Petra, Heshbon, Avdat, Khirbet Tannur, and Mampsis.[7] Coins from the era of Trajan (97–117 C.E.) have been found in connection with the destruction material at Masada, Petra, and Avdat while coins of his successor are absent— the same pattern as at Bethsaida. This supports a conclusion of a major earthquake affecting all of Palestine and Syria in 115 C.E.[8]

Archaeological evidence at Bethsaida corresponds to the data assembled for this earthquake. However, once again one is faced with the question of why the city was not later rebuilt. The answer comes from geological study in the Jordan River gorge. Two major landslides have been discovered north of Bethsaida. It appears that extensive rains and earthquakes caused these landslides which extended across the gorge to dam up the Jordan River, perhaps for as long as a week. With continually

---

6. Dio Cassius, *Roman History* 68.24. 1–3.
7. Kenneth W. Russell, "The Earthquake Chronology of Palestine and Northwest Arabia from the 2nd through the Mid-8th Century A.D." *Bulletin of the American Schools of Oriental Research* (1985) 37–60, esp. 40–1.
8. Russell is suspicious of literary evidence for the 128–30 C.E. earthquake because of a possible confusion of names with cities in Anatolia and prefers to speak of one major second century earthquake.

Twisted wall in "Winemaker's House"—earthquake damage

built up pressure, the force of the water then broke through with such a force that massive debris was carried down river. Huge boulders 130 feet above the present river level confirms the force of the water breaking through the landslide.⁹ This also corresponds to the report of Dio Cassius about the situation around Antioch:

> Even Mt. Casius itself was so shaken that its peaks seemed to lean over and broke off and to be falling upon the very city. Other hills also settled, and much water not previously in existence came to light, while many streams disappeared.¹⁰

On the basis of probes taken in the Beteiha plain, it has been confirmed that such debris from the landslides filled in the area at the mouth of the

9. John F. Shroder, Jr., and Michael Bishop, "The Geological Background for the City of Bethsaida," Paper presented to the 1995 International Meeting of the Society of Biblical Literature, Budapest, Hungary.
10. Dio Cassius, *Roman History,* 68.25.6.

Jordan. Here gravel deposited from moving water covers silt deposited from earlier quiet waters beginning a process which presently leaves et-Tell over a mile from the water's edge. Carbon-14 dating suggests a date about eighteen hundred years ago or a date which is consistent with the reports of a major earthquake in 115 C.E. and the evidence from archaeological excavations at Bethsaida.

2 Esdras 1:11 and the Destruction of Bethsaida

There is one final piece of literary evidence which confirms Bethsaida's destruction by earthquake at the beginning of the second century.[11] In the apocryphal work 2 Esdras the fate of Bethsaida is compared to that of the cities Tyre and Sidon:

> Did I not destroy the city of Bethsaida because of you, and to the south burn two cities, Tyre and Sidon, with fire, and kill those who hated you? (variant reading 2 Esdras 1:11).

While the author speaks of the burning of Tyre and Sidon, corresponding to historical fact, the Latin verb *everto* is used to describe the end of Bethsaida.[12] One might expect the verb *perdo* in speaking about destruction by war. However, the verb is *everto* which commonly refers to a natural, violent agitation of the sea or the uprooting of trees or even the ploughing up of land. What then is the significance of this reference to Bethsaida's destruction? When was it written? What does it mean?

The Book 2 Esdras

2 Esdras is a book which is not well known to many. It is part of the pseudepigrapha which means that it is connected with a famous biblical figure—in this case the scribe Ezra who helped rally the returning exiles in the fifth century B.C.E. around the law. Second Esdras is actually a composite work for which the core is a Jewish apocalyptic work dealing with the significance of the destruction of Jerusalem by the Romans in 70 C.E. For this reason it is sometimes included in the Old Testament apocrypha although it was for the most part written at the close of the New Testament era perhaps slightly before 100 C.E. This dating fits the author's own remarks setting Ezra's speech to "the thirtieth year after the destruction of the city" (2 Esdras 3:1). This work survives in one form under the title "Fourth Ezra" and contains 2 Esdras chapters 3–14.

11. Fred Strickert, "The Destruction of Bethsaida: The Evidence of 2 Esdras 1:11," *Bethsaida: A City by the North Shore of the Sea of Galilee*, eds. Rami Arav and Richard Freund (Kirksville, Mo.: Thomas Jefferson University Press, 1998) 2:249–74.

12. *Nonne propter vos Bethsaidam civitatem everti, et ad meridianum duas civitates, Tyrum et Sydonem, igne cremavi, et eos qui adversum vos fuerunt male interfeci?*

Fourth Ezra, however, was not included in the Septuagint—the Greek translation of the Old Testament—and its place in the apocrypha came about because of Christian additions to the work. These Christian additions, known as Fifth Ezra and Sixth Ezra, were appended at the beginning and end of the document so that the present 2 Esdras is structured as follows:

5th Ezra = 2 Esdras 1–2
4th Ezra = 2 Esdras 3–14
6th Ezra = 2 Esdras 15–16

Although this document was included in many manuscripts of the Vulgate of the Middle Ages, it was not accepted as either canonical or deuterocanonical by the Council of Trent in 1563. The Clementine revision of the Vulgate in 1592 incorporated deuterocanonical works within the Old Testament, but placed 1–2 Esdras along with the Prayer of Manasseh as a supplement following the New Testament. Therefore, 2 Esdras often occurs in the apocrypha of Protestant Bibles, although it is not usually included in either the Orthodox or Roman Catholic Bibles.

The Christian edition known as 2 Esdras 1–2 or Fifth Ezra was probably written in the middle of the second century. Just as 2 Esdras 3–14 was written as a reflection on the significance of the destruction of the Temple in 70 C.E., so this later section seeks answers and comfort in the face of further developments during the Bar Kochba revolt in 132–135 C.E. Second Esdras 2:6 speaks of Jerusalem as destroyed and her people scattered. The revolt came about shortly after a visit to the area by the emperor Hadrian around 129–131 C.E. Two of his actions brought about the revolt. He attempted to rebuild Jerusalem as Aeolia Capitolina and to establish a pagan shrine on the site of the Temple and he issued an edict forbidding the practice of circumcision.[13] Like the Old Testament prophets (Isa 1:10-17; Amos 5:21-24; Jer 7:1-15), the second-century writer speaks out in the strongest terms against the Temple:

> When you offer oblations to me, I will turn my face from you; for I have rejected your festal days, and new moons, and circumcisions of the flesh (2 Esdras 1:31).

However, he goes beyond the concerns of these prophets and, like other Christian writers since Paul, condemns also the practice of circumcision. Since Antonius Pius, who became emperor in 138 C.E., lifted this ban, it is likely that 2 Esdras 1–2 was written around 135–140 C.E.

According to Justin Martyr this second Jewish revolt was a time of persecution against Christians by those who recognized the messianic

---

13. Dio Cassius, *Roman History* 69. 12.1-2; *Vita Hadriani* 22.10.

claims of Bar Kochba.[14] Thus 2 Esdras 1–2 notes how his community has experienced hardship and persecution (2:23-32), yet they have endured through their confession of the Son of God (2:42-48). It shows evidence that the "separation of the church from Israel is felt so keenly in 5 Ezra that it may well have been a recent event."[15] Thus the metaphor of mother and sons occurs a number of times (2:10, 15, 17, 31) so that it is clear that Christian and Jews have shared the same mother (Jerusalem) and now a coming people inherit the privileges of Israel.

Second Esdras 1–2, therefore, opens with Ezra commissioned as a prophet to speak out against the misdeeds of the people in contrast to the gracious mighty acts of God. These deeds begin with the Exodus and include the deliverance through the sea, guidance through a pillar of fire, feeding of manna and quail, and providing water from a rock. In addition God shows his strong arm destroying "many kings because of them" and culminating in the destruction of Tyre, Sidon, and Bethsaida. According to this author, Israel's rejection of the Lord, however, leads to their own house becoming desolate. "I will give your houses to a people that will come, who without having heard me will believe" (1:35). Following this prophetic indictment of God's people, assurance of redemption is offered for the new people (2:10-48).

2 Esdras 1:11 and Manuscript History

The use of 2 Esdras 1–2 as a source for reconstructing the history of the destruction of Bethsaida is complicated by the fact that there are two manuscript recensions for these two chapters. In the case of 2 Esdras 1:11, there is extensive variation between the two recensions as can be seen as follows:

Recension # 1—I destroyed all nations before them, and scattered in
  the east the peoples of two provinces, Tyre and Sidon;
  I killed all their enemies (NRSV).
Recension # 2—Did I not destroy the city of Bethsaida because of you,
  and to the south burn two cities, Tyre and Sidon, with
  fire, and kill those who hated you? (variant NRSV)

As can be seen, only the second recension mentions the destruction of Bethsaida. This is significant since this reading cannot be accepted as very helpful if it is a medieval scribal addition.

The manuscript history of 2 Esdras 1–2 is quite complicated with nine Latin manuscripts surviving from the ninth to the thirteenth centuries. The

---

14. Justin Martyr, *First Apology* 33.6.
15. G. N. Stanton, "5 Ezra and Matthean Christianity in the Second Century," *JTS* 28 (1977) 71.

two earliest, which are often referred to as the French family of manuscripts, are reflected in the first recension and the rest, referred to as the Spanish family of manuscripts, are reflected in the second recension. Since the French text was used in the 1592 Clementine revision of the Vulgate, it has generally been used uncritically in modern translations. Even in the New Revised Standard Version is the Spanish text reflected only in a series of footnotes. Nevertheless, there is a long history of scholarship which challenges the preference for the French text and which today is calling for a critical edition of 2 Esdras 1–2 which takes seriously the Spanish text. Although it is impossible to treat this complicated argument in detail here, the work of Theodore Bergren gives the most thorough analysis of these issues.[16]

It is becoming apparent that variations between the two recensions is not simply the matter of scribal error and a few intentional changes here and there.[17] Rather the changes originate at the time of translation from Greek to Latin. It perhaps can be said that the Spanish recension reflects a fairly literal translation while the French recension adapts the text for Western Christendom. As an example, 2 Esdras 1:38-40 includes a long list of Old Testament figures who will lead a return to Palestine from the east. While the Spanish recension lists in a haphazard order a number of prophets, apocalyptic figures, and twelve angels, the French recension includes only the twelve minor prophets in the exact order of the Septuagint. In other words, while the text originally spoke of a return to the land from Mesopotamia, the medieval translator has shifted the meaning to speak of the movement of Christianity from Palestine to Europe.

A similar thing has happened in 2 Esdras 1:11. The French recension offers the perspective of a European writer who understands Tyre and Sidon as "provinces" located "in the east." The Spanish recension correctly understands Tyre and Sidon as "cities" and, writing from the perspective perhaps of Syria, speaks of them "to the south." It is not difficult to understand that a medieval writing would also omit reference to Bethsaida since its destruction seems out of place in a book which fits more with the Old Testament. The opposite argument is less convincing that a medieval writer wanted to include Bethsaida because of familiarity with the woe saying of Jesus. This does not explain why only Bethsaida is mentioned and not the more familiar Capernaum or Chorazin, whose fourth-century destruction was in fact mentioned by Eusebius. The Spanish

16. Theodore A. Bergren, *Fifth Ezra: The Text, Origin, and Early History*. Septuagint and Cognate Studies 25 (Atlanta: Scholars Press, 1990).
17. Robert A. Kraft, "Towards Assessing the Latin Text of '5 Ezra': The 'Christian' Connection," *Harvard Theological Review* 79 (1986) 158–69.

recension of 2 Esdras 1:11 is to be preferred. In other words, this reference to Bethsaida's destruction by earthquake was probably written about twenty years after the event itself.

The Significance of Bethsaida's Destruction in 2 Esdras

Earthquakes are commonly mentioned in apocalyptic literature (Mark 13:8; 2 Baruch 27.7) among the final cosmic signs. In the earlier written portion of 2 Esdras, such earthquakes will precede the great return of God's people to the land (2 Esdras 6:14; 9:3). Along with earthquakes, this writing looks forward to another mighty act of God which will alter the courses of rivers making possible such a return. This belief is built upon the ancient intervention of God to bring about safe passage such as the stopping of the Red Sea at the time of the Exodus and the stopping of the Jordan River at the time of Joshua. It also includes a tradition that after King Shalmaneser of Assyria took the exiles "across the river" into another land (2 Esdras 13:40), the people resolved to keep the laws of God and therefore chose to travel even further to the north away from possible corruption and assimilation. Therefore, God performed a "sign" by stopping the channels of the Euphrates so that they crossed over to safety (2 Esdras 13:41-45). The descendants of these exiles remained faithful until the last times when God would bring about a new Exodus from the north.[18] How would this take place?

> The Most High will stop the channels of the river again, so that they may be able to cross over (2 Esdras 13:47).

Just as in the first Exodus God dried up the Red Sea and the Jordan River, so God would bring about a latter day return by diverting the waters again.

The later writer of 2 Esdras 1:11 was very much aware of the traditions in 2 Esdras 13. The destruction of Bethsaida, along with landslides which blocked the Jordan, was understood then as that final sign. It is important to note that this reference to Bethsaida comes at the end of a brief summary of defeats brought about by the hand of God (2 Esdras 1:4-11). Then the author continues describing in detail the various mighty acts throughout the Exodus period (vv. 12-23). Most significantly, the reference to Bethsaida's destruction in verse 11 is followed directly (in the Spanish recension there is no verse 12) by a report of the passage through the sea:

---

18. Theodore A. Bergren, "The 'People Coming from the East' in 5 Ezra 1:38," *JBL* 108 (1989) 675–83.

is I who brought you through the sea, and made safe highways
where there was no road; I gave you Moses as leader and Aaron as
[prov]ided light for you from a pillar of fire, and did great wonders
[yet] you have forgotten me, says the Lord (2 Esdras 1:13-14).

[ex]pression "on account of you" in verse 11 and "for you" in verse 14 link the Exodus and destruction of Bethsaida together as great wonders of God.

2 Esdras 1–2 and Matthew

The reference to the mighty acts of God in 2 Esdras 1–2 is reminiscent of the words of Jesus speaking woe to Bethsaida and other cities because they did not respond to the deeds that Jesus worked in those communities. The parallel is even more closely drawn because the Bethsaida miracles portray Jesus as the new Moses who crosses the sea (walks on water) and feeds the multitude in the wilderness with bread from heaven in a new Passover meal.

It is clear that 2 Esdras is dependent upon the Matthean version of the Q saying (Matt 11:20-24).[19] In verse 11, only three of the six cities are mentioned, Bethsaida, Tyre, and Sidon. However, in 2 Esdras 2:9 the description of Sodom and Gomorrah "whose land descends to hell" reflects knowledge of the Matthean version since this description was connected with the woe against Capernaum and only indirectly with Gomorrah. The connection is not made in the Lukan version which is likely closer to Q. However, 2 Esdras 2:9 replaces the word of woe against Capernaum with a condemnation of Assur, likely referring to Syria, the context in which 2 Esdras was writing. For 2 Esdras 1–2, the condemnation of Syria and the destruction of Tyre and Sidon to the south prepare for the community to return to the land by way of Bethsaida.

G. N. Stanton has demonstrated a very close connection between the writer of 2 Esdras 1–2 and the Gospel of Matthew, even to such a degree that the second-century writer shows no knowledge of other New Testament works.[20] Of special concern to 2 Esdras 1–2 is the section of Matthew 21–25 where the focus is on the kingdom of God "taken away from you and given to a people that produces the fruits of the kingdom" (Matt 21:43). The events of the Bar Kochba revolt therefore have been interpreted in terms of the "people to come" (2 Esdras 1:35, 38) who will take the place of Jacob and Judah (1:24) and inherit the "kingdom of Je-

---

19. Fred Strickert, "2 Esdras 1:11 and the Destruction of Bethsaida," *Journal for the Study of the Pseudepigrapha* 16 (1997) 113–23.
20. G. N. Stanton, "5 Ezra and Matthean Christianity in the Second Century," 67–83.

rusalem" (2:10). Earthquakes and landslides in the year 115 C.E. serve as an ideal prologue to the writing of 2 Esdras 1–2 shortly after 135 C.E. The destruction of Bethsaida, along with the geological changes at the mouth of the Jordan, are a sign that the time had come for this return.

The Abandonment of Bethsaida

It is not uncommon for cities destroyed by earthquake or war to be rebuilt and reinhabited. This was the case for most sites affected by the 115 C.E. earthquake. Inscriptions from Jerash and Petra suggest that Hadrian may have provided funding for such rebuilding projects.[21] However, the pattern does not follow for Bethsaida. After three thousand years of occupation, with stages of building and rebuilding, et-Tell was abandoned after 115 C.E. Why was Bethsaida different from the other rebuilt cities? The likeliest explanation is that the geographical and geological changes rendered it no longer profitable to rebuild at et-Tell. Bethsaida's history had been connected to its access to the sea as a center for the fishing industry and as a stopping-off point for travelers heading north and south. With its harbor destroyed, both means of livelihood had come to an end and et-Tell was abandoned.

The abandonment of the Tell should not automatically lead to the assumption that all activity in the area around Bethsaida came to an end. It is reasonable to assume that some inhabitants moved to other fishing villages around the sea while others decided to rebuild at another location.[22] General surveys of the region have noted evidence of a dozen Jewish communities within four miles of Bethsaida.[23] Following Josephus' description of the encampment of Sulla's army, one might expect a settlement to be established almost a mile to the north of Bethsaida near the east-west Roman road. With the destruction of the harbor, this would also connect with the main north-south routes. The importance of this location would likely increase with the influx of population into the Golan region in the second through fifth centuries. A 1905–7 excavation in this general vicinity, in fact, uncovered a synagogue known as Khirbet ed-Dikke.[24] This points to the need to expand excavations in the area around Bethsaida.

21. Russell, "The Earthquake Chronology," 41.
22. It may be that some inhabitants who saw this destruction as the fulfillment of Jesus' words, migrated north to the community of Matthew in Syria and served as a catalyst for the composition of 2 Esdras 1–2.
23. Dan Urman, "Jews in the Golan," *Ancient Synagogues: Historical Analysis and Archaeological Discovery*, eds. Urman and Paul V. M. Flesher (Leiden: E. J. Brill, 1995) 2:382.
24. Heinrich Kohl and Carl Watzinger, *Antike Synagoguen in Galilaea* (Leipzig: J. C. Hinrichs, 1916) 112–24.

: *Home of the Apostles*

the Rabbis

...es to Tzaidan in Rabbinic literature, still being debated ... to Sidon or Bethsaida, may in fact refer to such a relo-... to the north. Especially interesting is the passage datable to ...me of Rabbi Judah ha-Nasi which speaks of a debate about work and the Sabbath. At the end it is stated that "the incident took place on the highway of Tzaidan and it was completely inhabited by Israel."[25] The reference to the highway of Tzaidan seems more fitting to this location to the north. This location was still not that far removed from the sea, and thus the fishing traditions recorded in the rabbis are appropriate. A fifth-century source, however, employs Ezekiel 47:8, 11 to speak of the marshes and swamps around Bethsaida. It refers to some of the waters which will be healed and others which will not be healed. In other words, this passage includes information which supports the decline of the fishing industry in the postbiblical period.[26]

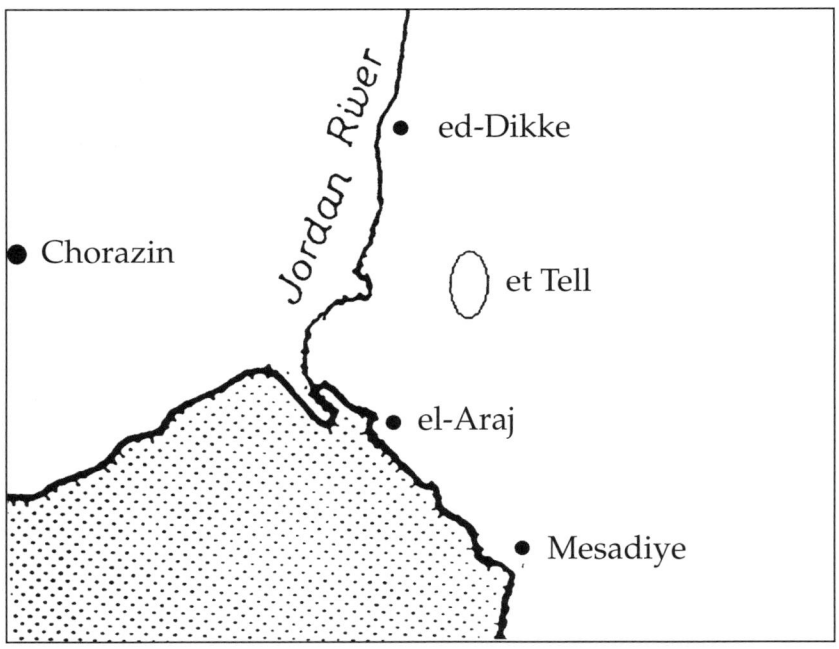

Later Sites Near Bethsaida

25. PT *Avodah Zarah* 5:5, 44d.
26. PT *Sheqalim* 6.2, 50a. Richard A. Freund, "The Search for Bethsaida in Rabbinic Literature," *Bethsaida* (1995) 286–90.

Bethsaida and Pilgrims

While the Jewish community may have relocated to the north, later pilgrims from the Byzantine period built villages closer to the sea, perhaps wanting to preserve the memory of Bethsaida as a fishing village. Today the remains of villages el-Araj[27] and Mesadiye are located on the Beteiha plain close to the water's edge and for centuries they brought confusion to visitors about the history and location of biblical Bethsaida.

There is also one other connection between the city Bethsaida built on the top of et-Tell and these later Jewish and Christian sites. The destroyed city provided ready-made building stones and architectural fragments which could easily be transported and reused in later building. This is the best explanation for the presence of a dozen coins discovered among the ruins of the public buildings—in stark contrast to the lack thereof in the residential sections. It is not surprising, therefore, to find remains from biblical Bethsaida scattered among these other villages. Bethsaida therefore continued to live on after the abandonment of et-Tell through memories preserved in these nearby locations, through written traditions, and through visitors who wanted to get a glimpse of this important New Testament city.

For well over a millennium, there is no evidence for further settlement. Only during the thirteenth through the fourteenth centuries did the Egyptian Mamluks apparently use et-Tell as a military post. Even later the site became a Bedouin cemetery (eighteenth through the nineteenth centuries), and a Syrian military position in the twentieth century until modern biblical scholars returned to uncover the ancient city.

---

27. Rami Arav, "Et-Tell and el-Araj," *IEJ* 38 (3) (1988) 187–8.

Index of Ancient Sources

Aristophanes, *Plutus*	130	17.80-2	79, 94
Virgil, *Fourth Eclogue*	79	17.134-41	94
Strabo, *Geography* 16.2.46	94, 95	17.188	79
		17.189	77, 79
Philo, *Embassy to Gaius*		17.219-20	102
38.299	84	17.220	94
38.300	84	17.224	79
38.305	85	17.321	94, 95
		17.342-4	95, 102
Josephus *Antiquities*		18.4-6	2, 89
8.37	112	18.27	92, 94
13.318-319	86	18.28	1, 13, 20, 91
13.393-397	17, 77		
13.397	86	18.31	94, 95
15.199	93	18.55-62	84
15.342-3	79, 94	18.106	80, 82
15.361	93	18.106-108	2, 82, 89
15.363	86	18.107	80-1
16.6	94	18.109	82
16.78-86	94	18.136-7	82
16.285	79	18.143-9	90
16.290	93	18.143	89, 94
16.338	93	18.146	89
17.10	94	18.156	94
17.14	79, 82	18.165	89, 94
17.21	79	18.237	89
17.23-29	79, 112	19.343-52	90, 148
17.26	86	19.360	94
17.27	80	20.138	90
17.29-31	81	20.51-53	148

Index of Ancient Sources

Josephus *Life*	
37	164
86	39
96	57
155-178	59, 60
167	60
187	164
304	57
398-400	39
398-406	3, 31, 57, 123, 164

Josephus *War*	
1.104-105	17
1.404	86
1.557	82
1.566	94
1.603	79
1.641-3	94
1.672	79
2.15	94, 137
2.20	79
2.67	95
2.95	79
2.98	94
2.111	95
2.167	94, 95
2.167-77	84
2.168	2, 31, 77, 92, 94
2.503-4	65
2.573-574	90, 164
2.632-646	59, 60
2.639	60
3.43	82
3.57	2, 17, 20, 86
3.392-408, 530	60
3.506	41
3.515	2, 31
3.618	57
4.4-10	164
4.454	2
4.87-92	39
6.422-7	143

Pliny, *Natural History*	
5.15.71	3, 21, 31, 165
30	130

Ptolemy, *Geographia*	
5.16.4	4, 21

Tacitus, *Annals*	
1.8.14	93
3.24	92
5.1-2	98
Histories 4.81	130

Dio Cassius, *Roman History*	
46.1	93
55.27.6	95
56.32.1	93
56.41	98
57.12.2	93
58.2	98
60	99
65.271	130
68.24.1-3	167
68.25.6	168
69.12.1-2	170
69.14.1-2	165

Suetonius, *Augustus* 101.2	93
Suetonius, *Tiberius* 51	98
Suetonius, *Claudius* 11	99
Suetonius, *Vespasian* 7	130
Vita Hadriani 22.10	170

Old Testament

Exodus 12:48	143
Exodus 29:27	152
Leviticus 11:9-12	53
Numbers 32:32-3	112
Numbers 34:11	48
Deuteronomy 3:8	112
Deuteronomy 3:17	48
Deuteronomy 4:43	77
Deuteronomy 4:47	112
Joshua 12:3	48
Joshua 13:27	48
Joshua 19:35	15, 47, 48

180   *Index of Ancient Sources*

Joshua 20:8	77	10:37	158
2 Samuel 3:3	16	10:39	158
2 Samuel 12:30	14	11:2-6	110
2 Samuel 13:37-39	16	11:4-5	127
1 Kings 15:2, 10, 13	16	11:7-8	110
2 Chronicles 11:20	16	11:16-17	110
2 Chronicles 15:16	16	11:19	110
Ecclesiastes 9:12	48	11:20	110, 136
Job 19:6	48	11:20-21	22
Isaiah 1:10-17	170	11:20-24	4, 131–132, 141, 149, 166, 174
Isaiah 9:9	67		
Isaiah 14:13-14	136		
Isaiah 23	135	11:21	110
Jeremiah 7:1-15	170	11:22	133
Jeremiah 47:4	135	11:23-24	133
Ezekiel 9:3-8	151	11:24	133
Ezekiel 17	159	12:22	126
Ezekiel 26–28	135	13:47	53
Ezekiel 26:5, 14	48	13:47-50	48
Ezekiel 32:2	48	13:58	126
Ezekiel 47, 8, 11	176	14:3	82
Ezekiel 47:10	48	14:11	82
Daniel 4	159	14:13	33, 88, 114, 119, 120
Joel 4:4-8	135		
Amos 5:21-24	170		
Habakkuk 1:15	48	14:13-21	115–118
		14:19	120

The New Testament

The Gospel according to Matthew		14:22	33, 118
2:6, 20, 21	133	14:22-34	115
3:1	111	14:23	120
4:13	22, 26	14:34	33, 118
4:15	133	15:39	33
4:18-22	22	16:17	19
8:5-13	27	17:24-27	48, 55
8:11	159	19:1	114
8:14-15	24–25	20:29-34	126
8:18	35	21:25	174
8:20	22	21:43	174
9:1	35	22:1-14	159
9:11-15	110	27:8	133
9:18-26	27	28:15	133
9:27-31	126	28:16-20	141
10	133		
10:2-4	19, 29	The Gospel according to Mark	
10:15	132, 133	1:14–6:13	88

Index of Ancient Sources 181

1:14–8:30	128	6:45	5, 33, 35, 115, 118, 119, 126
1:16	22		
1:16-20	26, 48, 50, 57	6:45-52	88, 115
		6:45-53	60
1:19	54	6:46	120
1:20	59	6:48	124
1:21	22	6:52	118
1:29	26	6:53	33, 35, 118
1:29-31	24–25	6:53–7:23	88
1:30-31	26	7:24–30	88
2:1	26	7:31	35
2:1-12	27, 137	7:31–8:12	88
2:4	67	7:33	126
2:14	19	8	39, 47, 126, 158
3:16-19	19, 29		
3:18	19	8:1-10	127
3:19-35	27	8:10	33, 126
4:1	48	8:11-13	127
4:35	35	8:12	127
4:36-41	58	8:13	31, 127
5:1-20	77, 123	8:13-26	88
5:1, 21	35	8:14-21	127, 128
5:21-43	27	8:17-18	128
5:22	27	8:22	33, 127
5:38	27	8:22-26	5, 125, 126, 128
5:40	27		
6–8	115	8:23	107
6:3	107	8:26	126, 129
6:5	126	8:27–9:1	88
6:14-16	88	8:29	128
6:17	82	8:31–10:52	128
6:17-29	88	8:34-35	157
6:22	82	9:2-13	88
6:28	82	9:30-31	88
6:30-32	88	10:1	88, 114, 120
6:31-44	115–118, 127		
		10:28	26
6:31	114, 120	10:35-45	128
6:32	33, 120	10:46	129
6:33	119, 120	10:46-52	126, 128
6:33-44	88	11–15	88
6:35	120	11:1–16:8	128
6:39	120	13:8	173
6:41	123	16:7	21, 128, 141
6:44	33		

The Gospel according to Luke

3:1-2	77
3:3	111
3:7-9	159
3:16-17	159
3:18	127
3:19	82
4:31	22
4:38-39	24–25
5:1-11	22, 48, 63
5:6	54
5:7	53
6:14-16	19, 29
7:1-10	27
7:18-23	110, 159
7:22	127
7:24-26	110, 159
7:26-28	110
7:32	110, 159
7:33-34	159
7:35	110
8:22, 26, 40	35
8:41-56	27
9	39, 131, 158
9:10	33, 107, 115
9:10-11	5
9:10-17	115–118
9:11	119
9:12	120, 122
9:18-22	35
9:58	22
10	131, 134
10:12	132
10:13	110, 132
10:13-15	4, 22, 131–132, 141, 149
11:14	126
13:18-19	159
13:29	159
14:15-25	159
14:26	158
15:8-10	66
17:22-36	65
17:33	158
18:35-43	126
23:12	85

The Gospel according to John

1	30, 157
1:28	39, 109, 111, 112
1:35-37	159
1:35-51	21
1:37	109
1:40	109, 122, 159
1:43	21, 109, 159
1:43-44	5, 39
1:44	20, 107, 137, 141, 143, 155, 156
1:45	20
2:1	39
2:22	156
3:23	111, 112
4:46-54	27
5:1-18	137
5:2	1, 6, 137
6	6, 157
6:1-14	115–118, 142
6:1	33, 118
6:2	119, 144
6:3	120
6:4	144
6:5	141
6:6-8	156
6:9	57
6:10	120
6:11	142
6:14	144
6:15	120, 123
6:16-17	33
6:16-21	115
6:17	118
6:19	124
6:21	33

Index of Ancient Sources   183

6:22	124	10	140, 144
6:22-24	56, 118	10:9	67
6:23	45, 142	11:19-21	144
6:26-35	123	11:27	149
6:47-51	123	11:27-29	148
6:49	120	12	148
6:59	118	12:1-19	90
9	130	12:20-23	90, 148
9:1-7	126	21:20	139
9:2	129	26:11	144
9:6	126		
10:40	114, 120	1 Corinthians 15:36-37	145
11:18	111	Galatians 2:7	140
12	157	Galatians 2:9	141
12:16	156	Hebrews 6:19	152
12:20	141, 143		
12:20-22	6	2 Esdras	
12:20-24	20	1–2	170–5
12:21	5, 20, 21	1:4-11	173
12:21-22	156	1:11	6, 169, 171, 172, 173, 174
12:22	137		
12:24	144, 145, 147, 152, 157	1:12-23	173
		1:13-14	174
12:25-26	157	1:24	174
14	157	1:31	170
14:8	141, 156	1:35	171, 174
14:10	156	1:38	174
14:25-26	156	1:38-40	172
19:12	85	2:6	170
19:35	109	2:9	174
21	30, 48, 63, 136, 141, 142, 148	2:10	171, 175
		2:10-48	171
		2:15	171
21:1-2	53	2:17	171
21:1-14	48	2:23-32	171
21:2	20, 59, 142	2:31	171
21:4	143	2:42-48	171
21:6	54	3–14	169, 170
21:8	53	3:1	169
21:11	53, 63	6:14	173
21:12	143	9:3	173
21:13	136	13:40	173
Acts 1–12	141	13:41-45	173
1:13	29	13:47	173
9:31	140, 144	15–16	170

2 Baruch 27.7	173
2 Baruch 41.3	140
2 Baruch 83.8	140
Didache 9:4	142
Papias of Hierapolis	155
Justin Martyr, *Dialogue* 38	140
Justin Martyr, *First Apology*	171
Pistis Sophia	156
Origen, *Against Celsus*	48
Jerome, *Commentary on Isaiah* 8.14	140
Eusebius, *Ecclesiastical History* 1.7.13	140
Epiphanius, *Haer.* 29.7	112
Epiphanius, *Haer.* 30.2	112
Orosius, *History* 7.6.12	149
3 Q15 xi 12-13	137

Rabbinic Literature

Mishnah Avodah Zarah 3:7	8
Mishnah Gittin 7:5	8
BT Gittin 75a	8
PT Avodah Zarah 5:5. 44d	9, 40, 176
PT Sheqalim 6.2,50a	49, 176
PT Sheqalim 6.2,50c	8, 57
Sifrei Devarim 4.39	48
Sifrei Devarim, Reeh 80:4.80	7, 36
Sifrei on Deuteronomy 42	67
Tosefta Avodah Zarah 3:7	8
Tosefta Erubin 4.5	38
Tosefta Hullin 22	140
Tosefta Shabbath 4:11	74
Genesis Rabbah 31:13; 32:9	35
Song of Songs Rabbah 1. 4:89	9
Midrash Kohelet Rabbah 1.24	140
Midrash Kohelet Rabbah 2.8	47
Midrash Rabbah Leviticus 34:16	67
Midrash Rabbah Leviticus 35:12	67
Baba Bathra 6:4	65

Index of Names and Places
(Map pages in italics)

Absalom, 16, 30
Acco, *37,* 39–40, 47, 49
Agabus, 149
Agrippa 1, 2, 82, 89, 90, 94, 99, 102, 103, 113, 145–9, 158, 162
Agrippa 2, 3, 21, 90, 94, 162–3
Akiba, 7–8
Alexander (Herod), 94
Alexander Jannaeus, 16, 77, 86
Andrew, 5, 6, 19–21, 25–30, 48, 109, 117, 122, 141–4, 148, 155–9
Antioch, 21, 140, 149, 167
Antipas, 2, 21, 35, 40, 79, 82–90, 92–5, 102–3, 107, 110, 114, 118, 123, 162
Antipater, 94
Antonia, 89
Antonius Pius, 162, 170
Archelaus, 79, 83, 87, 94, 95, 102, 162
Aristobulus (Hasmonean), 86
Aristobulus (Herod), 82, 89, 94
Asclepios, 130
Assyria, 15–16, 173
Athens, 16
Augustus, 2, 60, 77, 85–7, 92–9, 101–3, 105
Azotus, 94

Babylon, 77, 81, 86, 112, 136
Bar Kochba Revolt, 6, 50, 105, 170–1, 174
Bartholomew, 30
Bartimaeus, 126, 128–9
Bashan, 40, 112
Batanea, *37,* 112–4, 120
Bernice, 89, 94, 102
Beteiha Plain, 41, *42,* 63, 91, 111–2, 168, 177
Bethany (beyond Jordan), 109, 111, 114, 120
Bethany (Judea), 1, 39, 111
Betharampta, 93–4, 111
Beth Shean, 37
Bethzatha, 6, 137

Caesarea, *78,* 85, 90, 103, 140, 148, 167
Caesarea Philippi, 1, 2, 35, *37,* 39–41, 58, 77, *78,* 80, 83, 86–9, 91–3, 101–5, 107, 118, 127–9, 157
Caligula, 90, 94, 102
Cana, 20, 30, 39, 112
Capernaum/Cepharnocus, 1, 3–4, 6, 22–31, 33, *34,* 35–6, *37,* 38, 40–1, 45, 51, 62, *78,* 118–9, *121,* 131–8, *135,* 141, 149, 158, 163, 172
Chorazin, 4, 6, 22, 28, 36–9, *37–8,* 41, *78,* 119–20, *121,* 124, 131–8, *135,* 141, 149, 158, 165, 172, *176*
Claudius, 94, 99, 102, 146–8
Cleopatra of Jerusalem, 79
Constanine, 28, 151

185

Dabura, 39
Dalmanutha, 33, 45, 127
Damascus, 16, 36, *37, 78,* 140, 144
David, 16
Decapolis, 35, *78*
Demeter, 145–7
Drusus, 89, 93, 102

ed-Dikke, 40, *44,* 175, *176*
Egeira, 22, 24, 28, 62
el-Araj, 10, *44,* 80, *176,* 177
Eleazara ben Shamoa, 7, 36

Gaius, 93
Gamla, 3, *37–38,* 39, *42,* 61, 77, 86, 121, 163
Gaulanitis, 2, 31, *32,* 35, 77, 89, 92
Gennesaret/Gennesar/Ginnosar, *34,* 35, *37,* 45, 57–60, *61,* 118, 124
Geshur, 16, 30
Gischala, 39
Golan, 9, 10, 13, 17, 21, 35–7, 39–41, 47, 60–1, 65, 67–77, 79, 88–90, 122, 129, 135, 163, *166,* 175
Gratus, Valerius, 83, 95, 96

Hadrian, 47, 170, 175
Hananya, Kefar, *37,* 39–40
Hasmoneans, 17, 77, 86–7, 162
Haurun, 40, 72, 81
Helena, 149
Herod the Great, 77, 79–80, 82, 86–7, 93–4, 103, 112, 162
Herodias, 82, 103
Hippos/Susita, 3, 31, *32, 34, 35,* 37

Idumea, *78,* 79
Iturea, 77, 86

Jairus, 27
James (son of Alphaeus), 17, 30
James (of Jerusalem), 139
James (son of Zebedee), 6, 17, 19, 21, 25–6, 28–9, 48, 54, 59, 90, 141, 148, 155
Jeremiah, 3, 163
Jerusalem, 1, 6, 14, 17, 78, 84, 87, 90, 102, 126, 137, 139, 141, 148, 169–70

John the Baptist, 82, 88, 107, 109–14, 120, 127, 133, 159
John (son of Zebedee), 6, 17, 19, 21, 25–6, 28–9, 48, 54, 59, 109, 141, 155
Josephus, 3, 38–9, 90, 163
Jotapata, 39
Judah ha-Nasi, 9, 40, 176
Julia (daughter of Augustus), 1, 91–3, 99, 106
Julia (see Livia)
Julias (= Livia in Perea), 2, 92–3, 95, 102–3, 107

Khader, Tell, 119
Kursi (Gerasenes), *34,* 35, 51, 77

Livia (= Julia), 2, 60, 85, 87, 92–106, 113, 123–4, 145–9, 157–8
Lucius, 93

Malthace, 102
Mariamme, 79, 82
Matthew, 155–6
Mesadiye, 10, *44, 176,* 177
Migdal (= Magdala = Magadan = Tarichaeae), 3, 31–3, *32, 35, 37,* 45, 51, 57–8, 60, *61*
Mount Hermon, 36, *78,* 80, 88

Nabatea, 40, 81
Naphtali, *15,* 48
Nathanael, 19–21, 30
Nazareth, 1, 6, 19–20, 27–8, 107, 126–7

Paneas, 1–2, 6, 28, 47, 49, 77, 86–7, 91–2
Papias, 155
Paul, 139–40, 144–5, 152
Perea, 2, *78,* 79, 93, 114
Peter, 5, 17, 20–30, 48, 55, 67, 88, 90, 117–8, 122, 127–8, 136, 141–2, 148, 155, 157–8
Philip (Disciple), 5–6, 17, 20–1, 28–30, 81, 109, 116–7, 122, 141–8, 155–9
Philip (Tetrarch), 1–2, 12–13, 20, 35, 40, 61, 77, 79–95, 98–103, 105–6, 110, 113, 162
Philip (son of Zamaris), 81

Index of Names and Places

Phoenecia, 16, 56, *78,* 140
Pilate, Pontius, 83–6, 89, 95–9, 113, 145
Pollio, C. Asinius, 79
Ptolemies, 16, 162

Rabbah bar Hanah, 8
Rama, 37
Rome, 21, 79, 89, 93–4, 99, 102, 151

Salome (daughter of Herodias), 82, 102
Salome (sister of Herod), 94–5, 102
Samaria, 14, 140
Scribonia, 93
Sebaste (city), 103
Seleucia, *38,* 39, 77, 163
Seleucids, 16, 162
Sepphoris, 4, 28, *78,* 92–4, 103, 107, 110, 158
Si, 40, 81
Sidon, 4, 6–7, 35–6, 49, *78,* 132, 134, 140, 169, 172, 174, 176
Simeon ben Gamaliel, 8–9, 49, 57
Simeon ben Yohai, 8, 9
Sodom, 4, 132–3, 136, 174
Sogane, 163
Soreg, 16
Sulla, 3, 38–9, 90, 163, 175

Syria, 16–17, 20, 30, *78,* 86, 90, 140, 172, 174

Tabgha, 6, 28, *34,* 62–3, 119
Talmai, 16, 30
Theodosius, 6, 28, 41
Thomas, 155–6
Tiberias, 2–4, 28, 31, *32,* 35, *37,* 45, 57, 59, 60, *78,* 83, 90, 92, 94, 102–3, 107, 110, 118
Tiberius, 2, 84–5, 87, 89–90, 92–100, 102, 106, 113, 145
Tiberius Nero, 93
Titus, 39
Trachonitus, 2, 77, 89
Trajan, 162, 165–8
Tyre, 4, 6, 16, 35, 37, 49, *78,* 86, 132, 134, 169, 172, 174
Tzaidan, 7–8, 36, 40, 47, 57, 63, 176
Tzer, *15,* 74

Vespasian, 130

Willibald, 6, 29–30

Yehudah ben Batayrah, 7, 36
Yohanan ha-Sandlar, 7, 36

Zamaris, 79, 81, 112
Zenodorus, 87